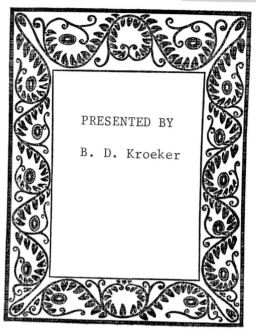

TWO VIEWS OF FREEDOM
IN PROCESS THOUGHT
A Study of Hegel and Whitehead

American Academy of Religion
Dissertation Series

edited by
H. Ganse Little, Jr.

Number 28

TWO VIEWS OF FREEDOM IN PROCESS
THOUGHT
A Study of Hegel and Whitehead
by
George Ramsdell Lucas, Jr.

George Ramsdell Lucas, Jr.
Two Views of Freedom in Process Thought

Scholars Press

Distributed by
Scholars Press
PO Box 5207
Missoula, Montana 59806

TWO VIEWS OF FREEDOM IN PROCESS THOUGHT
A Study of Hegel and Whitehead
George Ramsdell Lucas, Jr.

Library of Congress Cataloging in Publication Data

Lucas, George R.
  Two views of freedom in process thought.

  (Dissertation series - American Academy of Religion ;
no. 28)
  Bibliography: p.
  1. Hegel, Georg Wilhelm Friedrich, 1770–1831.
2. Whitehead, Alfred North, 1861–1947. 3. Liberty.
4. Process philosophy. 5. Organism (Philosophy)
I. Title. II. Series: American Academy of Religion.
Dissertation series - American Academy of Religion ; no.
28
B2949.L5L82   193   79–12287
ISBN 0–89130–285–9
ISBN 0–89130–304–9 pbk.

Printed in the United States of America
1 2 3 4 5
Edwards Brothers, Inc.
Ann Arbor, MI 48104

TABLE OF CONTENTS

DEDICATION

Dr. Tyler Thompson
Professor of Philosophy of Religion

Garrett Theological Seminary
   1951-1974

Garrett Evangelical Theological Seminary
   1974-1978

   The present study merely supports certain ideas which he
has long held to be the case.

PREFACE

In many respects, as the reader will discover, this work represents yet another attempt to expound Hegel. If one wishes to approach Hegel at all, why attempt to do so through Whitehead? Surely previous, longstanding interpretations as offered, for example, by existentialists, phenomenologists, Christian theologians and Marxists adequately display the many-sided complexity of Hegel's own thought.

While I respect, and have borrowed heavily on occasion from these major "received" interpretations, I find nonetheless a certain selectivity pervading all of them. Almost without exception, these interpretations altogether ignore an important dimension of Hegel's own interest: *viz.*, cosmology and the philosophy of nature. I personally regard such omissions as a fatal criticism of these alternative interpretations. In utilizing a Whiteheadian perspective to correct such deficiencies, the reader will note that I endeavor to identify the present work as a sustained development of another equally-longstanding, distinctive, but decidedly minority tradition of Hegelian scholarship.

In this regard, sympathetic critics of the present study on occasion have complained that my use of the category of "organism" --and especially "organic mechanism" as a descriptive label for Hegel's philosophy of nature--are ill-advised. While granting that my usage of these concepts is unorthodox, I feel nonetheless that such usage is justified in that it points up the marked similarities of discussions by both Hegel and Whitehead of reciprocal internal relatedness. In addition, "organism" and "organic mechanism" call attention to the criticisms by both philosophers of the use of reductionistic analysis and mechanistic explanation in the natural sciences, and underscore their similar attempts to exhibit these as relatively trivial and restricted forms of a more adequate and inclusive variety of teleological explanation, which Whitehead recognized as implicit in the metaphysical foundations of contemporary evolutionary biology and statistical physics.

For their influence and assistance, I am indebted to my teachers, friends and colleagues: Errol E. Harris, George L. Kline, Lewis S. Ford, William Earle, James E. Will, Tyler Thompson and the late Robert W. Browning. None of these persons are liable, of course, for my errors and excesses. Carolyn and Jessica, however, on numerous occasions have been victims of both! For their toleration of this project I can only reply with gratitude and love.

G. R. L.

Ashland, Virginia
February 15, 1979

ABBREVIATIONS AND SPECIAL NOTES

1. Abbreviations of Whitehead's Works.

CN	*Concept of Nature*
SMW	*Science and the Modern World*
RM	*Religion in the Making*
PR	*Process and Reality*
AI	*Adventures of Ideas*
MT	*Modes of Thought*
Key to PR	*A Key to Whitehead's Process and Reality*

2. Abbreviations of Hegel's Works.

Phenomenology, Phen.	*Phänomenologie des Geistes* (1807)
GL, "Greater" or "Larger Logic"	*Wissenschaft der Logik*, 2 Vols. (1812, 1816)
Enc., *Encyclopedia*	*Encyclopädie der Philosophischen Wissenschaften im Grundrisse* (1817)
"Lesser Logic"	*Enc.* Sections 1 - 244, with *Zusätze*
"Philosophy of Nature"	*Enc.* Sections 245 - 376, with *Zusätze*
"Philosophy of Mind"	*Enc.* Sections 377 - 577, with *Zusätze*
Phil. R., *Philosophy of Right*, or *Rechtsphilosophie*	*Grundlinien der Philosophie des Rechts* (1821)
Zusatz	One of the *Zusätze*, or explanatory comments or elaborations, based upon Hegel's class lectures, and distilled from student lecture-notes. These were inserted into the texts of posthumous editions of the *Encyclopedia* and the *Rechtsphilosophie*.

3. Special Notes.

A. Whenever possible, citations of primary sources appear in the body of the text, rather than in footnotes.

B. Numerals following the abbreviated citations of Whitehead's works refer to the pagination of the editions of those works listed in the Bibliography.

C. Numerals following abbreviated citations of Hegel's *Phenomenology* and "Larger Logic" (GL), refer to the *page numbers* in the English-language editions of those works, as translated by A. V. Miller. Consult Bibliography for particulars.

D. Numerals following abbreviated citations of Hegel's *Encyclopedia* and *Philosophy of Right*, however, refer to the enumerated *sections* of the original text, rather than to the pagination of any particular edition.

E. Unless otherwise noted in a specific citation or footnote, the English translations of quotations from Hegel's works are from the editions or translations cited in the Bibliography. [I have chosen to use Mr. Miller's more recent translation of Hegel's *Phänomenologie des Geistes* in place of the older Baillie translation.]

F. In all cases, I have taken the liberty of substituting "Concept" for the translation by both Wallace and Miller of *Begriff* as "Notion."

I.   INTRODUCTION

> I have never been able to read Hegel: I initiated my attempt by studying some remarks of his on mathematics which struck me as complete nonsense. It was foolish of me, but I am not writing to explain my good sense.
>
> -Alfred North Whitehead-[1]

Section 1.   Whitehead, Hegel and Hermeneutics: On the Purpose, Organization and Rationale of the Present Study

This essay represents an encounter with Hegel's thought on the part of a student of Whitehead's philosophy. It is intended for consumption primarily by Whiteheadians and other varieties of "process" philosophers. Those acquainted with Hegel's philosophy may find the following discussions of modest interest as well. Indeed, such persons may find here upon occasion a novel treatment of some familiar Hegelian themes. By and large, however, the present work will endeavor to demonstrate certain points which thoughtful Hegelians long have believed to be the case, even if they have not heretofore succeeded in proving them. Principally, this work is intended as a demonstration of the similarity of methodology, content and results exhibited in the metaphysical systems of Whitehead and Hegel.

Freedom is the central theme in both metaphysical systems. Accordingly, I shall outline the respective doctrines of metaphysical freedom developed by Whitehead and Hegel individually. Each of the two doctrines is significant because : (i) each was derived in close dialogue with a broad range of empirical data and scientific theory; and (ii) each attempted to understand and articulate a theory of causality consistent with (rather than opposed to) a meaningful doctrine of freedom. The resultant doctrines of metaphysical freedom are compatible in the main with the empirical observations and theoretical structures of contemporary physics and biology. This is to be expected in the case of Whitehead, whose metaphysics was developed in dialogue with, and as one possible interpretation of many of those data and theories. For those unfamiliar with Hegel's cosmology and the extensive empirical and analytic dimensions of his thought, however, such a judgment with respect to his metaphysics may come as a surprise.

The judgment of Hegel's modernity with respect to the problem of freedom is not surprising, however, when one takes the trouble to interpret and develop Hegel's cosmology. As one whose former interest lay in the field of nuclear and elementary-particle physics, I have found this exercise to be a fascinating and rewarding one. A study of his cosmology and philosophy of science dispels the common myth of Hegel as a thinker unacquainted or unconcerned with the natural world and with the attempts by scientists to understand that world. Quite the contrary, Hegel emerges as one passionately interested in, and intimately acquainted with the scientific enterprise.

Hegel was uncomfortable with--and on occasion, criticized or rejected--certain scientific procedures and conclusions. His "bad press" with scientists and empirical philosophers is due in large part to this tendency. It is interesting to note, however, that many of the features of nineteenth-century science which Hegel criticized were precisely those abandoned by scientists themselves less than a century later. Some of Hegel's suggested alternatives bear marked resemblance to the theories subsequently adopted.

On the other hand, certain of Hegel's criticisms--such as his apparent rejection of temporal evolution and of the atomic theory of elements and compounds--fail this test of modernity. It is sophistry to suggest that good philosophers are precisely prescient in every respect. It encourages likewise a recurrence to the more naive and destructive dimensions of medieval science to suggest that adequate scientific theories may be developed without ever taking leave of one's armchair.

For the most part, however, such criticisms and evaluations of scientific theory as Hegel offers are based upon extensive knowledge and considered judgment. The philosophy of nature, and the broader metaphysical position developed in partial dialogue with this interest in science has much to recommend it. And, in particular, I shall wish to argue that Hegel's views on freedom are in keeping with the more contemporary features of this general cosmological orientation of his thought.

Unfortunately, among the numerous Continental, British and American writers who acknowledge Hegel's influence upon their own work, it would appear that only R. G. Collingwood and Errol E. Harris share with Hegel this comprehensive and holistic approach to metaphysics--an approach which embraces both a lively interest in, and an extensive knowledge of the methodology and content of the natural sciences. In the present century, however, no writer has expressed more thoroughly and profoundly this all-encompassing and holistic approach to metaphysics than Alfred North Whitehead. It is this common dimension of the thought of Hegel and Whitehead which I wish to explore.

It is possible, of course, to develop a variety of self-consistent approaches to Hegel's thought. My own interpretation obviously is shaped by a prior acquaintence with Whitehead, and by an interest in science and the philosophy of nature. Beyond the legitimate differences in interpretation which hermeneutics reveals, however, it is often the case that various interpreters of Hegel have seen in his philosophy only what they wished to see. Marx, for example, perceived in Hegel the economics and politics of alienation and revolution. For Heidegger, Sartre and Tillich, Hegel is the first to discern the threat of non-being and to develop the theme of that suffering which is identical with existence. These, at least, are developments entirely consistent with Hegel's own views. In Great Britain, however, the emphasis by McTaggart and Bradley on Hegel's *Logic* together with a deliberate de-emphasis of his philosophy of nature, led to a rather obscure ontology and theology which simply ignored the cosmological features which also were part of Hegel's own essential "Spirit." Such interpretations have done serious damage to the understanding of Hegel himself, as J. N. Findlay so eloquently and forcefully has indicated.[2]

Students of Whitehead's thought are familiar with a similar phenomenon. Few of Whitehead's expositors share his training or interest in mathematics and physics. Many, if not most, however, have their own private agendas with respect to philosophical theology. For Whitehead, as for Aristotle and Hegel, God is a necessary and integral feature of the more general cosmology which God enables, and in which God participates (or, more correctly, through which God is more fully actualized). Most Whiteheadians have chosen to concentrate on the theistic dimension of

Whitehead's thought to the detriment of the wider considerations
which informed Whitehead's own philosophical development. In so
doing, they create a threat to the understanding and interpretation of Whitehead similar in many respects to the actual damage
done Hegel by several of his interpreters. In some cases this
procedure has been justified by suggesting, as did Victor Lowe
and Ivor Leclerc,[3] that Whitehead later adopted metaphysical
interests different from his earlier preoccupation with the philosophy of nature. In my judgment, this interpretation suggests
too narrow a view of metaphysics. Whitehead's interests and
investigations, like Aristotle's, broaden as he encounters new
difficulties, questions or problems which cannot be resolved
strictly within the domains in which they are raised.

As noted, the theme of freedom is integral to the general
metaphysical positions of Whitehead and Hegel, respectively.
This doctrine thus suggests itself as the issue to consider for
purposes of comparison. I develop and subsequently utilize
individual expositions of their respective theories of freedom
in order to lend substance to the suggestion of striking similarity between the broader metaphysical systems of Whitehead
and Hegel. The place of freedom itself in the individual philosophies of Whitehead and Hegel has been the topic of much writing
and research. For this reason I feel compelled as well as enabled
not only to summarize these respective doctrines, but also to
offer criticisms and suggest certain modifications where appropriate. In the main, however, the present essay is offered as
the first attempt at a sustained comparison of the metaphysics
of Whitehead and Hegel.

Such a comparative study lends itself to interests which
are other than purely academic. Several theologians and philosophers from the United States and Western Europe, for example,
have found in process philosophy and theology a useful vehicle
for mutual understanding between themselves and the varieties
of Marxism and liberation thought current among the philosophers
and theologians of Eastern Europe, Latin America, and other parts
of the Third World.[4] The present discussion could serve to demonstrate that such mutual understanding is not merely coincidental
or fortuitous, but proceeds as a result of the fundamental similarity and compatibility of the metaphysical infrastructures
upon which Marxism and process theology are grounded.

In a slightly different vein, those concerned with the development of a system of ethics grounded in process thought may find certain of Hegel's insights--concerning, for example, the dialectical tension of love and justice, of rights and mutual responsibilities among individuals, the family and the state-- helpful at precisely the points of Whitehead's greatest ambiguity. Whitehead, in turn, serves as the basis for certain novel and interesting discussions of metaethics--such as the nature and importance of discrete individual "decisions," the concept of moral (and especially of "derivative") responsibility, the pos- sibility of tragedy and suffering as well as of unanticipated joy in consequence of certain realized moral possibilities--all of which provide a helpful supplement to Hegel's theory of ethics. All of these possibilities are among the larger ramifications of the basic metaphysical affinities between Whitehead and Hegel which I shall discuss here.

Certain features of the following treatment should be noted in advance. The table of contents reveals that the form of treat- ment utilized is virtually identical for the two philosophers. That is, following an overview of the argument to be pursued and a discussion of essential terminology, I have given major at- tention to the development of the micro-ontologies of freedom developed by each philosopher. In Whitehead's case, this amounts to a fairly straightforward discussion of the theory of actual entities, along with certain current objections to, and modifi- cations of that theory. With Hegel the treatment is more com- plex and extensive, involving a lengthy discussion of his organic mechanism in the *Naturphilosophie*. The latter is a doctrine which appears to be relatively unfamiliar, even among Hegelians. In both cases the discussion then shifts to macro-ontology--the application of the technical metaphysical argument to problems of ethics and metaethics, concluding in each case with some general remarks on the respective understandings of human his- tory and of philosophical theism.

Not surprisingly the content and style of discussion differ considerably between the two chapters. Whitehead and Hegel have two very different styles of philosophizing and of writing. Both styles have contributed in no small measure toward the misunder- standing of each individually. Furthermore, the radical differ- ence between the two styles of philosophizing has all but obscured

certain essential points of similarity in the metaphysical systems of Whitehead and Hegel.

There is a frustrating tendency when discussing Whitehead
to depend heavily on his own highly specialized and technical
vocabulary. I have refrained from this excess as much as possible. Selective use of that terminology, however, permits exact
understanding and concise discussion of Whitehead's thought--
which, of course, was part of his intention in developing it.

When discussing Hegel, one is tempted instead to *expound*
him in a manner consistent with his own prolix style. I have
not entirely succeeded in avoiding this pitfall--nor is it really
possible to do so. One can understand Hegel only by retracing
the ground he has covered (although, unfortunately, understanding is not thereby guaranteed). For this reason, my treatment
of Hegel differs both in length and in style from my treatment
of Whitehead.

The understanding of Hegel is complicated further by his
insistence, throughout his mature works, on waging a running
battle against what he terms "school logic"--the self-certain
and self-assured judgments regarding the nature of truth (and
the proper methods for its discovery and exhibition) offered by
logicians, analytic philosophers, and some scientists. There is
a serious, as well as a light-hearted interpretation of this
polemic. The serious dimension involves Hegel's conviction,
shared by many existentialists and phenomenologists, that a
certain irreducible measure of contradiction, opposition, alienation and paradox is rooted in the nature of reality itself. Such
tensions never can be resolved fully through logical analysis
alone. Indeed, the fallacy of logical atomism, so far as Hegel
is concerned, is that the method of analysis provides a false
and inadequate portrait of truth: by appearing to circumvent
contradictions, logical analysis divests reality of its fundamental character of tension, opposition and negation. By implication, such analysis thus makes light of the tragedy of real
existential alienation.

Hegel seriously suggests that the German language is suited
by nature for philosophical expression, since its vocabulary inherently embodies such contradictions (GL 32). In a more frivo-
lous vein, however, Hegel seems to delight in overstating this
case by engaging in occasional word-play--creating more antitheses

and contradictions in the course of his argument than legitimately can be found in the topics under discussion.[5] This is done deliberately in order to ridicule the tenets of formal logic. This activity demonstrates Hegel's modernity in a less-positive light, reflecting the contemporary opposition between logicians and analytic philosophers, and those of a more diverse philosophical persuasion.

This debate is not worthy of the vocation of philosophy. We shall not dignify it further here, save to say that Hegel's involvement in this pastime further contributes to an obscure and frequently abstruse mode of expression. Indeed, one can become sufficiently frustrated with the obscurity of Hegel's exposition, so as to concur finally with the judgment of logicians and analytic philosophers: "If this be metaphysics, then no sense can be made of it!" In defense of Hegel, I can only reply that if one is willing to understand some of the reasons behind this mode of exposition, and so suffer the pain and endure with patience this labor of the negative, then one is assured of reaping those "new and surprising thought-dividends" which Professor Findlay (among others) has promised.[6]

Whitehead is by no means absolved of similar charges of obscurity and internal contradiction. But these cases of obscurity and contradiction occur less frequently and for different, and perhaps more justifiable, reasons. Indeed, careful application of Whitehead's terminology aids in the elimination of unnecessary contradiction and obscurity. Accordingly, in order to clarify certain of Hegel's positions, and in order to highlight certain points of similarity between the two positions, I have throughout the treatment of Hegel inserted such "Whiteheadian" expositions of the Hegelian doctrines as seemed particularly appropriate. In the concluding chapter of this essay, I provide both a summary of the points of similarity I have detected, as well as a discussion of the major objections to the enterprise in which I have engaged.

Section 2. On the Relation of Hegel to Whitehead

None of what precedes or follows should be taken as an attempt to argue for a direct influence of Hegel on Whitehead. Such influence is denied expressly by Whitehead himself, as our

opening quotation reveals. That Whitehead even felt called upon
to make such a dissociation of his thought from Hegelian idealism,
however, is indicative of the relationship which other contemporaries discerned between the two.

Those familiar with Hegel's thought, for example, cannot
escape the conviction when reading Whitehead's *Adventures of
Ideas* that they are encountering a work of decidedly Hegelian
character.[7] Indeed, the bulk of Whitehead's nonsystematic writings on history, culture and civilization suggest numerous comparisons with the generalized philosophy of culture which may
be derived from Hegel's writings. The comparisons which might
be advanced on such grounds, however, are easy to suggest but
difficult to define or defend with precision. In any case, the
more superficial similarities which can be detected at such
points proceed, I argue, as a result of the more basic metaphysical affinities exhibited between Whitehead and Hegel. Accordingly, it is the more difficult but decisive metaphysical
comparison which we shall wish to consider in the present essay.
In so doing, I conclude finally that, in spite of certain differences, Whitehead and Hegel represent two distinct schools
within a single tradition of process philosophy.[8]

The literature discussing specific connections between
Whitehead and Hegel is sparse. William Ernest Hocking gives a
charming account of Whitehead's growing interest in Hegelian
themes as a result of the influence of Josiah Royce and other
American Hegelians during Whitehead's tenure at Harvard University.[9] In addition to the acknowledged influence of F. H.
Bradley[10] and the unacknowledged influence of Royce and Hocking,
the name of Whitehead's colleague at Boston University, Edgar
Sheffield Brightman,[11] should be included among the list of
those who gradually persuaded Whitehead of the elements of
Hegelianism latent in his own views.

R. G. Collingwood, in his profound treatment of the philosophy of nature, suggests that the contemporary view of nature
is characterized by a recovery of a modified form of teleological explanation. This modified teleology, he suggests, replaced
the outmoded and discarded model of mechanism which had served
as the paradigm for classical physics. Collingwood dates this
transition to the modern view of nature with Hegel, and suggests

that this view is developed subsequently by Bergson, Alexander and Whitehead.[12] Errol Harris concurs with this view of the importance of "internal" teleology in contemporary science,[13] and suggests further that, despite his ignorance of this Hegelian tradition, Whitehead himself represents its most contemporary exponent.[14]

Beyond such general comments, however, very few thorough or systematic studies of this relationship have been published. Gregory Vlastos, in 1937, suggested that Whitehead and Hegel both were "dialectical" philosophers, concerned with understanding the processes of becoming. The major difference, he noted, was that Hegel's dialectic was "homogeneous": i.e., all the categories of existence were derived in terms of *Geist*. Whitehead's "heterogeneous" dialectic, by contrast, was based upon diverse categories of existence derived from "eternal objects" and "actual entities."[15]

Robert Whittemore, inspired by Collingwood and Harris, offered a number of comparisons in an article discussing "Hegel's 'Science' and Whitehead's 'Modern World'."[16] Specifically, he suggested that Whitehead's notion of process corresponded closely with Hegel's understanding of dialectic, and that both embraced panentheism. Theologian Daniel Day Williams saw further important similarities in the respective attempts by Hegel and Whitehead to develop a philosophical interpretation of Christian faith, and of religion in general.[17]

All three of these articles are brief and relatively specific. None purports to offer the kind of in-depth metaphysical treatment which is necessary to establish fully their suggestive comparisons. An excellent beginning toward a comprehensive metaphysical comparison, however, recently has been developed by Professor George L. Kline.[18] We shall have frequent occasion to refer to Kline's study during the course of the following argument. The preceding materials provide both background and justification for the present study.

Section 3. A Note on Freedom

It is imperative that I define the kind of "freedom" which we shall have occasion to consider and compare in our study. The *Oxford English Dictionary* in fact lists some fifteen different definitions of freedom as these occur in the ordinary-language usage of English-speaking peoples. These may be organized, however, into three distinct classes.

We may speak of freedom as a physical state, as freedom from physical constraints and obstructions. In quantum and classical mechanics, for example, one speaks of "degrees of freedom" in reference to the number of coordinates in a given system in which unrestrained movement is, in principle, possible. In a similar vein, an animal may be described as possessing the freedom to move unrestrained through its natural environment--unless, for example, it is caught, caged and exhibited in a zoo, in which case the animal is no longer described as free.

This last example suggests a second and related class of meanings for freedom, especially as applied to the human social condition. In this second sense of the term, physical constraints are surely involved, but are included as a subset of constraints which are social, economic, legal or political in character. Freedom as liberty is a social condition in which unreasonable constraints of these sorts on human existence and behavior by other persons, by governments, or by other socio-economic or political institutions are minimized. It is an important task in ethics and political philosophy, for example, to identify potential or actual origins of such constraints, and to clarify the point at which these cease to be reasonable and become instead "unreasonable."

It is possible to hold that the problem of freedom consists only in the discussion of this issue, and that all other descriptions of freedom are meaningless and result in "pseudo-problems." The early-American theologian Jonathan Edwards borrowed heavily upon the arguments of John Locke and David Hume in maintaining that freedom consists entirely in the empowerment of one's choices, originating from one's natural desires. If none of the constraints outlined above operate so as to inhibit an agent from the normal pursuit of his natural inclinations, such an agent may be described properly as "free."[19] This is precisely the point made by Moritz Schlick (with reference to Hume) in defense of the premise that the problem of free will is a "pseudo-problem."[20]

There is, however, a third sense or usage of the term "freedom," implying "the quality of being free from the control of fate or necessity; the power of self-determination, attributed to the will."[21] It is this usage or connotation which is implied in discussions of "freedom of the will."

The phrase "freedom of the will," however, is fraught with ambiguity. Before one properly can treat the question of whether or not the will is free, one must first establish one's usage of the term "freedom," and define what is meant by the "will." The latter is itself problematic, since for example, "the will" means something very different for Aristotle and Aquinas on one hand, and for Schopenhauer, Nietzsche and Martin Luther on the other. In the historical terminology of faculty psychology, one must decide whether or not the will is indeed distinguishable from the intellect, and if so, whether the latter tends to "dominate" the former (as most classical and medieval rationalists held), or whether in fact the opposite relation obtains (as, for example, William of Ockham, Martin Luther, Schopenhauer and Nietzsche maintained).

Furthermore, an examination of some of the historical Latin texts in which "freedom of the will" is discussed and debated reveals that, for many of the philosophers and theologians mentioned above, most frequently it is *arbitrium* ("choice" or "action") rather than *voluntas* ("will," "volition" or "desire") which actually is examined. Thus, many historical arguments purportedly favoring free will are in fact discussing only the issue of freedom of choice and action. This gives further credence to claims, such as those of Edwards and Schlick, that unrestrained action, liberty and the empowerment of choice are the sum and substance of the matter of freedom.

Use of the phrase "metaphysical freedom" avoids such ambiguities by indicating that the problem of freedom is potentially independent of any particular doctrine of the will. This term also suggests, however, that freedom (whatever it may be) is in some sense a general property of being--or even (as Satre would maintain) *constitutive* of one's existence. As we shall see, it is just such a view of freedom to which both Whitehead and Hegel subscribe.

In ascertaining just what this term might entail, it is normally assumed that metaphysical freedom is in some sense the opposite of determinism--indeed, that these represent two contradictory and mutually-exclusive concepts. Freedom (according to this view) is seen as some mysterious contra-causal force which, upon certain occasions, interferes with, suspends, or overrides the normal operation of causality in the natural world. Determinism is a rigid interpretation of causality which suggests that for every event there exist certain antecedent conditions (the "causes" or "reasons") which, when fully known, are necessary and sufficient explanations of the occurrence of that event. Philosophers who eschew metaphysics, for example, naturally hold that contra-causal freedom is a meaningless term. Thereupon they either dispense with the problem of freedom altogether, or agree with the reconciliationist position of Schlick, Edwards, Bertrand Russell and others, for whom freedom means only the personal and civil liberty requisite to the empowerment of choice and the consequent realization of one's desires.

Acceptance or rejection of this Laplacian interpretation of determinism[22]--i.e., what William James called "hard determinism"--pits necessitarians and/or believers in strict theological predestinationism against libertarian defenders of this mysterious contra-causal freedom.[23] The debate customarily is joined within the discipline of ethics, but is in fact always a metaethical or metaphysical problem. Naturalistic (i.e., non-theistic) opponents of contra-causal freedom, for example, will utilize data and theories drawn from the natural or social sciences to discount the possibility of freedom in the non-human world. They proceed to argue that the "contra-cuasal" freedom of the libertarian is epiphenomenal and wholly unsupportable. This line of argument obviously entails a whole series of un-criticized metaphysical assumptions concerning the nature of determinism and the applicability of "scientific" theories out-side the domain of science.

The libertarian is thereby forced either to recant or "do metaphysics" in order to demonstrate how contra-causal freedom can be rendered consistent with the theories of the contemporary natural and social sciences. This proves difficult, if not im-possible to accomplish, however, since such contra-causal free-dom in nature would amount to little more than randomness and indeterminism, and would fail to account for the order and structure which *are* in fact encountered in the natural world.

In between these extremes one encounters the reconciliation-ists--those whom William James called "soft determinists," such

as Schlick and Edwards--who argue that this entire debate is
irrelevant. These hold to a metaphysical view of determinism
(whether theological or naturalistic), and deny that freedom
(by which they mean "contra-causal freedom") exists. What is
significant is liberty, the lack of physical or civil restraints
towards the realization of one's desires (however these may
originate). The existence of liberty is all that is necessary
to render intelligible a doctrine of moral responsibility in
philosophical or religious ethics.

The entire range of debate, however, rests upon a fundamental misapprehension of the nature of determinism. No such doctrine of determinism as necessitarians support and libertarians
oppose is in fact derivable from contemporary scientific theory.
This "Laplacian" determinism, based as it is upon a mechanistic
interpretation of nature and of natural law, no longer is thought
to be an adequate interpretation of causality. Causality is
interpreted *statistically* in terms of an ensemble of real possibilities for a set of future events as ascertained from a
knowledge of past and present conditions. This "causal efficacy"
as understood in contemporary science is not necessarily inimical
to freedom--which, in turn, need not be restricted in its con-
ceptualization to some sort of mysterious "contra-causal" force.[24]
It is possible to articulate a doctrine of conditional, finite
or "quasi-causal" freedom which is perfectly compatible with
the current understanding of causality in physics and biology,
and which is sufficient to render intelligible a notion of moral
responsibility in ethics.

As we now shall observe, precisely such a doctrine of freedom is developed by both Whitehead and Hegel. Furthermore, the
freedom which is encountered at the level of human moral experience (which freedom is, for both philosophers, an undeniable
dimension of human experience), is *grounded* on, or "built up
from" a more generalized phenomenon which is pervasive, and in
some sense constitutive of all reality. That phenomenon, for
both philosophers, is teleological self-determination.

II.   WHITEHEAD'S CATEGORY OF CREATIVITY

> The passage of time is the journey of the world
> towards the gathering of new ideas into actual fact.
>
> (RM 159)

Section 1.   Preview of the Argument

Freedom qualifies in Whitehead's metaphysical system as one
of the "stubborn and irreducible facts" of existence. The proper
task of metaphysics is neither to question nor to justify freedom, but rather to explain its operation in a manner consistent
with all other general facts of existence.[1]

Whitehead's concept of freedom is to a large extent presupposed rather than systematically developed and defended. In
accordance with the methodology of *Process and Reality*, the concept of freedom is simply introduced and then dialectically developed: i.e., referred to successively in different contexts
of discussion with the effect that, in each such reference, the
concept is more fully and adequately elucidated.[2]

The value of Whitehead's contribution to the understanding
of freedom lies in his analysis of this concept in close dialogue
with many striking features of contemporary scientific theory.[3]
Consequently, freedom is not restricted to the phenomenon of human agency. Rather, freedom becomes in Whitehead's metaphysics
the principal ontological category defining all things which
truly exist, all *res verae*. Indeed, Whitehead's category of
creativity is the principal criterion by which what is actual
may be distinguished from what is merely abstract and derivative.[4]

This last point is most significant. Whitehead's concept
of freedom represents no suspension of, or special exemption from
other general metaphysical principles. There is no "bifurcation
of reality" into classes of entities which exhibit freedom, as
opposed to others which are subject to a strict deterministic
description. Instead, Whitehead's explanation of freedom is
grounded in an understanding of *degrees* of determinism in nature,
most especially a description of "causal efficacy" that views
the past as a necessary, but not sufficient condition for the
description of present events. This doctrine facilitates

15

explanations of the role of spontaneity in statistically-governed systems and processes, describing the novel incorporation of spontaneous events into the larger systems of growth, change and becoming within which these occur.[5] Such creative process is operant even at the most fundamental or elementary levels of being.

Whitehead does not, however, equate creativity or freedom with mere spontaneity or indeterminacy. Creativity is this *systematic reaction* to spontaneity, issuing in unique and novel occasions of experience. Insofar as this creativity involves a "subjective decision," it is proper to speak of freedom as teleological self-determination. The mechanisms of transmission and of spontaneous mutation of genetic traits in biology, for example, aid in illustrating the role of spontaneity in the world. It is the creative reaction to, and incorporation of spontaneous events by the organic systems within which they occur which produces novel developments within the evolutionary process.[6]

Whitehead sought to understand such contemporary theories within a comprehensive metaphysical framework. Like Leibniz and the Greek atomists, Whitehead sought to explain variety and change by appeal to a fundamental quantitative pluralism. Unity is discerned within diversity, however, in that all *res verae* (Whitehead's "actual entities") are subject to the same set of metaphysical principles.[7]

Thus, Whitehead's system represents a quantitative pluralism exhibiting qualitative unity. The unifying feature is that all entities which are deemed actual are individual instances of the general metaphysical feature of creativity (PR 31).

Actual entities are processes of becoming. They are "concrescences," the "growing together" into a novel unity of data inherited from the past. Thus, what is finally actual is not a "thing"--a passive, inert substance in which certain qualities are said to inhere--but a "creative process." Creativity is Whitehead's "Category of the Ultimate" (PR 31). For Whitehead, "esse est non percipi et non intelligi; sed esse est creare." His description of this process of creativity constitutes the genetic analysis of actual entities.

Section 2. The Terminology of Freedom in Whitehead's Thought

Delineating Whitehead's understanding of freedom presents linguistic difficulties. There are four classes of terms which are relevant to an understanding of freedom. Some of these are further sub-divided by systematic versus nonsystematic uses of the terms.

i) "Spontaneity" is a term which occurs predominately in *Adventures of Ideas*. By spontaneity we shall intend "chance" or "randomness" in the sense of individual events with no discernable causal antecedents. This is, in general, Whitehead's intention. His usage of the term is nonsystematic, however, and occasionally overlaps a second term, novelty.

> Sporadic spontaneity is composed of flashes mutually thwarting each other . . . In so far as the mental spontaneities of occasions do not thwart each other, but are directed to a common objective amid varying circumstances, there is life. The essence of life is the teleological introduction of novelty, with some conformation of objectives.
>
> (AI 81, 266)

In the initial "conformal" phase of concrescence of a Whiteheadian "actual entity," the entity is indeterminate with respect to the final outcome of its synthesis of data inherited from its past. As we have noted, the causal antecedents of an entity are *necessary* to explain its concrescence, but not *sufficient* to determine the outcome of its synthesis.[8]

The passage from indeterminateness to the determinateness of "satisfaction . . . marking the evaporation of all indetermination" (PR 323, 71) will be discussed at length in the following section. We note here only that Whitehead's "indeterminateness" is not to be equated with the philosophical doctrine of "indeterminism," which in certain situations asserts the operation of chance and randomness in denial of causal efficacy. Whitehead never *denies* causal efficacy. He merely analyzes and explicates every phase of its meaning. Despite the occasional ambiguity engendered by his nonsystematic use of the terms "spontaneity" and "novelty," Whitehead never attempts to found his assertion of freedom on the basis merely of randomness or spontaneity. He thus does not embrace a doctrine of "indeterminism" which, according to C. D. Broad, cannot be equated with an intelligible definition of "freedom."[9]

ii) The "decisions" effecting its self-determination constitute the salient feature of the passage of an actual occasion from "indeterminateness" to the "satisfaction" of determination (PR 68). Thus actual entities are "creative processes." More properly, they are individual manifestations of what Whitehead initially called "the general metaphysical character of activity" (SMW 255), and subsequently designated "Creativity."

> In all philosophic theory there is an ultimate which is actual in virtue of its accidents . . . In the philosophy of organism this ultimate is termed 'creativity'. . . .
> Creativity . . . is the pure notion of the [generic] activity conditioned by . . . the actual world. . . .
> (PR 10ff., 46ff.)[10]

Creativity is always a systematic term in Whitehead's metaphysics It is understood as applying solely to this subjective-teleological process of concrescence comprising the "being" of actual entities.

iii) Whitehead compares creativity with the principle of novelty. The latter term has a systematic connotation, referring to the uniqueness and "newness" of the resulting contribution of every actual entity to the world process. The "novelty" of an actual occasion represents a contribution which cannot be wholly anticipated on the basis of that actual occasion's antecedents.

> 'Creativity' is the principle of *novelty*. An actual occasion is a novel entity diverse from any entity in the many which it unifies.
> (PR 31)[11]

Novelty, as mentioned above, also carries connotations of spontaneity, randomness and indeterminacy which should be rigidly distinguished from the systematic Whiteheadian definition of the term. Whitehead himself contributes to the ambiguity by occasional lapses into incautious use of this term.[12]

iv) The final Whiteheadian term to be considered is "freedom," which must be understood in its relationships to "purpose" and "teleology." "Novelty" is a judgment of the uniqueness of the outcome of each concrescence. "Creativity" is the universal principle manifested in every concrescence. The process of concrescence itself is always purposive, involving "decisions" based upon individual subjective aims. Thus, concrescence is a teleological process.[13]

My view in the present essay is that freedom is to be understood as this process of teleological self-determination or self-causation in every actual entity. In Whitehead's words, "To be *causa sui* means that the process of concrescence is its own reason for the decision . . . by which any lure for feeling is admitted to efficiency. The freedom inherent in the universe is constituted by this element of self-causation" (PR 135).

Freedom also has wider, nonsystematic connotations in Whitehead's thought. Some of these are entailed in his more sweeping generalizations, such as "Life is a bid for freedom. . . ."[14] More correctly, according to Whitehead, life is a bid for, or entertainment of "novelty." And novelty is the *issue* or result of free decisions by actual occasions.

Such occasional ambiguities as do occur in Whiteheadian terminology need cause no great difficulty, provided they are kept in mind and utilized to qualify the implications of various expressions encountered which purport to discuss the concept of freedom. It seems evident, for example, that the wider use of the term "freedom" as cited is dependent upon (even if not identical with) the systematic definition of the term. Further, while distinctions in systematic definitions can be made, it is likewise apparent that freedom, creativity, and novelty are interdependent terms. All are associated with different phases of one microscopic process: the coming to be and the perishing of actual entities. There is, then, justification for equation and interchanging these terms in certain contexts. This set of terms (ii-iv), however, should be distinguished from the set of terms represented by "spontaneity," "chance," and "randomness" as mentioned earlier (i). The latter are included in Whitehead's understanding of freedom, to be sure. But these concepts are not the sole basis for his defense of freedom. Rather, that defense is based upon the teleological, self-creative activity of actual entities as *causa sui*.

In the following section, we shall consider Whitehead's "microscopic" analysis of the freedom of actual entities as creative processes.[15] According to Whitehead's Ontological Principle, all other relevant descriptions and explanations of the

phenomenon of freedom must be referred to the analysis of actual
entities, since these are the only "reasons" for things as they
are. In subsequent sections of this chapter, the "macroscopic"
applications of these concepts are discussed.[16]

Section 3. Whitehead's Microscopic Doctrine: The Freedom of Actual Occasions

Whitehead's metaphysical system represents a search for the
ultimate matters of fact--what Descartes earlier had termed the
res verae and Aristotle, even earlier, *ousia*. Whitehead terms
his ultimate matters of fact "actual entities," in order to avoid
etymological or historical confusion of his description with
other terms--such as "substance"--which have been used to describe
such entities.[17]

We have noted Whitehead's Ontological Principle, whereby all
experience shall be referred ultimately to, and explainable in
terms of actual entities (*vide supra* p. 16, n.7). It remains,
then, to discuss some principal features of actual entities themselves.

The most distinctive feature of actual entities is the fact
that each is an individual manifestation of the "generic activity," the fundamental metaphysical principle of creativity.
Whitehead argues that an entity is actual if, and only if, it
is self-creative, functioning in respect to its own self-determination. In Whitehead's words: "An actuality is self-realizing
and whatever is self-realizing is an actuality" (PR 340).

Actual entities are not to be understood as passive "things,"
but as events or processes, whereby many elements of the past are
synthesized into a unique occasion of experience. In *Process and
Reality*, Whitehead terms this process a "concrescence"--a growing
together of many data acquiring "an individual unity in a determinate relegation of each item of the 'many' to its subordination
in the constitution of the novel 'one'" (PR 321). In *Adventures
of Ideas*, however, Whitehead criticizes his choice of the term
"concrescence" as a description of this process, in that "it
fails to suggest the creative novelty involved" (AI 303).

Whitehead is not entirely fair to himself in this criticism.
While it is true that "concrescence" etymologically implies a
passive "growing together" of inherited data, Whitehead also

takes pains to point out that actual entities are always to be
understood as creative, self-determining entities. In Spinoza's
phrase, actual entites are *causa sui*.

> An actual entity is at once the product of the
> efficient past, and is also, in Spinoza's phrase,
> *causa sui*. Every philosophy recognizes, in some form
> or other, this factor of self-causation in what it
> takes to be ultimate actual fact.[18]

Two clarifying remarks are in order at this point. First,
Whitehead's specific reference to Spinoza is most intriguing.
Spinoza is frequently described as a determinist because, in his
system, human beings were not considered "free" in the sense of
causa sui. Only the one underlying "substance," identified as
God, is in fact *causa sui*.

Whitehead shares Spinoza's conviction that the "universe"
(in order to merit that title) must exhibit, or be explicable in
terms of one unifying principle. But for Whitehead, that "principle" is not a simple, underlying substance, varying modes of
which account for all facts of experience. Instead, the unifying
principle is the generic activity or process of creativity, the
"universal of universals characterizing [all] ultimate matter[s]
of fact" (PR 31). Thus for Whitehead, *all* actual entites (and
not merely God alone) are instances of creativity, in that all
are describable as *causa sui*.

Secondly, in describing all actual entities in terms of
their activity of self-determination, Whitehead is clearly moving
toward a doctrine which would confirm the thesis of libertarians
that freedom is a real phenomenon. Yet important differences
should be noted. There is no attempt by Whitehead to dismiss
the role of external causal antecedents in the final determination
of the concrescence of actual entities, or otherwise to establish
a "contra-causal" freedom. Furthermore, Whitehead is not limiting
himself to human experience in contrast to other, nonhuman modes
of existence. Rather, his is a description of self-causation as
both characteristic and constitutive of the most elementary or
primary facets of being. According to his Ontological Principle,
human freedom must characterize a special case derived from an
understanding of the freedom of actual entities.

Whitehead does not argue for a doctrine of creativity which
could be interpreted as "contra-causal freedom." Neither does

he embrace the other extreme of a rigid, deterministic interpretation of causality which denies efficacy to any explanation of events in terms of freedom. For Whitehead, a deterministic treatment of causality is not possible because future states depend in part upon the creative action--the "decisions"--of present entities. The significant element of Whitehead's doctrine of creativity is, then, that it is "quasi-causal." Causal antecedents are necessary for the understanding of the process of concrescence in the present. They provide the data--the "decided conditions"--necessary for that concrescence. But the data alone, while they thus condition the possibilities open for that concrescence, are not sufficient finally to determine its final outcome. As Whitehead remarks: "it is to be noticed that 'decided' conditions are never such as to banish freedom. They only qualify it. There is always contingency left open for immediate decision" (PR 435).

The aspect of the conditioning of creativity by inherited data is vitally important. It is this dimension which prevents Whitehead's theory from being appropriated (or merely dismissed) as an apology for a theory of contra-causal freedom. Creativity is "bounded" by the past. Certain ranges of possibilities are open to an actual occasion by reason of its past, while certain other "abstract" or "ideal" possibilities may not, in fact, be relevant to the activity of *that particular* actual entity. But *which* of the ensemble of possibilities in principle open to an actual occasion finally is *actualized by* that entity is dependent upon its own creative activity as *causa sui*.

This is the full implication of Whitehead's "Ninth Categoreal Obligation of Freedom and Determinism," in which he indicates that the process of concrescence is "internally determined and externally free" (PR 41). This statement can be fully interpreted in terms of our present discussion. The issue of fixing the standpoint of observation from which the differentiation of "external and internal" is to be made, however, is rather complex.

Viewed externally, the only data available for the determination of an actual occasion are the circumstances given in its immediate past history. According to a strict deterministic interpretation of causality, the resultant actual entity is the "effect" of that immediate past which is its "cause." The resultant actual entity should be fully accounted for, or "explained," retrospectively in terms of its causal antecedents. Indeed, if a rigid deterministic causality obtains, the actual entity should be subject to complete *a priori* prediction of its outcome as well. But it is Whitehead's assertion, repeatedly stressed, that every actual entity is a *novel* synthesis, never accounted for wholly in terms of its antecedents.

By the Ontological Principle, the "reasons" given for any actual entity must ultimately refer to other actual entities. If the inherited data are not sufficient reasons for a given actual entity, then the only other explanation for its being what it is, is itself. In Whitehead's words: "every actual entity--since it is what it is--is finally its own reason for what it becomes" (PR 71). Herein lies Whitehead's basis for equating creativity (or, at least the ultimate issue of creative process) with "novelty," and for describing actual entites as "externally free."

Viewed internally, the process of concrescence which is an actual occasion involves three phases (not temporally distinct, or "coordinately divisible"). During the first, or "conformal" phase, circumstances of the past are received, and are either "positively prehended" ("felt") or "negatively prehended" (omitted or rejected as potential data for the concrescence).[19] This process involves a subjective "decision" on the part of the occasion itself.

In addition, in its genetically subsequent phases, the occasion is able conceptually to "prehend" (or "feel") so-called "eternal objects"--forms of definiteness unconditioned by any particular, past finite realization in actual fact. The actual occasion utilizes these prehensions as further ingredients in the final synthesis.[20] Such pure conceptual prehensions are made possible by the actual occasion's prior experience of those "universals" or "forms of definiteness" in their various finite actualizations in the actual entities of that occasion's own unique past. The passage from the initial "conformal" phase to this subsequent "conceptual" phase of concrescence involves the direct conceptual entertainment of pure possibilities irrespective of their past actualization. This creates, in principle, a situation for the envisagement of totally new and unique experiences by the present actual occasion. As Donald Sherburne notes, "with the emergence of conceptual prehensions there is . . . the possibility of liberation from the tyranny of the given."[21]

Whether in fact such liberation is achieved is finally dependent upon whether the given occasion merely reiterates patterns of experience previously actualized in other individual occasions in its past (in which case, creativity and resultant novelty are minimal, as in the ongoing experience of a stone), or instead undergoes what Whitehead termed "conceptual reversion." In the latter instance, totally new actualizations of novel forms are achieved in accordance with the occasion's "subjective aim" toward a maximization of the intensity and harmony of its own experience.[22]

Whatever the final outcome, this general pattern of concrescence obtains with respect to every actual entity, from God to the "most trivial puff of existence in empty space." And every phase exhibits some element of subjectivity, and of self-determination. Thus Whitehead designates every actual entity as "internally determined."

An actual entity is, then, more than merely the sum of its inherited data. It involves, in addition, some element of subjectivity and of agency--evidently affecting "decisions" and entertaining "aims," goals and purposes. Without this element of subjectivity inherent in every actual entity, argues Whitehead, we would be faced with the alternative of a "static monistic universe," devoid of real change, novelty, or becoming (PR 72). Since the facts of our common experience and history discount such an observation, it must be that some element of subjectivity, however faint and primitive, is constitutive of the very nature of reality. Such an assumption is required in order to explain creativity at all levels of being, and to account for the gradual evolutionary development of complex forms of subjectivity evident in the more complex "regnant societies" of actual occasion--such as in animals and humans.[23]

Some selection or "decision" must be involved in the process of concrescence, establishing at least a graded relevance of importance among the inherited physical data for the concrescence. And in some actual occasions, such "decisions" must govern the conceptual prehensions of the occasion's mental pole, issuing in novel finite actualizations of new forms of definiteness. To explain this necessary element of subjectivity, Whitehead postulates a "subjective aim," a principle of organization or purpose, unique to each actual occasion. Decisions are effected with reference to the subjective aim regarding the inclusion or exclusion of the welter of physical and conceptual prehensions in the process of synthesis.

> The concrescence is dominated by a subjective aim, which essentially concerns the creature as a final superject. This subjective aim is this subject itself determining its own self-creation . . . the 'subjective aim' at 'satisfaction' constitutes the final cause, or lure, whereby there is determinate concrescence.
>
> (PR 108, 134)

In this element of subjectivity at the heart of all things lies the key to the Whiteheadian doctrine of freedom. I conclude that freedom in Whitehead's metaphysics, founded upon the subjective aim of each occasion as to what it shall become, amounts to a creative process of teleological self-determination. It is essential, therefore, to understand fully the origin and properties of the Whiteheadian "subjective aim." Specifically: (i) where does the subjective aim originate; (ii) where does it "reside" in the process of concrescence; and (iii) how does it function during that synthesis to guide the occasion toward its ultimate issue in novel experience?

(i) Whitehead himself gives a straightforward response to the first question. The subjective aim of each occasion is derived from the ideal envisagement of possibilities for the world in God's "Primordial Nature."

> The initial stage of [the subjective aim] is an endowment which the subject inherits from the inevitable ordering of things, conceptually realized in the nature of God . . . Thus, the initial stage of the aim is rooted in the nature of God. . . .
>
> (PR 373)

This result followed from Whitehead's discovery, in his earlier metaphysical synthesis of "organic mechanism," that creativity alone was not a sufficient principle to account for the actual world. Unbounded possibility could not explain how or why particular possibilities had in fact been actualized as the present world at the expense of other, "equally possible" worlds.[24] Actuality, Whitehead discovered, required some

limitation, some principle of ideal order imposed upon the "unbounded freedom within which the actual is a unique categorical
determination" (SMW 253).

Creativity accordingly is "conditioned" by "a general fact
of systematic mutual relatedness which is inherent in the character of possibility." That is, different possibilities, as well
as the specific realization of conceptual possibilities ("eternal
objects") in actual entities, are not isolated and abstract, but
exhibit mutual or reciprocal relations with one another. Creativity is further conditioned by an ultimate, ideal ordering of
all possibilities in terms of this mutual relatedness. This
ideal ordering allows a valuation of different possibilities,
determining *which* possibilities are most appropriate or more
desirable for actualization. This ultimate "antecedent limitation among values, introducing contraries, grades and oppositions"
Whitehead called the primordial "principle of limitation" and
identified as "God . . . the Principle of Concretion."[25]

By locating the ground of finite freedom ultimately in the
nature of God, Whitehead leaves himself open to numerous charges
--such as "radical finalism" (according to which God *alone* is
the final determination of the outcome of all process), and even
the charge that Whitehead has produced a *deus ex machina* to explain certain inconsistencies in his general metaphysical outlook. We might wonder further whether Whitehead, like Spinoza,
seems to have removed the sphere of ultimately free, creative
activity from the creatures of the actual world and located it
solely in the divine nature.[26] We shall give attention to these
objections to Whitehead's doctrine of freedom presently.

For the moment, however, we shall lay aside the question of
the grounding of subjective aims and of freedom in God's own
being. The individual subjective aim originates initially as
the subjective form of an initial hybrid prehension, entertained
by the nascent mental pole of every actual occasion, of the most
ideal-possible order for the universe.[27]

(ii) The question of "where" the subjective aim may be said
to "reside" in an actual occasion involves a fundamental Whiteheadian metaphysical principle. There is no underlying "stuff"
or substance *in* which qualities "inhere," or *to* which certain
events happen. It is Whitehead's "principle of process" that

an actual entity is a "concrescence of prehensions" whose "'being' is *constituted* by its 'becoming'."[28] There is, according to Whitehead, no underlying "subject" of change or becoming, remaining itself unchanged and self-identical throughout the process of becoming. Instead, the "subject" which is an actual entity is understood as "emerging" in the process of its own becoming. It cannot be understood apart from its process of development.[29] Indeed, the very term "subject" as a description of an actual occasion is found to be inadequate.

> It is fundamental to the metaphysical doctrine of the philosophy of organism, that the notion of an actual entity as the unchanging subject of change is completely abandoned. An actual entity is at once the subject experiencing and the superject of its experiences.
>
> (PR 43)

The subjective aim thus does not reside in the "subject." Rather, the subject emerges from the activity of deciding, according to the pattern of its subjective aim, for or against inclusion of various inherited data in the novel synthesis. Further, as we have observed, this subjective aim—this purpose or principle of organization for the actual occasion—is *conceptual* in nature. It is a hybrid physical prehension by that occasion of some independent, ideal order or pattern. It thus cannot be among the data, nor in any sense *derived* from the data physically prehended from the past. These data can impart no *basis* for a decision, selection or synthesis from among themselves —not, at least, without violating Whitehead's Ontological Principle.[30]

The subjective aim is logically and temporally prior to any concrescence of data, since it is *with* that aim that the concrescence initiates. The subjective aim is the "central kernel" or the "catalyst" of the process of concrescence, around which the physical and conceptual data coalesce. That process of coalescence constitutes the becoming of the actual entity. Thus, the subjective aim resides in no part of the actual occasion. Rather, the subjective aim belongs to the concrescence as a whole, and the occasion has its being in the process of becoming patterned after its subjective aim.

At this point we encounter difficulties in reconciling Whitehead's theory of finite freedom with his understanding of

God. The initial conformal phase of an actual occasion apparently consists in a "convergence" of inherited data from the past around an initial subjective aim derived from God's own primordial envisagement of ideal possibilities for the world. As Whitehead himself describes it:

> Each temporal entity . . . derives from God its basic conceptual aim, relevant to its actual world, yet with *indeterminations* awaiting its own decisions. This subjective aim, *in its successive modifications*, remains the unifying factor governing the successive phases of interplay between physical and conceptual feelings . . . Thus the primary phase [of concrescence of an actual occasion] is a *hybrid physical feeling* of God, in respect to God's conceptual [ordering of possibilities] which is immediately relevant to the universe 'given' [i.e., the data 'inherited'] for that concrescence . . . In this sense, God can be termed the creator of each temporal actual entity.
>
> (PR 343; emphases added)

This explanation is open to several interpretations. First, God can be understood as somehow providing or "implanting" initial aims in each actual occasion, thereby initiating the process of concrescence. Actual entities are thus initially *passive*, inheriting data from the past, and deriving a subjective aim as a result of God's direct intervention--becoming active, self-creative concrescences only consequent upon this stage of total passivity. This would appear to replace the determinism of mechanism and efficient causality with the determinism of "radical finalism."[31]

The image of God as initiating the concrescence of each and every actual occasion by the direct activity of implanting "initial subjective aims" in each, does indeed seem to suggest difficulties for our understanding of freedom. Ironically, the image is, in certain respects, reminiscent of the variety of deism held by Newton.[32] More significantly, this view threatens to compromise the spirit of autonomy and creative activity which Whitehead maintains as generic to *every* actual entity. For these reasons, I harbor serious reservations concerning the adequacy of this interpretation.[33]

In that case, one possible alternative is that, while initially "conformal," the actual occasion is *not* entirely passive. Instead, *it actively prehends* (or "feels") the ideal envisagement of possibilities in God's Primordial Nature, resulting in the individual subjective aim governing that concrescence.

According to this neo-Whiteheadian analysis, the actual occasion, while in its initial conformal phase of concrescence,
would nonetheless be portrayed *not* as entirely passive, but as
exhibiting initially at least the faintest glimmer of the other
portion of its dipolar nature--its mental or conceptual pole
(cf. PR 165). As an individual instance of the generic activity
of creativity, every actual occasion would begin, *not* passively,
but *actively*, as instinctive "grasping" both for data and for
design. The initial subjective aim in the actual occasion's
conformal phase, in any case, is still a "hybrid physical feeling
of God." According to my interpretation, "Creativity" (Whitehead's "Category of the Ultimate") itself serves as a sufficient
"reason" or explanation for concrescence. Actual occasions do
not "pop into the actual world" from nowhere. Rather, each is
an "emergent subject," a finite particularization of the generic
activity of the universe. Concrescence initiates in every epochal
duration during which there are data to be unified--during which
there is a possibility for "the many" to "become one" and be
"increased by one" (PR 32).

This alternative interpretation is not without its own problems. In particular, it is necessary to specify that this modification constitutes no return to a doctrine of subject as underlying ·substance, antecedent to the process itself. Rather, all
I have suggested is a doctrine of the *active* self-actualization
of the "subject-superject": data and ideal pattern constitute
the initial phase of the one, whole actual entity and (as Whitehead remarks) presuppose one another. As John Cobb suggests:

> The coming into being of the ingredients presup-
> poses the *self-actualization* of the *whole synthesis*
> just as much as the self-actualization of the whole
> presupposes the coming into being of the ingredients.
> Thus, the *whole* is *active* in the becoming of its parts.
> Whole and parts *come into being together*. The whole
> is equally the subject of the one act of becoming and
> the superject or outcome.[34]

Indeed, Whitehead himself provides grounds for such a modification of his doctrine, suggesting that the term "superject"
must also convey a purposive aspect of actual entities, emphasizing the embodiment of their subjective aims as final causes:

> The philosophy of organism *presupposes* a *datum*
> which is *met* with feelings, and progressively attains
> the unity of a subject. But with this doctrine,

> "superject" would be a better term than "subject". .
> . .The subject-superject is the *purpose* of the process
> originating the feelings. The feelings are inseparable
> from the end at which they aim . . . as their final
> cause . . . This final cause is an inherent element
> in the feeling, constituting the unity of that feeling.
> An actual entity feels as it does feel in order to be
> the actual entity which it is. In this way, an actual
> entity satisfies Spinoza's definition of substance:
> it is *causa sui*.   (PR 234, 339; emphases added)

This suggestive ambiguity in Whitehead's doctrine of the
"superject," involving its active as well as its objective dimension, to my knowledge has not been engaged by Whiteheadians.[35]
For admittedly Whitehead's central intention was, through the
"principle of relativity," to overcome the subject-object dichotomy. The doctrine of the "subject-superject" primarily stresses
that what is a subject with respect to its own experience subsequently functions as an object in the experience of other subjects, for "it belongs to the nature of a 'being' that it is a
potential for every 'becoming'" (PR 33).[36] The actual entity as
superject functions as the potential for every subsequent becoming, as the object for every new subject:

> An actual entity is to be conceived both as a
> subject presiding over its own immediacy of becoming,
> and a superject which is the atomic creature exer-
> cising its function of objective immortality . . .
> To be actual must mean that all actual things are
> alike objects, enjoying objective immortality in
> fashioning creative actions [i.e., serving as ob-
> jective data for new concrescences]; and that all
> actual things are subjects, each prehending the
> universe from which it arises.
>   (PR 71, 89; cf. PR 374)

According to Whitehead's own arguments, however, the term
"subject" is *passive*. The "subject" does *not* "preside over its
own immediacy of becoming." Rather, it *emerges* during the course
of such a process (PR 135ff., 228, 234). The active, purposive
character of an actual occasion presiding over its own becoming
is inadequately conveyed by speaking of its "subjective" (i.e.,
emergent, passive) character. Some active, transcendental perspective is precisely what is required--and Whitehead's term
"superject" could, in this secondary connotation, adequately
convey this meaning.

(iii) Utilizing my nuance of the "superjective nature of the mental pole" to modify Whitehead's overall doctrine of the actual entity, it is possible finally to settle the issues of the locus and function of the subjective aim in the actual occasion. According to this alternate formulation, we first hold fast to Whitehead's assertion that the active-passive and subjective-objective functions of an actual entity cannot be separated. All apply to the same entity, viewed from different temporal frames of reference. "Superject" expresses an element of the active, transcendental, purposive quality of actual entities at their inception. "Subject" expresses the emergence of a novel synthesis of data which results in the satisfaction of the creative urge, subsequently "perishing" and passing into objective immortality to function as a potential datum for every new concrescence. In this stage of its "post-becoming" the actual entity is more helpfully viewed as a "concretum" than as a "superject."[37]

It is the actual entity as "subject-superject" (i.e., in its integrated, inseparable dipolar mode) which physically "feels" data from the past as well as entertaining a hybrid "feeling" of God's general primordial envisagement of ideal order for the universe. The subjective form of this latter prehension constitutes the "subjective aim" for that individual occasion. The subjective aim is thus a characteristic of the actual entity's mental pole, initially but nascently active, as opposed to its passive character as emergent subject-in-process. In this sense, the organizing influence characterizing the process of concrescence arises in and with the process itself, as a result of its own nascent conceptuality or subjectivity. The organizing influence thus is throughout immanent in and conditioned by the process of concrescence, yet it remains identifiable throughout the process of change and becoming.[38] In this sense the "subject-superject" is the final source of decisions involving the graded relevance of inherited data, as well as itself initiating the lure and final cause of the synthesis through its active hybrid prehension of the Principle of Concretion. In this manner the actual occasion functions with respect to its own internal self-determination. The finite freedom of real subjective agency is thereby guaranteed.

A final note, prior to summarizing and concluding this section, is required regarding Whitehead's understanding of "interna[
relatedness" in relation to his concept of finite or "quasi-causa[
freedom. Two recent introductions to the theological aspects of
process thought stress that Whitehead's philosophy is distinguished, first, by its stress on the rejection of "static actuality" in favor of the doctrine that "all actuality is process."
This doctrine, however, is common to other "process philosophies,
such as those of "Hegel, Bergson and Dewey." Whitehead's theory
is "unique" because of its additional stress on the reciprocal
relatedness and interdependence of all things--prompting Whitehead's own designation of his metaphysics as a "philosophy of
organism."[39]

For the present, we acknowledge that Whitehead's commitment
to the reciprocal relatedness of all actual entities is as important as his commitment to pluralism and process.[40] Mutual or
reciprocal relatedness among actual entities and among eternal
objects was mentioned briefly as one of the factors conditioning
creativity (*vide supra*, pp. 46ff.). The question is, does Whitehead's stress on mutual relatedness compromise the autonomy and
hence the freedom of actual entities?

I have avoided using the qualifying term "internal" to describe Whitehead's doctrine of reciprocal relatedness and the
interdependence of all reality. Complete *internal* relatedness
among actual entities might well undercut Whitehead's commitment
to pluralism, as William Alston has critically remarked. Since
all actual entities would in some sense require one another for
their own existence, he argues, it seems logically contradictory
to affirm simultaneously the relative autonomy and freedom of
the individual actual entities.[41] Moreover, complete internal
relatedness among "eternal objects" likewise would compromise
freedom. Apparently the novel actualization of any new "pure
possibility" in the conceptual phase of an actual occasion would
require, in some sense, the actualization of *all* possibilities,
should this interpretation of internal relatedness obtain.[42]

The basic category describing reciprocal relatedness in
Process and Reality is that of "prehension" or "feeling" (positive prehension). Actual entities prehend one another as objective "physical" data. Additionally, in their conceptual phase,

many actual occasions prehend one or more eternal objects as well. In this sense they are mutually related. Eternal objects are also "internally related" in terms of their "relational essences" (SMW 227ff.). For example, a number of different abstract colors (as Sherburne notes) might bear the same "relational essence" to a certain abstract geometrical form in which they might, in principle, be actualized. Obviously, such "relational essences," as Whitehead himself observes (SMW 237), cannot involve the *individual* essences of the different eternal objects (what they are in and for themselves). For, as in the preceding example, the same relational essence obviously can apply to a number of different eternal objects.[43]

As Hartshorne and, more recently, Lewis Ford have noted, the key to understanding these categories of mutual relatedness lies in the fact that they are asymmetrical.[44] Hence my hesitancy to describe Whitehead's variation of reciprocal relatedness as "internal." Relations among actual entities and eternal objects are internal to some terms (the actual occasions) and external with respect to others (the eternal objects). That is, Whitehead's is a doctrine of asymmetrical mutual relatedness.

Temporally simultaneous actual occasions, of course, cannot prehend one another (AI 251, 255). A given actual occasion prehends only actual entities in its own past. Since the latter, as "objective data" or "concreta" are no longer actual, the resultant relations are *internal* with respect to the concrescence, and *external* to the non-temporal, abstract "forms."[45] Also, as Ford points out, eternal objects are internally related to their own relational essences (their own possibilities for finite actualization), but the relational essences are only *externally* related to any specific eternal object (to the actualization of any *specific* quality in the general relation they describe). Thus:

> The virtue of external relatedness is precisely that the existence of one entity does not entail the existence of another. This is the freedom of the universe: the past does not entail the present, although the present entails the past out of which it grows. The relation between past and present is external with respect to the past, but internal with respect to the present. This doctrine of asymmetrical relatedness, internal to one term but external to the other, preserves Whitehead's . . . commitment to pluralism and freedom. . . .[46]

The point of this extended digression has been to suggest
that it was Whitehead's peculiar genius to demonstrate how a
doctrine of metaphysical holism stressing interdependence and
reciprocal relatedness, could be developed without sacrificing
freedom, pluralism, and a relative individuality for every actual
entity in the system. Whitehead's doctrine of "asymmetrical relatedness" thus gives us holism without determinism (see Ch. IV
below).

The concept of freedom in Whitehead's metaphysics is closely
aligned with the concepts of creativity, novelty and self-determination, involving a description of actual entities as *causa
sui*. "Freedom" for Whitehead represents a subjective decision
(or co-ordinated set of decisions) by each actual occasion pertaining to the relative importance of its inherited objective
data in determining precisely what it shall become. As Whitehead
remarks:

> [An actual] occasion arises as an effect facing
> its past and ends as a cause facing its future. In
> between there lies the teleology of the universe.
>
> (AI 249)

The kind of freedom here adumbrated is not merely the random
variation of chance and spontaneity. It is, in fact, the mid-
point between strict deterministic causality and a radical contra-
causal theory. The concept of freedom in Whitehead's thought is
defined by the purposive agency of the actual entity with respect
to its unique subjective aim. Freedom consists, for Whitehead,
in teleological self-determination of the discrete "microscopic"
organic entities. This final determination of the actual entity
is achieved by reference to a purpose, goal, or organizing principle. The principle is immanent in the process of concrescence
itself, and governs how the concrescence shall be carried out in
terms of the desire or expectation of that actual occasion as to
what it shall become. As Whitehead comments, the decisions effected with regard to this final determination are in every case
"the reaction of the unity of the whole to its own internal determination" (PR 41).

The "free decisions" of actual occasions governing their
own concrescence do not proceed independently of external factors
(as would be the case were Whitehead advocating freedom of the

contra-causal variety). Nor does the synthesis consist of chance, random combinations of the data without regard for their importance or relevance to the specific synthesis in question. Rather, the data are from the outset assimilated in the process of concrescence according to an initial pattern, purpose, intention or structure immanent within the totality of the given actual occasion of which each inherited datum becomes a part. That pattern or purpose alone is "responsible" for the final outcome of the synthesis, and is unique to each actual occasion (cf. PR 339).

This understanding of freedom does not exclude the alternative notion of novelty as merely random, chance variation (the "spontaneity" which one observes in genetics and statistical physics, for example). Rather, such chance occurrences as result from spontaneity are assimilated into the larger structure or system within which they occur according to the pattern of the structure or its organizing principle. As Whitehead comments: "The whole determines what it wills to be, and thereby adjusts the relative importance of its own inherent flashes of spontaneity" (AI 59). Thus chance and spontaneity constitute but one dimension of the larger concept of freedom--albeit a very crucial one, which functions to impart newness and novelty into established systems and structures.

Because "freedom" includes this dimension of arbitrariness, it is not always beneficent. Randomness may indeed serve as a principle source of evil, tragedy and suffering. It likewise may be the source of unanticipated joy. But it is important to stress that random events do not occur, for good or ill, apart from the reaction, adjustment and assimilation of these as novel data by the larger system within which they come to be. This analysis precisely parallels that of modern genetics and elementary-particle physics. Both of these describe the manner in which random events within systems and structures in time may come to modify, and even radically to change the function of the systems in which they occur--not merely by their chance occurrence itself, but as a result of the adjustments made by their larger system to accomodate the influence of their spontaneous existence.

Section 4. Objections to Whitehead's Doctrine

So central does the concept of freedom appear for Whitehead that it is surprising to encounter the objection that his metaphysics amounts to a *denial* of the efficacy of freedom. Such a sustained objection has surfaced, however, and is worth examining. It capitalizes on at least two weaknesses in Whitehead's position already noted in passing: *viz.*, (1) the troublesome aspects of the role of God in the process of concrescence, with respect to the imminent danger of lapsing into a radical finalism; and (2) the Whiteheadian doctrine of the "superject" with respect to the "subjective aim" and the real subjective agency of each actual occasion.

Edward Pols[47] argues that: (i) Whitehead is ambiguous regarding the possibility of successive modifications of the "initial aim" as received from God; and (ii) more significantly, no intelligible meaning can be attached to Whitehead's notion of the "self-causation" of actual entities; and finally (iii) "creativity," consisting of a "flux that issues in a determinate togetherness of eternal objects"[48] implies that eternal objects themselves ultimately determine passively (by their "participation") the internal constitutions of every actual entity. Pols concludes with a charge of Platonism against Whitehead, arguing that it is finally *not* the activity of the world, but rather the constitution of "eternal Forms" which in fact conditions the world. In this sense, Pols concludes, freedom is denied in Whitehead's system.[49]

(i) The issue of the possible non-modifiability of the initial aim suggests severe difficulties. Pols implies (and I would agree) that Whitehead frequently is ambiguous--occasionally to the point of carelessness--regarding the language utilized to analyze this feature of the subjective aim.[50] Suppose, Pols argues, that the initial aim is derived from God and is not modifiable, but constant throughout the process of becoming. Then it would appear, as we noted earlier (*supra*, pp. 50-52), that Whitehead is faced with a problem of radical finalism, whereby God (or, rather, God's activity) alone determines the final outcome of all process.

Even allowing for a certain unfortunate ambiguity in Whitehead's own exposition of this issue, Pols' objections may be

overcome in terms of the argument I have pursued to this point.
I have advanced the case that Whitehead's is a teleological version of freedom. In that case, however, we must demand that the
subjective aim (the "locus of purpose") be able to undergo successive modifications during the concrescence, as Whitehead himself seems to suggest (e.g., PR 343). That is, the subjective
aim must truly be immanent in, and at least in part generated by
the process of becoming itself. In order to qualify as "teleological" the subjective aim cannot in any sense be independent
of the process it enables. Were the subjective aim both exter-
nally-given and unmodifiable throughout the process of concrescence, we would be faced with a long-outmoded, trivial and discredited version of teleological explanation not in accordance
with present theory. According to the contemporary understanding
of teleological explanation, which both Collingwood and Errol
Harris equate with the development of the contemporary scientific
worldview (cf. Ch. I, pp. 8ff. above), a teleological process,
properly speaking, is "a process in which the outcome is all
along immanent and potential, [one] through which the final
state is being generated, or is generating itself."[51] Therefore,
regardless of any confusion in his exposition or failure on
Whitehead's part to clarify and rigorously demonstrate this
point, it simply *must* be the case that the subjective aim *is*
subject to modification during the concrescence. Pols admits
himself that Whitehead is emphatic on the point that the subjective aim must undergo several modifications in the course of
concrescence, and waives his initial objection.[52]

(ii) Pols' central contention is that Whitehead is confused
regarding his support for the *self*-causation of every actual
entity. Pols discerns two meanings of this term: (1) self-
causation is the reaction or interaction of *determinate* elements
of the concrescence (physical feelings, the subjective aim, etc.),
in which case the actual entity is merely the sum of its components; or else self-causation refers to (2) some "active power
indeterminate as to its exercise, capable of choosing arbitrarily
among the entities" to be synthesized. Pols finds these two
meanings in conflict, and suspects Whitehead of opting in fact
for a third, completely *causal* description (i.e., one which does
not admit of real subjective agency), by his repeated stress on

the ongoing influence in the future of the "superject" (the
"concretum," the objective *outcome* of the synthesis). This influence must be had at the expense of the factor of real subjective agency in the concrescing "subjects" themselves.[53]

One especially relevant passage from Whitehead, apparently
supporting the description (2) of self-causation as some mysterious "active power," states:

> The doctrine of the philosophy of organism is
> that, however far the sphere of *efficient causation*
> be pushed in the determination of components of a
> concrescence--its data, its emotions, its apprecia-
> tions, *its purposes, its phases of subjective aim--*
> *beyond* the determination of these components there
> always remains the *final reaction* of the *self-crea-*
> *tive unity of the universe.* This final reaction
> completes the self-creative act by putting the de-
> cisive stamp of *creative emphasis* upon the *determi-*
> *nation* of *efficient cause.*
>
>   (PR 75; emphases added)

I have emphasized here the phrases which outline the tension between efficient causality and creativity.

This passage, at very least, justifies Pols' frustration
with Whitehead's occasionally careless or ambiguous use of his
own systematic terminology, against which we cautioned in Section
2 above.[54]   I feel, however, that Pols himself has been seriously
misled by such language from Whitehead's central--and for the
most part, clear--exposition of the meaning of freedom.

The passage quoted above suggests that purpose and subjective aim are among the factors of efficient cause, and that
(as Pols puts it) there is some further, mysterious active power
to which freedom must be attributed in each actual entity. This,
of course, is not the case, Whitehead's own description notwithstanding. We have clearly seen that purpose and subjective aim
are *not* among the factors of efficient cause, but are the unique
property of, and indeed are the *source* of the real subjective
agency of every actual entity. The occasion's own purpose in
synthesizing the "factors of efficient cause" are what comprises
its finite freedom.[55] There exists no source of subjective
agency *other* than the subjective aim, which is fully sufficient
to account for freedom. Indeed, that freedom is "finite" only
because the individual subjective aim itself is a finite (yet
entirely unique and modifiable) derivative of the primordial
Principle of Concretion.

It is thus true that Whitehead upon occasion utilizes confusing language to describe self-causation. But his theory, when properly exegeted, is not in the least ambiguous. Pols' attempts to dismiss it finally do not obtain.

Lewis Ford suggests that such ambiguity as we have here encountered may be occasioned by Whitehead's "shift of perspective" associated with his principle of relativity.[56] From an *internal* point of view, determinateness of outcome is achieved by means of the creative process of concrescence and integration (subjectivity), whereas from an *external* perspective of the completed actual entity as "superject" (objective "concretum"), an analysis of the process of its becoming appears as a growing together of all the components--what Pols calls (p. 114) a "mixture of radical finalism and radical mechanism" (i.e., involving what I have described as a parallel to Newtonian deism; *vide supra*, p. 28, n.32). It is important to remember that such a deterministic analysis of causality may only be carried out retrospectively-- no prior prediction of the outcome of concrescence is possible, since that final "superjective" determination is a consequence of the actual occasion's own agency with respect to its subjective aim. As Ford notes:

> Freedom is precisely the subjective experience
> of this interplay of physical and conceptual feelings.
> In a free decision, a given multiplicity of factors
> is reduced to determinateness by the adjustment of
> these factors to one another.[57]

(iii) This discussion, I feel, disallows Pols' final objection to Whitehead, that, since "creativity" cannot provide for active agency and power in actual entities, then eternal objects in their role as pure potentials for the ingression of any and all actual occasions must finally be the only agency remaining to account for actuality. Creativity is *not* merely the "determinate togetherness of eternal objects," as Pols suggests in his book. The latter phrase describes in fact a retrospective analysis of the issue or result of the creative process from the standpoint of the "superject" ("concretum"). Creativity, however, applies exclusively to the process of teleological self-determination in the present--a process involving subjective "decisions" with respect to the actual occasion's subjective aim. Thus, there is no need to resort to eternal objects to

account for real subjective agency, involving an "agent who is
both actor and outcome,"[58] necessary for an understanding of
freedom.

Pols' most valuable criticism occurred after the publication
of his book. Beyond the questions there raised, he later indicates that even if Whitehead *has* produced a successful explanation
of self-determination with respect to actual entities, then:
(1) it is still very difficult to give a *concrete example* of an
actual entity; or (2) to describe how its freedom can generate
a successful doctrine of *human* freedom.[59]

Whitehead himself is once again the source of much frustration in this regard. He does indicate by implication how a human
person might be understood as a highly complex structure of living
and non-living nexūs and societies (especially "structured societies") of actual entities. Whitehead frequently leaves the impression, however, that freedom and creativity as described for
actual entities somehow "carry over" by analogy to "higher grades
of experience" (cf., for example, PR 339, 74).

Whitehead's doctrine obviously provides grounds for a truly
thorough doctrine of human freedom, agency and responsibility.
There remain certain difficulties, however, especially regarding
an adequate definition of the "person." The refinement of a
Whiteheadian doctrine of *human* freedom has been the focus of
much recent scholarship, the results of which we shall now briefly
consider.

Section 5. Freedom and Human Agency

Discussion of human freedom as a special case derivative
from the more comprehensive metaphysical scheme moves us from
the realm of metaphysics to the special case of ethics. This
shift prompts several remarks. First, a brief outline of the
salient features of the special case of human freedom illustrates
the general metaphysical principles just treated. Such a discussion provides a useful test case of Whitehead's fundamental empirical grounding of speculative philosophy--that its doctrines
shall be found generally exemplified in our common experience
(PR 4).

Secondly, as we have intimated, the strength of Whitehead's
doctrine of freedom lies in the fact that it is derived in a

formal and perfectly general context. Customarily, freedom is conceived as a phenomenon having a highly restricted domain--that of human behavior. The doctrine is developed for this special case. Subsequently, difficulties are encountered when that concept of freedom is "extrapolated" to the larger sphere of nature, where supposedly different laws hold. The marked contrast between the human subjective experience of freedom and the objective deduction of a deterministic concept of nature leads finally to a bifurcation of nature: a radical dualism of objectivity and human subjectivity. It was Whitehead's particular contribution, through his "reformed subjectivist principle," to avoid such pitfalls.

In developing his doctrine of actual entites, however, Whitehead concluded that all the "enduring objects" of our normal experience are *derived* from these actual entities. None of our direct experiences are experiences of individual actual entities, and hence, formally speaking, none of our human experience is "actual." The risk involved here is the potential for judging all common (but more complex) experience as in some sense epiphenomenal. At very least it is evident that the pronouncements on freedom offered in Section 3 cannot merely be assumed to apply to the complex structured societies of actual entities constituting human beings. Whether in fact the doctrines regarding freedom and creativity are transferable by analogy is a point we shall wish to consider. Accordingly, we shall treat in brief compass Whitehead's doctrine of the "self," and possible resultant interpretations of human freedom and agency.

Lynne Belaief, in attempting to formulate a Whiteheadian ethics, points out that the requisite features for an intelligible system of process ethics are a value theory, a concept of freedom, and finally a notion of "self-identical individuality" defining the entities to whom the ethics applies.[60] Whitehead recognized the latter as a particular source of difficulty for his system.

> Personal unity is an inescapable fact . . . Any
> philosophy must provide some doctrine of personal
> identity. In some sense there is a unity in the life
> of each man, from birth to death. The two modern
> philosophers who most consistently reject the notion
> of a self-identical Soul-Substance are Hume and Wil-
> liam James. But the problem remains for them, as it

> does for the philosophy of organism, to provide an
> adequate account of this undoubted personal unity,
> maintaining itself amidst a welter of circumstance.
>
> (AI 239ff.)

Whitehead himself, however, does not belabor this point.
To avoid any return to a metaphysical dualism and the bifurcation
of reality, personal unity must be explainable in terms of some
feature of the flux of actual occasions. The human body, as
partial locus of "personal" events is unquestionably an enduring
structure immersed in the wider environment of nature. We are
scarcely aware of many of its most important functions, unless
these are unnaturally hampered. Indeed, it is difficult precisely to discern where the human body "ends" and the external
environment "begins." So far as continuity of "self" with respect to the physical, bodily aspect is concerned, as Charles
Hartshorne notes, "spatio-temporal continuity connects one not
with oneself in the past or future so much as with the environment, that is, other individual beings, in the past or future."[61]

For this reason, Hartshorne agrees with Whitehead's implied
position that this relatively abstract feature of our experience
is not to be overstressed at the expense of the general compre-
hensiveness and coherence of the metaphysical system.[62] For
Whitehead, the phenomenon of self-identity is explicable in close
analogy with Plato's doctrine of the "receptacle" in the *Timaeus*,
the "natural matrix for all transitions of life," the "locus
which . . . provides an emplacement for all the occasions of
experience." Plato's "receptacle," argues Whitehead, had as its
sole function "the imposition of a unity upon the events of
nature":

> These events are together by reason of their
> *community of locus*, and they obtain their actuality
> by reason of *emplacement within this community* . . .
> This is at once the doctrine of the unity of nature,
> and of the unity of each human life . . . our *con-*
> *sciousness* of the *self-identity* pervading our life-
> thread of occasions, is nothing other than a *knowl-*
> *edge* of a *special strand of unity within the general*
> *unity of nature*. (AI 240ff.; emphases added)

The salient features of Whitehead's doctrine of self-identity emerge in this passage. First, human self-identity is to
be seen merely as a special case of the more general feature of

the recognizable identity of general *groupings* of actual entities involving "a particular fact of togetherness," termed nexūs (PR 29ff.). In particular, the property of "identity amidst change" is the result of the genetic derivation by actual entities in a given nexūs of a "common element of form," by reason of which such a grouping of actual entities is called a "society" (PR 50ff.).

> The members of the society are alike because, by reason of their common character, they impose on other members of the society the conditions which lead to that likeness.
>
> (PR 137)

If that element of inherited form is preserved in a purely temporal series of actual occasions, in which no two actual entities are contemporaries, then the society is said to be "personally ordered," and the object thus presented to experience more or less continuously through time is called an "enduring object" (cf. PR 51ff.).

It is evident that the "structured" or "regnant societies" which constitute complex organic and inorganic entities common to human experience are complex, interwoven bundles of such personal societies or enduring objects. This is, in part, why the precise distinction between the human person and its immediate interrelatedness with its local physical environment cannot be sharply drawn. Donald Sherburne, in fact, has illustrated admirably the manner in which that thread of personal order-- shared serially along some temporal route of actual occasions which we collectively terms a person's spirit, mind or soul-- can be understood as a "living"[63] regnant society ("historically" or temporally ordered) "wandering" amidst a living, nonsocial nexus of occasions which "support" its existence.[64] That immediate, nonsocial nexus supporting the regnant society would be constituted by the living physical occasions of the brain.

Sherburne notes that the inheritance of some "common form" which defines any personal society in this case "corresponds to our sense of personal identity through time."[65] Whitehead himself notes that "an enduring personality in the temporal world is a route of occasions in which the successors with some peculiar completeness sum up their predecessors" (PR 531).

That particular subjective form which uniquely defines any actual entity is, as we already have noted, its "subjective aim." Utilizing Whitehead's observation above, I would supplement Sherburne's argument by suggesting that the inheritance of a common form in a living regnant society consists in the serial coordination of the successive subjective aims of the actual entities (i.e., the complete and peculiar "summation" of the series by each succeeding term) toward a final end or "satisfaction" of the society as a whole. It is precisely this historical thread of purposive activity which provides for a sense of continuing identity amidst change. As Whitehead comments:

> I find myself as essentially a unity of emotions, enjoyments, hopes, fears, regrets, valuations of alternatives, decisions—all of them subjective reactions to the environment as active in my nature. My unity—which is Descartes' "I am"—is my process of shaping this welter of material into a consistent pattern of feelings. The individual enjoyment is what I am in my role of a natural activity, as I shape the activities of the environment into a new creation, which is myself at this moment; and yet, as being myself, it is a continuation of the antecedent world. If we stress the role of the environment, this process is *causation*. If we stress the role of my immediate pattern of active enjoyment, this process is *self-creation*. If we stress the role of the conceptual anticipation of the future whose existence is a necessity in the nature of the present, this process is the *teleological aim* at some ideal in the future. This aim, however, is not really beyond the present process. For the aim at the future is an enjoyment in the present. It thus effectively conditions the immediate self-creation of the new creature.   (MT 228; emphases added)

Personal identity and self-consciousness are thus not attributable to some underlying and unchanging structure. Consciousness is rather an activity of organization shared serially, and thus continuously "carried on," by a living personal society of actual occasions. Identity is determined with reference to "structure," to be sure. But it is an emergent structure of common inherited purpose, of deliberate organization. Identity is a constant achievement of a serially-ordered process of becoming, not something which somehow underlies that process. And self-consciousness is simply the supervenient activity of the society's own awareness of its attempts at ongoing organization, synthesis and unification of diverse elements. For this reason, when describing the Whiteheadian "self" as "free," Belaief appropriately notes that self-identity is a *task* of freedom.[66]

There is a logical difficulty connected with the emergence of this last stage of complexity. Can that which is aware of, that which is *discerning* the various elements in a relation (i.e., that which is "conscious") simultaneously be itself one of the elements in the relation it discerns (and so be said to be "*self-*conscious" according to the present theory)? Whitehead would, of course, defend the affirmative of this position, since in his theory of actual entities the element which is "aware of" the other (physical) elements in their potential relations in concrescence (i.e., the subjective aim) is itself a datum synthesized (and modified) in that concrescence. Hence Whitehead's microscopic theory is termed "pan-subjectivism."

With respect to the more complex theory of the process of self-consciousness of regnant societies, however, the idea that self-consciousness renders a temporal process at every instant its own "object" (which is the meaning of "self-awareness") originates with Hegel. That is, Hegel can be shown to affirm the very position for regnant societies of actual entities that Whitehead himself was led to affirm by virtue of his analysis of individual actual entities themselves.[67]

We have, at present, a theory of freedom applicable to actual entities, as well as a description of how these entities which are the metaphysical *res verae* enter into a multitude of possible combinations, the successively more complex of which are observable as the organic and inorganic "objects" of normal experience. Lynne Belaief argues persuasively that, while we cannot literally and entirely carry over the description of features of actual entities and apply them to the more complex combinations and relations of actual entities, nevertheless we can proceed by analogy to determine the more abstract and limited properties of the nexūs, since to presume otherwise would be "to undercut Whitehead's foundational claim that the basic metaphysical categories are generally applicable to all actual things. . . ."[68]

Thus, for example, an actual entity exhibits freedom according to the relative dominance of the subjective aim of its mental pole. The further claim that "life is a bid for freedom" (PR 159) is based upon the fact that living and non-living actual

entities are differentiated, as we saw (43ff.), by the relative
"novelty of definiteness" introduced into the *living* concrescence
through its subjective aim. By analogy, a regnant society of
actual entities is "alive" insofar as it generates "initiative
in conceptual prehensions" in order to:

> . . . receive the novel elements of the environ-
> ment into explicit feelings with such subjective forms
> as conciliate them with the complex experiences proper
> to members of the structured society . . . In the case
> of the higher organisms, this conceptual initiative
> amounts to *thinking* about the diverse experiences. . . .
> In accordance with this doctrine of 'life', the primary
> meaning of 'life' is the origination of *conceptual*
> *novelty*.   (PR 155ff.)

If freedom in an actual entity is constituted by this dominance of its mental (conceptual) pole, then freedom in higher
organisms, by analogy, must consist in the relative dominance
of "conceptual appetition" (purposes, goals, and aims entertained
by the conscious mind) over the physical determinants. That is,
human freedom must originate in the intellectual entertainment
of unrealized possibilities (MT 36), coupled with agency. As we
saw in Section 4, real subjective agency must consist in a selection among and actualization of certain such possibilities in
accordance with a dominant purpose, plan or principle of organization of one's behavior. That is, freedom in human nature (comparable to the case of actual entities) is a process of teleological self-determination. Its issue is novelty of purposeful
action. Its exercise is a function of wisdom.

> It is the function of wisdom to act as a modi-
> fying agency on the intellectual ferment so as to
> produce a self-determined issue from the given con-
> ditions . . . there is a spontaneity of thought
> which lies beyond routine. Otherwise, the moral
> claim for freedom of thought is without meaning.
> This spontaneity of thought is, in its turn, sub-
> ject to control as to its maintenance and efficiency.
> Such control is the judgment of the whole, attenu-
> ating or strengthening the partial flashes of self-
> determination. The whole determines what it wills
> to be and thereby adjusts the relative importance of
> its own inherent flashes of spontaneity. This final
> determination is its *Wisdom* or, in other words, its
> *subjective aim* as to its own nature, with its limits
> set by inherited factors.   (AI 59)

A more striking confirmation of the thrust of this essay hardly could be produced than this discussion by Whitehead of the role of wisdom in human affairs. Freedom includes "spontaneity" as a necessary condition. Creativity, however, is not equated with mere spontaneity, but rather with the adjustment of the larger organic system to its own "inherent flashes of spontaneity." In human beings, that adjustment is effected (as it is in actual entities) with reference to a central principle of organization, intention or purpose. In the case of human behavior, what corresponds with the subjective aim of actual entities is the intellectual entertainment of purpose, which Whitehead terms "Wisdom."[69]

Furthermore, as an actual entity is distinguished by its subjective aim, and as a society of actual entities is defined by its genetic coordination of temporally-successive subjective aims, so is the human person identified uniquely by that maintenance of a particular pattern, purpose or unique organization of his or her own behavior through time. This is not to suggest that for human persons (any more than for actual entities) such a pattern or purpose is rigidly prescribed and without modification. Quite the contrary, as the successive modifications of the organization of one's behavior from childhood to adult maturity testify! Nor are persons in any sense "bound" or "determined" by this pattern of organization which they exhibit.

Rather, the point is that identity through time is discerned by references to the unique pattern of organization exhibited by one's actions and intentions, successive modifications of which customarily are an orderly, sequential, evolutionary function of time. Sudden departures from that customary pattern in response to inherent conceptual "flashes of spontaneity"--e.g., as when a person whose dominant principle of organization has been cautious self-preservation and equilibrium suddenly performs a selfless act of heroism in defense of another--precisely for this reason are met with the common-language judgment: "She was *not herself*" in performing this or that novel act, or "that [individual act] is not *characteristic* of his personality."

Such judgments, of course, are made with reference to the past history (usually the recently-past history) of the organism prior to the novel decision and act. If the subsequent "adjustment of the whole [person] to its inherent flashes of spontaneity"

is to *minimize* the importance of that individual act for the overall modification of the dominant principle of organization, then
the person may be observed to return to more "customary" modes
of behavior, prompting the common-language judgment: "He has
come to himself," or "she is *herself* again." On the other hand,
should the novel particular decision and its act be incorporated
by the organism as the basis for a radical modification of its
dominant principle of behavioral organization (e.g., as when a
person abandons a career or social position for an entirely "new
and different" life) the judgment is offered that "he is like a
different person."[70]

These traditionally perplexing and unaccountable moral and
social phenomena of freedom and self-identity are thus admirably
accounted for within the context of a Whiteheadian doctrine of
the self. This discussion highlights the appropriateness of our
doctrine of self-identity as an organizing, unifying activity
and achievement (rather than an underlying, static infrastructure
of the person). Our treatment further reveals that Professor
Belaief's admirable judgment--that self-identity is a continual
"task of freedom" (*supra*, p. 45)--is precisely to the point.

This Whiteheadian doctrine of human freedom enables an
interesting explanation of the development of "degrees of freedom" in differing kinds of organisms, as well as in different
stages of the development of a single organism. Whitehead provides the basis, in effect, for a quantitative measure of the
exercise of freedom. This is a problem, as Edward Stevens points
out,[71] which has plagued the traditional libertarian position on
"contra-causal" freedom--a variety of freedom which was judged
either "present" or "absent" in a given organism. Whitehead's
doctrine also implicitly distinguishes the metaethical problem
of "internal freedom" from the very different physical and political question, with respect to an organism's environment, of
liberty. He thereby dispenses with the indiscriminate charge of
some reconciliationists that the moral and metaphysical problem
of freedom is a "pseudo-problem," reducing finally to a question
of liberty.[72]

The most valuable feature of Whitehead's doctrine, however,
is its contribution, through its novel theory of the self, to
an understanding of the pivotal notion of moral responsibility--

which many would regard as the *sine qua non* of any normative
theory of ethics. Whitehead's remarks concerning actual entities in this regard obtain by analogy with respect to human behavior as well, as he indicates:

> The point to be noticed is that the actual enti-
> ty, in a state of process during which it is not fully
> definite, determines its own definiteness. This is
> the whole point of moral responsibility. Such responsi-
> bility is conditioned by the limits of the data, and by
> the categoreal conditions of the concrescence. . . .
> Further, in the case of those actualities whose immedi-
> ate experience is most completely open to us, namely,
> human beings, the final decision of the immediate sub-
> ject-superject, constituting the ultimate modification
> of subjective aim, is the foundation of our experience
> of responsibility, of approbation or of disapprobation,
> of self-approval or of self-reproach, of freedom, of
> emphasis. (PR 390, 74)

Coupled with our modified Whiteheadian notion of the "self"
who is thus responsible, this view proceeds directly as a consequence of the notion of freedom as teleological self-determination. In particular, Whitehead specifies with precision the
mechanisms for decision, and a concept of the agent necessary
for an intelligible theory of responsibility.

It is important to note also in passing that Whitehead allows for *two* concepts of moral responsibility: what I would
term "primary" and "derivative" responsibility. Any actual occasion as *causa sui*--or any living regnant society of actual
entities--finally is its own reason for what it becomes. Thus,
it is "responsible" (i.e., subject to praise or blame) for what
it is. It is *answerable*, in a sense, for what use it has made
of its inheritance and its own autonomy. This is the familiar
form of individual moral responsibility for one's personal behavior and the *direct* consequences of that behavior.

More troubling has been the formulation of a notion of
"derivative" responsibility. This notion customarily is presented in the form of the lofty religious conception of St. Paul,
that one is also "responsible" in a derivative sense for decisions and actions which, while not themselves "immoral" from the
standpoint of the immediate agent, nonetheless might cause *another*
person in some way to commit an act which *is* immoral: in St.
Paul's words, an act which might "cause one's brother to stumble"
(Romans 14:20ff.).

Moral custom dictates a recognition of the responsibility of "witness" and "example," as well as of the more immediate concern for direct consequences of acts. But formal moral theory is hardpressed to affix clear responsibility for the former, since the mechanisms of causality are difficult to discern--and, in any case, the second agent is himself or herself free and autonomous, and therefore likewise "responsible" in his or her own right for what he or she becomes. Whitehead's notion of the objective immortality of concreta, however, suggests a precise explanation for "derivative responsibility."

As we have seen, an agent's freedom and responsibility are both "conditioned" by the inherited data--the behavioral "constraints" of the immediate past environment. These place an inherent limitation on its exercise of freedom and the novel issue of its behavior. An organism, so to speak, may "do the best it *can* with what it *has*" (or is provided). Yet if the entire ensemble of possibilities open to the moral agent with respect to a given decision represents, from a moral point of view, a range of acts all of which are wrong or evil by reason of the dominance of negative influences inherited from the moral agent's past, the the organism's freedom has been unnecessarily restricted. As a consequence, its opportunity for novel behavior issuing in a good or praiseworthy result is practically negligible. Therefore Whitehead suggests:

> In our own relatively high grade of human existence, this doctrine of feelings and their subject is best illustrated by our notion of moral responsibility. The subject is responsible for being what it is in virtue of its feelings ["primary" responsibility]. It is also derivatively responsible for the consequences of its existence because they flow from its feelings [derivative responsibility].[73]

The point to be noticed here is that a subject, in addition to considering the direct consequences of its own activity, must *also* take account of the passage of its acts into "objective immortality" as concreta--as data for the becoming of every new concrescence. Consider, for example, an act which does not appear to be itself directly immoral. If the results of this act exert unnecessarily negative, restrictive influences on a subsequent becoming--if this action serves (in a crude sense) to unnecessarily "pollute" the "data bank" for future concrescences--

then the original act is itself immoral in a "derivative" sense. The originating agent of the act is thus (as St. Paul suspected) derivatively responsible for the subsequent negative effects of his or her act.

The historical weakness of St. Paul's argument has been that, lacking any precise analysis of this process, acceptance of the doctrine of derivative responsibility has always been value-dependent. That is, embracing the responsibility of serving as "my brother's keeper" historically has been subject to the simultaneous embracing of a value system (such as Christianity, or another religious orientation) in which such social responsibility was binding. From a normative point of view, such acceptance of derivative responsibility has been seen as an act of supererogation. Whitehead provides the necessary analysis of the process of derivative responsibility, showing it to proceed directly as a consequence of the nature of actual entities. A process ethics thereby establishes derivative responsibility as a deontological principle: i.e., as a formal, non-relative, universally-binding moral precept.[74]

As Lynne Belaief notes, what Whitehead called "derivative responsibility" forms, in essence, the basis of the *tragic* feature of human moral existence.[75] Every moral act must be seen as a *risk*--i.e., moral agents must bear the responsibility even for the unanticipated consequences of their existence when, in retrospect, their actions can be seen as the sufficient cause of a subsequent immoral situation. The paradox of the moral vocation is that *no* agent, no matter how desirous of "being moral," *ever* can predict with certainty the eventual effects of his or her moral decisions and acts. Tragedy as a theme in existentialist ethics thus can be tied to Whitehead's doctrine of finite or quasi-causal freedom and its attendant notion of derivative responsibility.

On the other hand, this "Nordic" approach to the moral vocation can be balanced with the recognition that "derivative responsibility" may also form the basis both for the *faithful* dimension, and for the *hopeful* dimension of moral action. Regardless of value-orientation, all persons are invited, through the doctrine of derivative responsibility, to honor the Kantian edict regarding the infinite value and worth of every human person.

In addition, faithfulness to such a demanding moral vocation can serve as the ground for hope in our common human future. We enjoy together the possibility, not only of tragedy, but of unanticipated joy through persevering in our mutually-shared moral tasks.

Section 6.   Concluding Summary

For Whitehead, history is a "creative advance into novelty." The "creativity of the world" (the record of which is its history) is understood as the "throbbing emotion of the past hurling itself into a new transcendent fact" (AI 227; PR 340, 524).   History is the generic name for the vast welter of events and groupings of events advancing into their own novel and indeterminate future.

Freedom is exhibited in the occasions of history.

> It is the definition of contemporary events that they happen in causal independence of each other. . . .[This] causal independence of contemporary occasions is the ground for the freedom within the Universe.   The novelties which face the contemporary world are solved in isolation by the contemporary occasions.   There is complete contemporary freedom.
>
> (AI 251, 255)[76]

Thus, the perspective of process philosophy focuses on the possibility of change and novelty as an integral part of the complete description of world history.[77]   Hence, it is possible to view the historical process as literally the "realm of freedom," actualizing itself successively and perpetually in the flux of actual occasions.[78]

It is important to note, however, that Whitehead embraces no particular eschatology.   There is no apparent goal or envisioned end-state for the historical process as a whole.[79] History is *merely* this "creative advance," the bare, perpetual exercise of creativity amid the bewildering welter of myriad data.   And yet history is not without issue.   We enjoy particular facts of experience, past and present, which are and have been actualized at the expense of alternative, equally-likely possibilities.   All things are possible in principle, but not all possibilities are "compossible."   Indeed, some possibilities are mutually contradictory.   Thus, only finite, particular possibilities have been actualized in history.   As Whitehead notes:

The evolution of history is incapable of [com-
plete] rationalization because it exhibits a *selected
flux* of participating forms. No reason, *internal to
history*, can be assigned why [this particular] flux
of forms, rather than another flux, should have been
[actualized].

(PR 74; emphases added)

Thus, the generic activity of Creativity alone is not *sufficient* to account for the particular facts of existence, for
"to be an actual thing is to be limited . . . Unlimited possibility and abstract creativity can procure nothing" (RM 150,
152). Whitehead, as we already have noted with regard to the
subjective aim, was led to postulate a principle of limitation
on creativity, "introducing contraries, grades and oppositions."
This limitation is imposed through the *evaluation* and relative
ordering of pure possibilities (eternal objects). Whitehead
termed this the "principle of limitation" and subsequently the
Principle of Concretion, "that actual entity from which each
temporal concrescence receives that initial aim from which its
self-causation starts" (PR 374; SMW 256ff.).

The problem of utilizing *merely* a principle of limitation
or concretion to explain the facticity of history--or of the
individual instances of creativity, the actual entities--is that
by Whitehead's Ontological Principle, actual entities themselves
must be the only reasons for what exists. Accordingly, Whitehead was led to give his ideal ordering of pure possibilities
an ontological grounding in a primordial, non-temporal actual entity, which he identified as God, "the actual but non-temporal
entity whereby the indetermination of mere creativity is trans-
muted into a determinate freedom" (RM 90).

We already have noted the role of "God" in the creative
process of actual entities. The necessity for a "hybrid prehension" of ideal order initiating each process of concrescence
was there readily apparent. In the present situation, the necessity for a grounding of metaphysical freedom in order to provide
for the definiteness of history is likewise admitted. As Whitehead indicates, "freedom" without the limitations of some organizing principle of order and inter-relatedness is not freedom
at all, but wantonness and chaos.[80] In the present case, Whitehead's defense of this need amounts to a poignant inversion of
the Argument from Design:

> It is not the case that there is an actual world
> which accidentally happens to exhibit an order of na-
> ture. There is an actual world because there is an
> order in nature. If there were no order, there would
> be no world. Also since there is a world, we know
> that there is an order. The ordering entity is a
> necessary element in the metaphysical situation pre-
> sented by the actual world.   (RM 104)

We must, I think, grant Whitehead this important point in
light of our analysis of freedom as creativity. We must further
grant with him the final observation that "the universe exhibits
a creativity with infinite freedom, and a realm of forms with
infinite possibilities; but . . . this creativity and these forms
are together impotent to achieve actuality apart from the completed ideal harmony . . ." (RM 119ff.).

I have deliberately omitted the final phrase, ". . . which
is God." Whitehead, to my mind, has established beyond a reasonable doubt that the coherent interpretation of experience in
terms of general metaphysical principles requires that there be
what Heraclitus and the ancient Stoic philosophers termed a
Logos--a rational, intelligible principle of order, harmony and
organization at the heart of all things. This principle is required in order to: (i) enable the creative process of becoming;
(ii) ground our understanding of metaphysical freedom; and (iii)
account for why there is, after all, anything in particular to
experience.

It was Whitehead's particular genius explicitly to realize
that this *Logos*, like his actual entities, must in some sense be
dipolar. That is, Whitehead recognized that the principle of
order which conditions creativity by an ideal valuation of its
possibilities, cannot be wholly external to the world process,
but must itself be immanent in and conditioned by that creative
process. The new and novel possibilities actualized by this
process in turn assume their place in the subsequent modifications and re-evaluations of the harmonious ordering and valuation
of the total ideal pattern. Only in this way could a meaningful
doctrine of freedom be preserved.

This dialectical and teleological process of successive
generation of forms is precisely the description of the process
according to which organisms live and develop. Organisms attempt to impose an internal unity and harmony on the diverse

elements incorporated and synthesized from their environment and, in turn, the organisms suffer successive modifications in that ideal pattern of organization which each possesses by reason of the dialectical tensions inherent in the elements of the environment which are synthesized according to that pattern. This process lies at the heart of all *organic* life. I find no reason to prescind from Whitehead's carefully-reasoned extension of this view: *viz.*, that something like this creative, generative, immanent, dialectical, teleological process must lie at the heart of *all* reality.

It is somewhat misleading, I submit, to identify the generated and generative "ideal pattern of harmonious order" as "God." It may be true that, to satisfy the Ontological Principle and maintain the coherence of his system, it appeared necessary to give this *Logos* specific ontological grounding in one unique actual entity (although this decision seems to have created as many difficulties for Whitehead's followers as it solved). The necessary "dipolar" nature of the *Logos*--its conditioned and its conditioning functions, its immanent and its transcendent characteristics--are, to be sure, symbolized in Whitehead's conception of the "Primordial and Consequent Natures" of God (cf. PR 525, 529).[81] But I am not fully persuaded that the extensive characteristics he develops there in a description of God are themselves strictly necessary to his metaphysical system.

Neither do I suggest that they are invalid or "incoherent." Obviously, from a theological standpoint, such a description of God has tremendous appeal, as the derivative development of a "process theology" bears impressive witness. Unfortunately, such developments have contributed to a severe imbalance of emphasis in subsequent process thought toward theistic argument, generating in turn a reaction against the excessive intrusion of such concerns within Whitehead's own system.[82] The details of that debate need not detain us here.

My point is that, *strictly* from a philosophical perspective, all Whitehead has succeeded in demonstrating as necessary to explain the full range of human and nonhuman experience is "process" and its ideal pattern or principle of organization. I refer to the latter more impersonally as the *Logos*, or, in Whitehead's own terms, the Principle of Concretion. Neither "process"

nor its inherent, teleological principle of limitation can be
viewed as independent, nor as "preceding" one another, either
logically or temporally. As in the case of Whitehead's symbol
of "God and the World," these mutually *require* one another (cf.
RM 108, 157; PR 528ff.). The ideal pattern does not create the
process, it *enables* it. The process of becoming is thus by
definition a *teleological* process, appropriately described by
Whitehead as "Creativity."[83] The *tension* between the exercise
of creativity and the limitations imposed on it by the pattern
it generates and seeks to embody, further defines creativity as
a *dialectical* process. Its issue is novelty. And these factors
in aggregate permit a proper description of the meaning of freedom. Thus, from the standpoint of metaphysics alone, Creativity
and the immanent *Logos* which Whitehead discerns are all that are
necessary to insure freedom and account for reality.[84]

III. HEGEL'S CONCEPT OF FREEDOM

> One knows generally of no idea which is so inde-
> terminate, ambiguous and capable of the greatest mis-
> understanding . . . as the idea of Freedom.
>
> (*Enc.* 482)[1]

Section 1. Essentials of the Argument

Freedom is a pervasive theme in Hegel's metaphysics. His
Phenomenology has been described as a "manifestation of freedom
as well as a morphology of the development of freedom itself."[2]
Hegel himself interprets his last personally-published work, the
Philosophy of Right, as "the realm of freedom made actual. . ."
(Phil. R. 4).

The sustained passion of the *Phenomenology* was inspirational
for Karl Marx, who saw in it a doctrine of freedom elaborated in
terms of the "self-creation of man as a process," through which
Marx was enabled to view human beings as essentially the result
of their own creative activities--their labor.[3]

In this century, the *Phenomenology* has proved of central
importance to existentialist defenders of freedom. Jean-Paul
Sartre, for example, suggests that the very essence of being
human lies in freedom of agency. Sartre's judgment of the negative or alienating dimensions of this freedom, that human beings
are "condemned to be free," elaborated an intuition of the *Phenomenology*, stated explicitly in the "Philosophy of Mind," that
freedom is the "principle of evil and pain" (*Enc.* 472).[4]

The *Philosophy of Right* on the other hand has long been
viewed as Hegel's principal treatise upon the topic of freedom,
largely because the realm of "objective spirit" analyzed there
covers the familiar range of terrain in which freedom is understood to be operant (or at least significant) in human affairs:
law, morality and political institutions. Thus, H. A. Reyburn
and subsequent commentators upon Hegel's view of freedom in its
relation to ethics have concentrated upon this work in formulating their interpretations of Hegel's doctrine.[5]

In all these cases, a number of partially-distinct themes
are gathered under the umbrella of "freedom." In the *Philosophy*

of Right, for example, Hegel describes the moral good as "freedom realized, the absolute end and aim of the world" (Phil. R. 129), and the ethical life of the community and nation as that "good become alive . . . the concept of freedom developed into the existing world. . ." (Phil. R. 142). "Freedom" in the *Philosophy of Right* is then the very "substance" of ethical life--it is *Geist* objectively embodied in human laws, and in the moral and political institutions of the state.

> The ethical order is freedom or the absolute will as what is objective, a circle of necessity whose moments are the ethical powers which regulate the life of individuals.
>   (Phil. R. 145)

This "substance" in the *Philosophy of Right* must bear some integral relation to that "substance" in the *Phenomenology*, "which . . .is the process in which Spirit *becomes* what it is *in itself*," namely "Subject"--by which Hegel intends "purposive activity," or the "pure actuality . . . [of] realized purpose" (*Phen.* 487ff., 10-12). Likewise the "circle of necessity" in the *Philosophy of Right* warrants some comparison with that famous "dialectical circle" in the *Phenomenology* which illustrates *Geist* or "Mind" coming to a self-conscious realization of its own, free, ongoing development. The latter process Hegel describes self-identically as "the labor which it accomplishes as actual History," whose consummation in the "assurance of self-knowledge" is characterized as "supreme freedom," a phase whose "externalization is still incomplete."[6]

The *Phenomenology*, in its description of "Substance as Subject" and *Geist* as "supremely free," thus alludes to certain metaphysical doctrines with respect to freedom which undergird and are largely presupposed in the *Philosophy of Right*. The *Phenomenology*, however, is not itself the best source for the understanding of the metaphysical doctrine of freedom (although its acquaintance is obviously a prerequisite for such an understanding). On one hand, the *Phenomenology* neither intends nor attempts to separate metaphysical principles from their concrete embodiment in history, culture, science and philosophy. On the other hand, its massive dialectical sweep renders any precise metaphysical statements derived from the *Phenomenology* alone highly suspect.

Hegel offers, for example, a significant and suggestive assessment of metaphysical freedom in the *Phenomenology*:

> Absolute essential being . . . is all *reality*, and this reality *is* only as knowledge. What consciousness did not know would have no significance for consciousness and can have no power over it . . . It is absolutely free in that it knows its freedom, and just this knowledge is its substance and purpose and its sole content. (*Phen.* 365)

As we subsequently shall see, this statement--so far as it goes --is indeed Hegel's view of the freedom which is constitutive of being.

This statement, however, is incomplete and dialectically flawed. The view here expressed *as is*, is characteristic of the Kantian view of moral freedom in the knowledge of one's duty. The flaw of the categorical imperative is its excessive individualism, which (as Hegel brilliantly illustrates) leads the partial truth of this view of freedom to degenerate into the dissemblance or duplicity of questionable or competing claims for moral certitude. This degeneration is symbolized finally in the puritanical self-righteousness of Jacobi's "beautiful soul," which, in its absolute knowledge of its own goodness, resigns itself to the hopelessness of realizing its goodness in the actual world. This presumably morally upright person, Hegel argues, will finally refuse to acknowledge competing claims or versions of goodness. Such a person likewise will refuse to forgive those who are unable to meet his or her own lofty standards of conduct.

It is no accident, by contrast, that Hegel's final theme in his discussion of the political institutions of *objektiver Geist* is forgiveness. For Hegel, it is forgiveness, compassion and reconciliation in the knowledge of finite moral inadequacy and competing moral claims which characterize the highest and most ethical phase of "objective spirit" in its dialectical transition to the higher sphere of "absolute spirit": Art, Religion and Philosophy (*Phen.* 364-383). The chief flaw in this partial truth of freedom, then, is that true freedom must involve not only *an-sich Sein*, but also *Sein für anderen*--being-for-others in a community of selves (*Enc.* 431).

It is difficult to depend upon an exegesis of the *Phenomenology* alone for an understanding of the metaphysical freedom which informs the more familiar moral, social and political discussion in the *Philosophy of Right*. The progressive development of self-consciousness traced in the *Phenomenology* is not itself intended as a systematic metaphysical treatise, although important elements of Hegel's metaphysics are prefigured in this "autobiography of *Geist*." An understanding of freedom based primarily upon an exegesis of the *Philosophy of Right* tends on the other hand to restrict freedom too narrowly and exclusively to the human condition: i.e., to moral freedom, human agency, and the historical development of a meaningful concept of political liberty as guaranteed in the ideal state. This is frequently accomplished without coming to terms with the metaphysical doctrine from which these macroscopic views are derived.

The problem posed here is the precise opposite of that posed in our analysis of Whitehead. Whitehead's metaphysical doctrine of freedom as constitutive of being itself was straightforwardly discernable and recoverable. The macroscopic application of that theory to the human condition, however, was vague. With Hegel an understanding of freedom in all its subtle phases in the human sphere is explicit in the *Philosophy of Right*, as well as in the *Phenomenology* and the "Philosophy of Mind." The metaphysical ground of those doctrines, however, is not always so clearly defined.

The *Phenomenology* is the *terminus a quo*, prefiguring the whole system. The *Philosophy of Right* is quite clearly the *terminus ad quem* from the standpoint of a doctrine of human freedom. Traditionally, these works are the primary foci for understanding Hegel's doctrine of freedom. But, to transplant Whitehead's phrase, these are merely the initial and final stages of the process, in between which lies the teleology of the universe.

Hegel's understanding of freedom cannot be fully appreciated apart from a thorough recognition of the role of *purpose* in his philosophy. Not since Aristotle ("the greatest single influence in Hegel's inspirational background"[7]) has any philosophy or philosopher been so thoroughly guided by a teleological conception of reality as Hegel.

For Hegel, however, teleology does not entail the trivial, much abused and discredited notion of "external purposiveness." According to this "external" interpretation of teleology, virtually any object or event can be demonstrated as having its proper place or function (usually in the service of human convenience) in the grand, divine design of the cosmos.[8]

More to the point, Hegel does not use teleology as the antithesis of mechanism or determinism. He thus did not directly engage the debate, central to the metaphysics of the post-Cartesian period, between defenders of God and/or freedom on one hand, and proponents of naturalism and/or strict deterministic causality (the twin pillars of "scientific materialism") on the other. Kant, of course, had dismissed this debate in its entirety as one of the frustrating "antinomies" of the Pure Reason. Hegel's use of teleology, however, is not pre-critical, but post-critical. He anticipates in many respects the current interpretation of the role of purposive, patterned, organized activity in contemporary scientific theory.[9]

Hegel, like Whitehead, does not attempt to deny mechanism or causal efficacy. Instead, he regards mechanistic explanations and deterministic interpretations of causality as inadequate to explain the processes of perpetual organization and self-maintenance characteristic of organic systems.[10] In the latter sections of the "Larger Logic" and in the portion of the *Encyclopedia* devoted to the "Philosophy of Nature," Hegel maintains that organic systems may be interpreted only in terms of their self-directed, purposive behavior. That is, organic behavior is observed to exhibit a pattern or organizing principle which is immanent in the living system, and to some extent generated by the organism itself. As such, organisms are self-determined, and to that extent (at very least) prefigure human freedom.

Mechanism and determinism are not refuted, but are shown to be insufficient principles of explanation. These are dialectically subordinated and superceded (*aufgehoben*[11]) in a philosophy of organism, or "organic mechanism." According to this latter doctrine, any organic system is governed principally by its *Begriff* or *Selbstzweckmässigkeit*--the "self-moderating end"-- the pattern, concept or organizing principle which the organism seeks more adequately to realize in each of its successive phases.

The self-unfolding of an inner principle or pattern is similar
to the Aristotelian doctrine of "entelechy" in biology.

The doctrine of the *Begriff* or Concept is the central ontological theme in Hegel's thought. The presence of a purposive,
organizing Concept in any process establishes Reality as through-
and-through teleological in character. Most notably for the present argument, Hegel defines a moderate, quasi-causal version of
the freedom operant in human affairs as grounded in the teleological self-determination of organic systems in nature.

> Teleology possesses . . . the [Begriff] in its
> Existence, which is in and for itself the . . . prin-
> ciple of freedom that in the utter certainty of its
> self-determination is absolutely liberated from the
> *external determining* of mechanism.   (GL 737)

Hegel's doctrine of organic mechanism is adumbrated in the
Phenomenology. There the category of organism is contrasted with
those (inorganic) objects whose relations to one another are
purely external, according to the "Laws of Nature."

> In the organic being, on the contrary, every
> determinateness through which it is open to another
> is controlled by the organic simple unity . . . Con-
> sequently what is organic maintains itself in its
> relation . . . [i.e., in] what is called a *teleo-
> logical* relation.   (*Phen.* 154-156; emphasis added)

In the *Phenomenology*, Hegel views the teleological relation as
differentiated from the concept of natural law, yet in one sense
comparable to that concept, in that the teleological relation
is still in a partial sense external to the related terms. That
is, the lower organisms of nature are not themselves aware of
the end or goal (*Zweck*) which governs their own individual behavior. Instead, the immanent Concept, the essence of actual
organic life, is discerned by "Reason in its role of observer.
. ." (*Phen.* 156).

The concept of metaphysical freedom as related to organic
mechanism is worked out in greater detail in the final section
of Hegel's massive *Science of Logic*, and in the "Philosophy of
Nature," whose "exposition constitutes the transition from necessity to freedom" (*Enc.* 381, *Zusatz*). These particular writings
of Hegel frequently either are ignored outright, or are given
only a cursory examination by those more interested in freedom

as a cultural, political and historical theme. The "micro-ontology" of organic mechanism with its attendant understanding of freedom as grounded in teleological self-determination, however, is absolutely necessary for an adequate comprehension of Hegel's "macro-ontology": in the realm of "objective spirit," freedom of thought and the human spirit are institutionalized and analyzed according to their respective embodiment of the organic, purposive *Begriff* discussed in Hegel's metaphysical writings.

It is the primary function of the following treatment to recover and consider Hegel's doctrine of metaphysical freedom. Section 2 analyzes briefly some key Hegelian terms and concepts requisite for this project. In Section 3, Hegel's ontology of process and freedom—his "logic of becoming" described in terms of the teleological development of the "free and immanent Concept"—is analyzed. Section 4 traces the development of organic mechanism in the *Naturphilosophie*, culminating in an understanding that freedom entails teleological self determination according to an immanent and self generating pattern or principle, together with a self-conscious awareness of that process (and consequently the governance of purpose by *Vernunft* or Reason). Only then do we turn to a discussion of the macroscopic application of this ontology to the customary sphere of human moral freedom and the relation of this theory to Hegel's doctrine of the Absolute.

Section 2. Hegelian Terminology

As George Kline notes, both Hegel and Whitehead share the fate that their formidable vocabulary has been "more often deplored than analyzed."[12] We consider in this section certain specific terms germane to an understanding of Hegel's doctrine of metaphysical freedom.

(i) The German *Freiheit* offers in translation no clear cut distinction between "freedom" and "liberty." Translations vary in part according to context—a discussion of *Freiheit* with respect to political theory primarily being understood as referring to "liberty," while a discussion of the *Freiheitsbegriff* deals more generally with what we understand in the present essay as Hegel's metaphysical doctrine. Hegel, of course, makes no sharp distinction between the ontological, historical or socio-political

treatment of freedom. His *Freiheitsbegriff* is a "concrete universal": it is understood primarily in terms of its mediation,
its successive finite particularizations in each of these varied
forms or modes (*Bestimmungen*). None of these particular determinations of the concept may be fully appreciated in abstraction
from the general concept of freedom, which, in turn (to borrow
Whitehead's phrase), owes its concrete "existence" to these, its
various "accidents."

Indeed, Hegel would view our present attempt to maintain a
distinction between metaphysical freedom and liberty as an abstraction (in a sense slightly at variance with Whitehead's use
of this term, as discussed below). Hegel would describe our
exercise condescendingly as a function of *Verstand* ("understanding," meaning empirical, reductionistic analysis) as opposed to
the higher critical function of *Vernunft* ("Reason") to illustrate
concepts in their "concreteness" (i.e., adequately-mediated many-
sidedness; cf. GL 28, 45). For Hegel, the methodology of the
Phenomenology is an example of the most adequate way to reach
an understanding of freedom through exhibiting that concept in
all its dialectical phases.[13]

I finally concur with this view. The present exercise is
clearly an abstraction (in Hegel's sense), completed only when
the various moments or determinations of freedom are allowed to
come together once again to exhibit their full inter-relatedness,
their "living concrete unity" (GL 48). Nonetheless this abstraction is, for our purposes, a necessary exercise. Formally, of
course, we must isolate Hegel's pure ontology of freedom in order
to see its similarities with Whitehead's doctrine.

There is yet another motivation for this exercise. Contemporary reconciliationists, as we noted, often assert that the
problem of freedom really only concerns the problem of liberty,
and that no metaphysical doctrine need be affirmed merely in
order to establish human moral "freedom" as political liberty.
A reconciliationist who found himself or herself in essential
agreement with Hegel's judgments regarding the nature of historical and socio-political liberty, might nonetheless suggest
that these doctrines could be affirmed without recourse to Hegel's
"obscure metaphysics." That is, such a person might accept the
Freiheitsbegriff while rejecting its necessary grounding in the

Freiheit des Begriffs. This, of course, Hegel would vehemently deny.

An analysis of the Hegelian position based largely or exclusively on the *Phenomenology* or the *Rechtsphilosophie*, however (and therefore making no clear distinction between the ontological, historical and socio-political doctrines of freedom), would be hardpressed to defend Hegel at this point. Our "abstract" analysis must then be made in order to demonstrate how, for Hegel, the "micro-ontology" of freedom is absolutely necessary for, and fully embodied in the various determinations of that concept in the more familiar historical and socio-political situations. Accordingly, unlike Hegel, we must for a time maintain a careful contextual distinction in translating *Freiheit* between freedom (the metaphysical doctrine) and liberty (its concrete, socio-political embodiment in the realm of "objective spirit").

(ii) *Geist* is a particularly difficult term in Hegelian literature, translated as both "mind" and "spirit." The latter suggests certain religious overtones which, on one hand, are important for a full understanding of Hegel's enterprise. On the other hand, "Spirit" suggests a mysticism and supernaturalism regarded with suspicion in some quarters, leading to a preference for "Mind" as a translation of *Geist*. Hegel's occasional reference to a *Weltgeist* (e.g., *Phen.* 17) as a distinct ontological entity (like the world-soul of Plato and Plotinus) seems to reinforce this suspicion. This supernatural or "supra-natural" connotation is clearly present in Hegel's writing, and should not be dismissed out of hand. I hope to suggest a modest and acceptable interpretation of these nuances.

"Mind," however, is not an adequate substitute translation (even though frequently used) in spite of its apparent advantage in playing down this latter dimension of *Geist*. I shall allow the use of this term in the present essay only where it seems especially appropriate in its own right, and where its use will not seem to sacrifice any of the important richness of the original term. For the present, that richness and multi-dimensionality is suggested in phrases such as *Zeitgeist* ("Spirit of the Age"), *Volksgeist* ("national or cultural spirit"), and *menschliche Geist* ("human spirit"). When utilized in one sense of the French *esprit* (as in *esprit de corps*), such phrases bring us closer to an adequate understanding of *Geist* for Hegel.

The central thrust of the entire Hegelian philosophy is towards a metaphysics of "community" (of "We") as contrasted with a purely atomistic or reductionistic metaphysics of pure individuality (of "I"). It is this fact which sets Hegel apart from his predecessors in German "absolute idealism," from the "objective subjectivity" of the Kantian transcendental unity of apperception to the "absolute Ego" of Fichte. His doctrine of *Geist* further distinguishes Hegel from his contemporaries in the German Romantic movement (including the idealist Schelling). All were, in his opinion, excessively individualistic or atomistic in some phase of their thought.[14] Hegel, by contrast, adopted an organic or holistic view, stressing both the process of becoming and the inter-relatedness of all reality. The former is encompassed in his doctrine of the self-unfolding of the Absolute Idea or Concept (*Begriff*) which we shall define presently. The latter aspect of organic holism and inter-relatedness is the principal feature of Hegel's doctrine of *Geist*.

Human community and the complete inter-relatedness of the world as a living, organic whole are definitely the thrust in Hegel's exposition of the emergence of *Geist* in the *Phenomenology* There we see that the fundamental unity of the "ethical order" is *not* the moral individual, but the family (*Phen.* 266-278). Likewise the basic unit of social, cultural and legal substance is the *polis*--a democratic community--and not the soul-less (*geist-los*) impersonal "empire."[15]

Indeed, for Hegel, the dialectical breakdown of every phase of history and human culture was in some sense to be traced to the loss or decay of its essential spirit, and its subsequent degeneration into some fallacious form of separateness. The culminating symbol of this degeneracy was, for Hegel, the debacle of the French Revolution, during which the noble ideal of absolute equality came to mean merely atomic individuality, devoid of responsibility. Each "unit" was found to be equally expendable and "the guillotine became thus the ultimate leveler" (*Phen.* 355-363).[16]

Even Hegel's interpretation of Christianity stresses this aspect of community as the *sine qua non* of the spiritual life. God--the vast, bare, impersonal Universal--becomes object to Himself, particularizes Himself, and makes Himself "concrete"

in one, finite individual ("the Incarnate Son"). The consequent
reunification of the particular with its Universal (death and re-
surrection) makes of God the "concrete universal." Hegel symbolizes this unity of finite human beings with the universal,
essential ground of Being as the "Holy Spirit" (*heiligen Geist*),
whose Being *is* the Christian community, the "koinonia," the Church
(*Phen.* 453-478).

A good many theologians, of course, would reject Hegel's
actual rendering of Christianity in so symbolic and suggestively
humanistic a form. Nonetheless, the fact that he understood the
Christian "Holy Spirit" not as a separate ontological entity,
but as the collective being of the Christian community, is a
dramatic example of the profound implications of *Geist* in Hegel's
thought.

Geist is Hegel's manner of expressing organic holism, in
which any given "whole" (family, nation, church, humanity or
whatever) may be said somehow to transcend the sum of its "parts"
(the finite, atomic individuals of which that whole is comprised).
Hegel formulates this position in the process of considering the
concept of organics in the *Phenomenology* (pp. 147-180). He is
able subsequently to apply the findings of this micro-ontology
to the macroscopic example of *Geist* in human affairs, concluding:

> The whole is a stable equilibrium of all the parts,
> and each part is a Spirit at home in this whole, a Spir-
> it which does not seek its satisfaction outside of it-
> self but finds it within itself, because it is itself
> in this equilibrium with the whole.   (*Phen.* 277)[17]

There is no metaphysical mystery or subterfuge involved in
the assertion that any (organic) whole is "more than the sum of
its parts." From the phenomenon of human community all the way
down the "scale of forms" to the relatively simple phenomenon of
wave diffraction and quantum-mechanical "scattering," the truth
of this assertion is evident. One basic and essential difference
between the whole and its individual parts is, quite simply, reciprocity or mutual relatedness. Pure atomism, empiricism and
other variations of reductionistic analysis dismiss reciprocity
and mutual relatedness as unimportant. The philosophies of Hegel
and Whitehead, the contemporary theory of quantum mechanics, and
all forms of human community (to name but a few examples) thrive
on mutual relatedness. Any "whole" differs from the sum of its

individual, atomically-isolated "parts" at least by the sum of
the relational terms of those parts with one another in the whole
--terms which are absent when the constituent parts are considered
in isolation.[18]

Hegel's *Geist* captures this essential and easily misinter-
preted truth. It is this interpretation (rather than the mystical or supernatural connotations) which is essential for a proper
appreciation of *Geist*. "Spirit" occupies the central position
in Hegel's thought: it is that "ultimate principle" which, as
Whitehead suggests (PR 10), is present in any philosophical system and is actual by virtue of its accidents. Spirit manifests
itself: (a) in finite (human) minds; (b) in select human com-
munities and their cultural, moral and political institutions
("objective spirit"); and (c) in an "Absolute" or universal sense
--"Spirit in its infinitude"--as revealed in art, religion and
finally in philosophy (cf. *Enc.* 553-577).[19]

In all its manifestations, *Geist* is what is self-actualizing.
Its "substance is freedom." It is the principle of striving, becoming, process and creativity (*Enc.* 381, 382, 384). Spirit creates itself according to the inner pattern of its own essential
Concept.

(iii) The other pivotal notion in Hegel's thought is the
Absolute Idea or Concept (*Begriff*). But, as Hegel warns, "What
the nature of the Concept is, can no more be stated offhand than
can the concept of any other object" (GL 577).

The strong Aristotelian flavor of Hegel's thought already
has been noted. It is with the doctrine of the *Begriff* that
Hegel's Aristotelianism takes its clearest form. For Aristotle,
every living entity possessed an inner pattern or principle which
it sought to actualize in its own development (entelechy), and
all things formed a hierarchy of being or "scale of forms"[20] according to their successively more adequate realization of the
Form of Perfection of the Universe--"Self-Thinking Thought"--
which Aristotle identified as God.[21]

. For Hegel, every organic entity likewise possesses its own
inner "concept" (or "notion")--the teleological pattern or principle which organizes the activity and the temporal development
of that organism. But it is also the case with Hegel that the
world process itself (which Hegel saw principally in terms of

the development of human history) possesses an immanent, gradually developing pattern or principle of intelligible order--the
Concept or Absolute Idea coming to its full realization in the
continuing flux of life and history.

Based upon our previous treatment of *Geist* and Hegel's close
affinity with Aristotle, we must expect that this all pervading
teleological principle--this "genetic code" of history, gradually
generating and more adequately realizing itself in the world-
process--will correspond finally to Hegel's vision of God's Will
and Purpose, working in and through the world. Again, it is difficult, if not impossible, to interpret Hegel's terminology and
involved categorical scheme (and thus glimpse what it is he is
trying to say about reality) apart from an understanding of the
profound religious symbolism his thought entails.

This is not to acknowledge Nietzsche's typically brash com-
plaint that Hegel and the German Idealists were nothing other
than frustrated theologians in the guise of philosophers. Hegel,
of course, did study theology extensively. The import of that
period for understanding his mature thought, however, is the profound impact that religious, and especially Christian doctrines
made upon him as symbols of the essential features of the actual
world process. These essential features themselves finally are
grasped only through the medium of reflective thought. These
features in themselves--entertained by the rational, self conscious mind apart from religious symbolism--are the proper subject matter of Absolute Knowledge (i.e., philosophy). The lengthy
process of coming to such a rational understanding of the Concept
is, of course, precisely what is traced in Hegel's *Phenomenology*
(*vide* especially pp. 485ff.).

Hegel's *Begriff* is the key to understanding his view of
freedom as grounded in the process of teleological self determination. Ultimately (i.e., from an ontological perspective) only
the *Begriff* is truly free because only the *Begriff* is self-suf-
ficiently and completely self determining. Accordingly Hegel
suggests in the *Encyclopedia* that the *Begriff* is "the principle
of freedom" (*Enc.* 160). Insofar as any finite entity embodies
its own internal concept, it is to that extent self-determining.

One final point must be borne in mind regarding Hegel's
doctrine of the *Begriff*. The finite manifestations of the Concept (its "mediation") in all things suggests that the universe,

despite its diversity of forms, exhibits an intelligible, ordered structure, a rational pattern or principle of organization. This *is* the Concept in its concreteness in the world. That there *is* a rational order--an intelligible set of relations among the flux of forms--is the pre-condition of all knowledge, whether scientific or philosophical. For to know is to discern the "order and connection of things" as related to the order and connection of our ideas of those things.

"Experience" is the encounter with individual "things." Knowledge is the discerning of a relation or set of relations among different "things." The central epistemological question was and is: Does the order and connection of our *ideas* about objects correspond in any sense with the objects themselves? Spinoza (whose phraseology I have utilized) asserts that the "order and connection" of ideas is identical with that of actual things, and that in this knowledge lies true freedom.[22] Kant's objections notwithstanding, it is the presupposition of all scientific investigation that the theories which result from systematic and empirically-grounded inquiry will result in greater knowledge of the world as it is in itself--i.e., that the order and connection of ideas is (or can be) equivalent to the order and connection of things.

It was Hegel's particular genius to grasp the full significance of this point. Rational order and structure--the set of intelligible relations among our ideas of things--cannot be merely a subjective construct superimposed upon the *Ding-an-sich*. Rather, the principle of rational order must *itself* be rooted in the very nature of reality. Mind and self-consciousness must be one special instance of, rather than some fantastic exception to, the general structure of nature. This principle of rational order Hegel calls the Concept. In this sense, Hegel's *Begriff* corresponds to the ancient Greek notion of the *Logos*. As Hegel himself suggests:

> This Concept is *not* sensuously intuited . . .
> it is solely . . . the absolute self-subsistent object, the *logos*, the *reason* of that which is, the
> *truth* of what we call things. . . .   (GL 39)

The *Begriff*, however, is not external to the process of becoming. It is immanent in the world, generating the process, and in turn being itself generated or actualized in the course of the world's development. *Geist* and *Begriff* are Hegel's twin principles of process, corresponding in many essential features to Whitehead's "Creativity" and "Principle of Concretion." *Geist* is the actualizing, energizing principle of flux and becoming. *Begriff* is *what* is coming to be, what is *determining* itself (and hence free) in all process--the pattern, structure or principle of organization which focuses all development and becoming toward a determinate issue in ultimate novelty.[23]

(iv) A note is in order at this point concerning Hegel's understanding of "negation" and the negative as the moving principle of his dialectic. Readers accustomed to a Marxist or existentialist interpretation of Hegel, stressing the dialectics of alienation and of non-being or nothingness will find little discussion of such interpretations in this exposition. This is due in part to my stress on Hegel's cosmology and philosophy of nature --dimensions of Hegel's thought apparently less familiar and less significant for Marxist and existentialist writers. This absence of negation as a dominant theme also is due to my impression that such emphases and interpretations of "dialectic" are not so integral to Hegel's own thought as is often supposed.

Negation, to be sure, is a pivotal notion for the understanding of dialectic. But negation, in my estimation, must always be interpreted in the context of *auf heben*: dialectic "unfolds" by means of the subordinating and superceding of certain tensions and oppositions which exist, say, between an organism and its environment.

Against the benign and optimistic interpretation of dialectic on the part of the "Hegelian right," however, Hegel himself suggests that the concept "sinks into mere edification, and even insipidity, if it lacks the seriousness, the suffering, the patience, and the labour of the negative" (*Phen.* 10). Just what such "suffering and patience" may entail is suggested in Hegel's famous vignettes of dialectical opposition: Master and Slave, the Unhappy or "Contrite" Consciousness, and the discussion of real alienation between Spirit and the objective (and sometimes oppressive) institutions it engenders in its quest for absolute freedom and self-knowledge. Contrary to many popular interpretations, however, one cannot suggest that these motifs are dominant for Hegel, insofar as they are seldom further discussed by

him beyond this early treatment in the initial sections of the
Phenomenology. The subsequent elaboration of these themes by
Marxists and existentialists represents a profound and original
contribution on their part. But it is important to note that
such themes neither were *ignored*, nor were they given central
prominence by Hegel himself.

For Hegel, the "power of the negative" is freedom. According to his terminology, to negate oneself is to render oneself
one's own object. This act of the will is at once the defining
act of self consciousness, of the transcendental ego or Absolute
Mind. This sort of negation comprises the essence of freedom
for Hegel, because nothing which was not free of external constraints ever could perform this ultimate act of self-consciousness. In that regard, freedom is much like the Cartesian *cogito*:
to doubt it is to affirm its existence in the skeptic. It is in
this sense that freedom is an activity or an *achievement* of *Geist*
alone.

It is this phenomenon of self consciousness as negation and
freedom which Hegel seeks to elaborate. It is this search which
dominates his own thought, rather than the theme of the dialectical power of alienation and non-being sometimes attributed to
him. And it is this understanding which both requires and proceeds directly as a consequence of his general metaphysical
position--specifically his cosmology, and even more specifically,
what I shall term his micro-ontology of organic mechanism. Finally, through pursuing this quest, one is led to understand the
remaining features or nuances of dialectic and negation entirely
in terms of the real and creative process of organic becoming:
i.e., the process by which elements alien and opposed to an
organism's own being are, in some sense, integrated and recon-
ciled. Those external oppositions are "sublated" into an intensity of internal contrasts within a harmonious unity.

This is to suggest that Hegel intends by dialectic and negation precisely what Whitehead intends by concrescence. This
point was perceived by R. G. Collingwood and Errol E. Harris
precisely as a result of their willingness to encounter the
Hegelian corpus entirely, rather than selectively. This interpretation is less adequately reflected in Bradley and McTaggart,
who were uninterested in Hegel's cosmology and philosophy of

nature. This interpretation is lost entirely upon (or perhaps rejected by) many Continental interpreters of Hegel--such as Marx, Kierkegaard, Nietzsche, Heidegger, Sartre and Tillich-- for the very reason that these apparently considered the essentials of Hegel's metaphysics as either unintelligible or unimportant, or both.[24]

My own interpretation of negation, alienation, dialectic-- and indeed, the whole of Hegel's thought--is *not* available as yet another exposition in behalf of the Hegelian right. Hegel, I feel, would justifiably resist appropriation of his thought by either side in that traditional debate. Indeed, Hegel in many respects anticipated and criticized both these interpretations of his thought. Against the right Hegel suggests that the reality of negation, and the pain, suffering and labor of dialectic are not sufficiently stressed.[25] Properly understood, the themes of forgiveness and reconciliation so essential to the final phase of objective spirit could never serve merely as a comfortable bourgeois apologetic for violent and authoritarian institutions and oppressive ideologies (see below, Sections 5 and 6).

On the other hand, Hegel would indict the Hegelian left for overstressing the role of alienation and negation. Pure negation --i.e., negative or abstract freedom--results for Hegel (as it did admittedly for Marx as well) in the "fury of destruction." This may be--and frequently is--a necessary dimension of freedom as liberation. And negative freedom indeed constitutes the partial truth of concrete freedom for Hegel. Where Hegel differs from Marx is in suggesting that the anger of this necessary retributive justice finally must be sublated (with all the emotional force which can be mustered in behalf of so awkward and archaic a term). That is, righteous and morally justifiable anger finally gives way to forgiveness, compassion and reconciliation in a new and higher synthesis, in which the unjust *causes* of that suffering and anger likewise are overcome.

Marx's theory of class struggle likewise stresses the eventual victory over oppression and injustice, to be sure. Yet one senses that in principle, as well as in actualization, the dimensions of love and trust which are essential to Hegel's view never quite reach an equal significance in Marx's interpretation.

This digression constitutes a warning regarding my less-conventional usage of negation in the exposition of Hegel's thought. The justification for this position finally lies in the exposition of the primary material which follows.

(v) Finally, we must point out the peculiarly Hegelian uses of the terms: abstract, concrete and objectivity. These terms are critical to a full understanding of Hegel's thought. His use of these terms differs slightly from common usage and from their use by Whitehead.[26]

For Whitehead, the distinction between abstract and concrete referred ultimately to actual occasions. These were concrete in the sense of being experient, subjective, and actively self-relating. The nineteenth-century concept of matter, by contrast, was an abstraction for Whitehead--i.e., it portrayed entities which were *non*-experient and *non*-active ("vacuous actuality"). These uses differ from ordinary language, in which concrete means definite, particular, down-to-earth, as opposed to abstract, which is normally understood as either vague or else conceptually difficult, abstruse, or up-in-the-air.

Hegel's use of the term is, on the surface, entirely different from the two preceding uses. As we have seen in several examples, abstract means, for Hegel, isolated, particular, one-sided, atomistic, and inadequately *related* or mediated ("*im*-mediate"). The concept of liberty advocated in the French Revolution, Kant's concept of individual duty, the concept of private and individual rights, and Jacobi's "beautiful soul" all are abstractions in this Hegelian sense. By contrast, as we have seen, an entity or concept is concrete for Hegel when it is multi-dimensional, many sided, and fully inter-related or mediated in its various finite moments or particularizations. *Geist*, *Begriff*, and the proper metaphysical concept of *Freiheit* are all concrete in Hegel's sense. Freedom, for example, is a universal concept which has many finite meanings. All of these, when taken in aggregate as mutually conditioning, limiting and relating to one another yield "freedom" in its full and complete meaning as a "concrete universal."

Finally, we must define Hegel's use of "objectivity." Recall that, for Whitehead, the categories of "subject" and "object" represented no fundamental ontological distinction. Rather, these were relative judgments of the *same* entity from different temporal frames of reference. What was a "subject" in its own active present would be an object, a "concretum" enjoying complete determinateness, and hence no longer active as viewed by another subject at a subsequent time. Hegel likewise eschews the absolute subject-object distinction as representing an unnecessary bifurcation of reality, one which he viewed as destructive of earlier metaphysical systems, such as Kant's (GL 62ff.).

Like Whitehead, Hegel sought to overcome the subject-object dichotomy by appeal to a relative distinction or definition of subjectivity and objectivity. But in Hegel's thought, the distinction is relative with respect to a hierarchy of being or "scale of forms," proceeding through various dialectical phases of complexity from immediate objectivity to fully mediated subjectivity. A "subject" for Hegel is what is *thinking*; an object is what is *thought about*, or entertained in thought. A subject is thus merely an "object experiencing" (i.e., in a state of consciousness). *Any* subject may be an object, and Hegel is particularly concerned with the case of "subjects" rendering themselves their own "object"--i.e., reflexivity or self-consciousness, the most complex and developed phase of sentience. Not all objects may be subjects, however, for not all objects can *think*, let alone undergo reflexive, self-conscious experience.

Thus, Hegel's only distinction of reality comes at the point of objects which *cannot* be subjects: namely, inorganic matter, subject to mechanistic physical laws. Only such objects may be described by "natural laws" external to the objects themselves (and even then not completely). *Organism* is the logical category which Hegel devises to describe objects which are simultaneously experiencing subjects, only partly and inadequately described by external mechanical laws.

Hegel's other sense of "objectivity," however, concerns the *Begriff* as "object." The Concept (like Whiteheadian "concrescences") during different stages of its self-determination is both subjective and objective.

> The Concept in the guise of immediacy constitutes the point of view for which the Concept is a subjective thinking, a reflection *external* to the

subject matter. This stage, therefore, constitutes
subjectivity or the *formal Concept*.   (GL 597)

When the *Begriff* is actually embodied or "mediated" in various
modes of being (thereby providing the form, structure and organization for being), it is said to be *objective*.

> Objectivity is the *real Concept* that has *emerged
> from its inwardness* and passed over into determinate
> being . . . the Concept thus has a *free* determinate
> being of its *own*. But this is still only an *immediate*
> . . . freedom.   (*Ibid.*)

Inorganic objects do not embody their own concept. Hence
they are not self-determining, but governed according to external
laws of nature. Organic objects embody their own concept, are
subject to teleological rather than mechanistic explanation,
and thus pre-figure freedom. As Hegel notes, their self-determination is only an "immediate" freedom, since organisms are
not self-conscious. This gradual emergence of self-consciousness
in higher organisms Hegel portrays as the "objective" Concept
"giving itself the form of subjectivity" (which it originally
possessed in its immediate, formal, "abstract" existence), culminating in *Reason*, through which the Concept has attained its
most adequate phase as the Absolute Idea, the realm of perfect
truth and freedom:

> In this consummation in which it has the form
> of freedom even in its objectivity, the *adequate
> Concept* is the *Idea. Reason*, which is the sphere
> of the Idea, is the *self-revealed truth* in which
> the Concept . . . is free, inasmuch as it cognizes
> this . . . objective world in its subjectivity and
> its subjectivity in its objective world.   (*Ibid.*)

A complete study of the phases of self-development of the
Concept, then, carries us all the way from the scientific realm
of inorganic objects to the realm of Absolute Spirit--universal
self-consciousness. This is the progress traced in Hegel's
Encyclopedia, which documents the very development of freedom
itself, a development which we shall now consider.

Section 3. The Doctrine of Metaphysical Freedom

The formal doctrine of metaphysical freedom is contained in
Hegel's *Logic*. The *Logic* has been described as a kind of metaphysical lexicon, in which one provisional definition of a given

concept leads on to another until the most complete term has been reached--the *Begriff*--sublating within itself the salient aspects of all the previous concepts.[27] In Hegel's words, the *Logic* treats only "pure thoughts, spirit thinking its own essential nature."[28] Hegel implies that the Concept cannot be defined or even presupposed. Instead, it must be discerned or discovered by tracing the phases of its own development. The *Logic* provides precisely this "genetic exposition of the Concept" (GL 577).

According to Hegel, however, the Concept itself is "the realm of *subjectivity* or of *freedom*" (GL 571). Thus, the goal of the analysis in Hegel's *Logic* is itself precisely what we seek in the present essay: the principle of metaphysical freedom. As developed in the *Logic*, however, this principle is purely formal: i.e., we can expect that whatever doctrine of metaphysical freedom is adumbrated will be perfectly general in all its features, and will therefore serve indiscriminately to describe the freedom encountered in Nature, human morals, politics or religion. The freedom of the Concept in the *Logic* is thus a "bare universal," whose subsequent moments or determinations in the various phases of spirit, as traced in the *Encyclopedia* renders it finally concrete.

The first half of the "Lesser Logic" is given over to statements concerning the proper aims of philosophy and logical inquiry, together with an historical assessment of the contributions to this task offered by previous modern philosophies. Hegel views the aim of philosophy, as the quest for absolute truth, to be the overcoming of the subject-object distinction--the dichotomy between the world as it is and our subjective experience of it. He writes: "the highest and final aim of philosophic science [is] to bring about . . . a reconciliation of the self-conscious reason with the reason which *is* in the world" (*Enc*. 6).

This last phrase is highly suggestive. Hegel anticipates Whitehead's "reformed subjectivist principle" by repudiating Cartesian ontological dualism. We know the actual world because the actual world is itself rationally ordered and is therefore intelligible in itself. The observing mind, itself an element in the process of nature, merely reflects in a conscious manner the rational structure of the larger world process in which it participates and of which it is a part. Hegel thus resurrects a pivotal doctrine of classical philosophy: the world embodies a *Logos*, an internal source or principle of development. This principle is rational, and when properly understood, it reveals the world to be a "free and unified whole" (*Enc*. 14; cf. GL 39).

The freedom and unity which characterize the internal self-development of the world-process, however, are not to be confused with the "abstract freedom" of Locke, Rousseau and the French Revolution (with which the young Hegel, like many of his German contemporaries, had been first fascinated, and ultimately horrified). The latter was an excess born in the error of failing to perceive that the individual "is also a member of a group" whose collective conceptions issue in the statutes of law, morality and religion. "All other men have it in common with me to be 'I' . . . to this extent, 'I' is the existence of a wholly *abstract* universality, a principle of abstract freedom" (*Enc*. 20).[29] Pursuit of this sort of freedom, which is not actual or concrete, results (as we have noted) in absolute terror rather than absolute freedom.

True freedom consists rather in breaking the bonds of individuality, of overcoming "bare particularity" and the isolated subjective immediacy of "I" in favor of "We." Freedom means participation in a community of selves in which "the abstract self, freed from all the special limitations to which its ordinary states or qualities are liable, restricts itself to that universal action in which it is identical with all individuals" (*Enc*. 23).[30]

Furthermore, Hegel argues, rationalist metaphysics (principally the thought of Spinoza and Leibniz) has demonstrated that a proper understanding of freedom reveals its dependence upon necessity or determinateness. Freedom and necessity require one another for their own essential definition. Each is unintelligible apart from its "opposite." Hence, freedom is (in some sense) "conditioned" by necessity.

> A freedom involving no necessity, and mere necessity without freedom, are abstract and in this way untrue formulae of thought. Freedom is no blank indeterminateness: essentially concrete, and unvaryingly self-determinate, it is so far at the same time necessary. Necessity, again, in the ordinary acceptation of the term in popular philosophy, means determination from without only . . . This however is merely external

necessity, not the real inward necessity which is
identical with freedom.   (*Enc.* 35, *Zusatz*)[31]

Finally, Hegel acknowledges a contribution of empiricism to
the subjective understanding of the principle of freedom. For
"the main lesson of empiricism is that man must see for himself
and feel that he is present in every fact of knowledge which he
has to accept" (*Enc.* 38). Indeed, Hegel's own criticism of empiricism is that it fails to immerse itself fully in the process
of knowing--it stops at the point of an epistemic dualism (such
as that of Locke and Kant) between what "really" exists and our
knowledge of this. Hegel argues that this position amounts to
"a doctrine of *bondage*: for we become free when we are confronted
by no absolutely alien world, but depend upon a fact which we
ourselves are" (*Enc.* 38, *Zusatz*).

By contrast, Hegel himself asserts that the categories of
his *Logic* are not only those principles which enable us to attain knowledge of the physical world, but are also "the real essence of things" (*Enc.* 41, *Zusatz*). It is thus Hegel's view,
rather than that of either eighteenth or twentieth-century empiricism, which is in fact held by the practicing scientist.
The scientist believes not only in the internal coherence of
his or her theories about nature, but also that those theories
do actually correspond in *some* sense to the way in which natural
events actually are related and structured.[32]

The process of ascertaining the doctrine of freedom in the
Logic itself is laborious. One must, of necessity, trace the
route of Hegel's "triad" of Being, Essence and Concept, only in
the latter of which will true freedom be found to reside.

(i) Hegel ascertains that the truth of existence lies in
neither traditional category of Being or Nothing, but rather in
their synthesis, the process of Becoming (GL 82ff.). Being is
merely that which we find "identified with what persists amid
all change, with *matter*, susceptible of innumerable determinations." But, argues Hegel, when we try to understand just what
is entailed in this "empty abstraction" of "pure being" we find
that we can give an answer only in terms of determinate examples
and characterizations--none of which exemplify "pure being" in
its simplicity. *Pure* being in its mere generality is "Nothing"
(i.e., it is an empty, immediate abstraction). There is no real

difference of meaning between the two traditional contraries,
"Being and Nothing." Both are relatively meaningless in isolation. "The truth of Being and of Nothing," Hegel writes, "is
accordingly the unity of the two: and this unity is *Becoming*"
(*Enc.* 87, 88).

> Becoming is the first concrete thought, and
> therefore the first concept: whereas Being and
> Nothing are empty abstraction. The concept of
> Being, therefore, of which we sometimes speak,
> must mean Becoming; not the mere point of Being,
> which is empty Nothing, any more than Nothing,
> which is empty Being . . . Being which does not
> lose itself in Nothing is Becoming . . . Becoming
> is only the explicit statement of what Being is
> in its truth.
> (*Enc.* 88, *Zusatz*)

It is worth commenting on the salient features of this well-
known but perplexing conclusion. What Hegel establishes is that
the concept of an underlying, unchanging substrate of all reality
("Being") is an empty abstraction, devoid of meaningful content.
We can make no sense of such a notion. The ideas of "some-thing"
which *is*, and "no-thing" which *is not*, individually are meaningless. That which exists or is actual only is that which is in
the process of development from a state of being "nothing" to
one of being a determinate "something." Whence, "Becoming is
only the explicit statement of what Being is in its truth."
While it may be objected that Hegel's is not the clearest statement of this principle, it is impossible, I feel, to escape the
conclusion that, for Hegel, being is constituted by becoming.

(ii) Dialectical consideration of "Being" leads to an ac-
knowledgement of the process of Becoming, issuing in determinate
manifestations--particular, finite things or existents. That
which traditionally is contrasted with determinate being as
Existence is Essence, those universal concepts which tell us
what a particular entity is.

To determine the essence of a particular thing, argues
Hegel, is to establish its Ground: a reason for, or cause of
any particular thing which embodies that essence. The ground
of, or reason for a thing is thus merely the *immanence* of the
universal essence in that particular thing (*Enc.* 120). Essence
is, in this sense, the truth of Being "passing over" into the
very existents (particular things) which it grounds (GL 389).

To establish the ground or reason of a particular thing is to establish how and why that thing is what it is--i.e., to determine "that for the sake of which" a particular thing exists. The essence has no concrete meaning apart from the partial, finite particularizations of itself in actual individuals, "in so far as essence as ground no longer distinguishes itself from itself as grounded" (GL 483).

All universals are thus "concrete" in Hegel's sense of that term: they are actual by virtue of their accidents, their finite particularizations. Universals are thus immanent in their actualizations, and transcend these only in the sense that they can be spoken of as forms of definiteness more general than any single *one* of their finite particularizations. The finite existents are, in turn, identifiable in terms of the general essence or form which they individually embody. An essence is thus that which is immanent in each actual individual, while yet transcending any one particular manifestation. The essence in its totality serves to give each of its actualizations a unique identity as a determinate form of being.[33]

The relation of essence and determinate being thus may be portrayed as a relation of a whole and its parts (GL 513ff.). An essence or universal as a ground of finite being is a "whole" subsuming each of its finite particularizations as a "part." The whole, however, is not some mystical absolute within which the relative autonomy of all finite determinations of being are sublated. Rather, the relation is *reciprocal*: finite things exist by virtue of the general Concept or pattern of organization which they embody as the ground of their finite existence. The Concept or pattern is in turn concrete or actual by virtue of its ingredience in its many "moments" or finite particularizations.

> *The whole is equal to the parts and the parts to the whole.* There is nothing in the whole which is not in the parts, and nothing in the parts which is not in the whole (GL 515).[34]

Thus Hegel asserts that an appeal to a modified form of teleological explanation is necessary to determine fully what a particular, finite entity *is* in terms of the pattern or principle of organization it strives to actualize in its own development. I term this appeal to teleological explanation "modified" due to Hegel's insistence on the reciprocity of pattern and entity, whole and part, being and its essence. The pattern or Concept is throughout immanent in, and rendered actual or concret by its finite particularizations.[35]

(iii) At this point, Hegel's consideration of being and essence have revealed that being is constituted by becoming, and *what* becomes is the essence, ground or Concept of a particular thing, more adequately and fully realized in each of the successive phases of its development. How is this rather formal and abstract discussion of teleological process related to our problem of metaphysical freedom?

Hegel makes several suggestions on the road to a complete answer to this question (contained in the concluding sections of the *Logic*). First, there is a sense in which freedom is a property of self-consciousness, of *für-sich Sein*, in contrast to mere *an-sich Sein*. Being-for-itself includes self-determination of one's activities; whence to be self-conscious is to be free.

> Man, it may be said, is distinguished from the animal world, and in that way from nature altogether, by knowing himself as 'I': which amounts to saying that natural things never attain a free Being-for-self, but as limited to Being-there-and-then, are always and only Being for an other.
>
> (*Enc.* 96, *Zusatz*)

Not much can be made of this, however, for even *für-sich Sein* is "immediacy" (*Enc.* 96), since it does not embody its own essence--i.e., it is not "self-related" (*Enc.* 112). In general, the first step toward the embodiment of an entity's own essence is the process of relating that allegedly self-subsistent, unitary existent with the many other, similar existents--the recognition that one "thing" is one among many things. In the human situation, this formalism translates into the need for the individual person to realize that he or she is a member of a communi of similar persons. The essence of human being is not individuality, but *Geist*-in-community. By this reasoning, self-subsistence, as Hegel argues, is the greatest possible error. The concept of abstract freedom which bare individuality entails, Hegel describes as in reality the principle of destructive evil (GL 172).

Nonetheless an important point is uncovered in the analysis of these first dialectical phases of being. True freedom entails a process of development from what is merely internal, potential, immanent and inadequately mediated (*an-sich Sein*) to what is explicit, actual, still immanent, but now adequately and fully mediated (*für-sich Sein*). A *Ding-an-sich* which becomes thus a *Ding-für-sich* is properly described as "free."[36] Thus, freedom is achieved by means of the process of self-development of an object's own inner nature (the Aristotelian "entelechy"), a process which is at once dialectical and teleological in the manner described.

It is clear that Hegel is speaking of freedom somewhat at variance with the traditional (historical) discussion of *liberum arbitrium* (freedom of choice or will). Indeed, the latter term involves for him some essential ambiguities, if not outright contradictions. These become apparent when one examines dialectically the meaning of the phrase "Freedom of the Will" or "free choice." Hegel offers such an examination in a lengthy *Zusatz*:

> Of contingency in respect of the Will it is especially important to form a proper estimate. The Freedom of the Will is an expression that often means mere free choice, or the will in the form of contingency. Freedom of choice, or the capacity for determining ourselves towards one thing or another, is undoubtedly a vital element in the will (which in its very notion is free); but instead of being freedom itself, it is only in the first instance a freedom in form. The genuinely free will, which includes free choice as suspended, is conscious to itself that its content is intrinsically firm and fast, and knows it at the same time to be thoroughly its own. A will, on the contrary, which remains standing on the grade of option, even supposing it does decide in favour of what is in import right and true, is always haunted by the conceit that it might, if it had so pleased, have decided in favour of the reverse course. When more narrowly examined, free choice is seen to be a contradiction, to this extent that its form and content stand in antithesis.
>
> (*Enc.* 145, *Zusatz*)

Hegel suggests that if free choice means merely chance or indeterminacy, then no sense can be made of the term. For Hegel, choice is (self) determined by a knowledge of conditions, constraints and obligations as mediated by an ultimate consideration of the goal, pattern or principle which the agent self-consciously strives to actualize. That principle (his "Concept" or "Idea"), however, does not determine the action or its outcome in a mechanistic sense. Such an interpretation would suggest the kind of causality which necessitarians or determinists assert to be operative, and which Hegel deems likewise incoherent.

Since the principle is immanent in the process itself, we have instead teleological self-determination of actions in pursuit of an end. As Hegel noted with reference to rationalist metaphysics, it is in this Aristotelian sense that freedom "requires necessity" in order to render it intelligible. And the freedom of the human moral agent is but a supervenient phase of the more-generally operative mode of teleological self-determination in the whole of the cosmic system.

In this regard, the "free choice" which Hegel sees as contradictory is that narrower definition (which he rejects) of equally possible, completely open alternatives. Hegel regards such possibilities as illusory, and this trivial explanation of freedom as a sham. Utilizing Whiteheadian terminology, what Hegel suggests is that the mere envisagement of abstract "pure possibilities" in any situation does not guarantee that all such possibilities are "compossible"--i.e., equally capable of harmonious and satisfactory alternative realization. Indeed, many apparent alternatives, were they actualized, would reveal themselves as contradictory, disharmonious, and self-refuting. These pure possibilities are thus not in fact "real" possibilities for the moral will.

It is Reason which, for Hegel, makes this discrimination between real and merely abstract possibilities in terms of the conditions and constraints operant at any moment of decision--such as those imposed constraints on his own actions discerned by Socrates by virtue of his choosing to see himself as a member of a community rather than merely an abstract individual. Furthermore, it is impossible for Hegel, as it was for Aristotle, to envision a situation in which healthy and fully-operant reason could make such a determination among possibilities and then fail to act upon it. Hegel, therefore, describes the "necessity of choice" or will in terms of the self-determination of reason, in contrast to the trivial case of merely random determination of action. The latter is the view of free choice which Hegel dismisses as a contradiction.

Hegel thus limits the abstract range of "pure possibilities" in principle open to the will to the relatively selective ensemble of "real" (i.e., rational or harmonious) possibilities, in terms of his doctrine of "internal necessity" (as established by the dictates of a healthy Reason). Is the doctrine too confining, however? In attempting to relate freedom and necessity, has Hegel in fact merely reduced freedom *to* necessity (as some critics would charge), providing only a convenient justification for the actual as the rational (and therefore, presumably, the Good or desirable)?

In elaborating his doctrine as outlined above, Hegel does indeed seem to suggest that his doctrine of conditional or "finite" freedom is, in fact, no more than a Stoic reconciliation of one's hopes and desires with one's determined lot in life.

> Necessity gives a point of view which has important bearings upon our sentiments and behavior. When we look upon events as necessary, our situation seems at first sight to lack freedom completely . . . But a close examination of the ancient feeling about destiny will not by any means reveal a sense of bondage to its power. Rather the reverse . . . the sense of bondage springs from inability to surmount the antithesis, and from looking at what *is*, and what happens, as contradictory to what *ought* to be and happen. In the ancient mind the feeling was more of the following kind: Because such a thing is, it is, and as it is, so ought it to be. Here there is no contrast to be seen, and therefore no sense of bondage, no pain, and no sorrow.
>
> (*Enc*. 147, *Zusatz*)[37]

We might, of course, re-assert that Hegel is here merely explicating more fully what is entailed by "conditioned teleology" or "finite freedom" with respect to any individual entity. In Section 148 of his *Encyclopedia*, Hegel offers a "typology of necessity" which seems to agree with later statements by, among others, Marx and Whitehead on the true meaning of freedom. Any activity, Hegel argues, presupposes some "conditions" as well as certain facts which the agent seeks to bring into being from the antecedent conditions. The "activity" is thus conditioned by the past in the obvious sense that the translation of conditions into facts through activity is dependent upon the nature of those antecedent conditions.[38]

Hegel further suggests the similarity of his position with that of Spinoza, in which the only "cause" of things as they are

is Substance, which is *causa sui*, and hence free (*Enc.* 153).
However, it appears that Hegel's ultimate formulation of the relation of freedom to necessity is given in terms of "Reciprocity,
the doctrine through which the subject-object dichotomy finally
is overcome.

> Causality passes into the relation of *action and
> reaction*, or *reciprocity* . . . the rectilinear move-
> ment out from causes to effects, and from effects to
> causes, is bent round and back into itself, and thus
> the progress *ad infinitum* of causes and effects is,
> as a progress, really and truly suspended . . . which
> transforms the infinite progression into a self-con-
> tained relationship.
>
> (*Enc.* 154)

Thus Hegel finally does suggest the notion that in a true,
holistic system every event or entity entails every other in the
sense that each individual entity or event exhibits relations
with and among all the other particulars in the whole.[39] These
relations are in some sense internal and partially constitutive
of each finite entity. The "false" infinite regress of linear
causality is thus transformed or "transfigured" [verklärt] into
the "true" or circular infinite of *reciprocity*. The true meaning
of necessity, for Hegel, is thus reciprocity (*Enc.* 157). And,
as we have noted, the finite freedom of individuals-in-community
is in part constituted by such reciprocity.[40] This re-interpre-
tation of necessity in terms of reciprocity finally clarifies
Hegel's ostensibly contradictory claim that the "truth of necessity, therefore, is *freedom*" (*Enc.* 158).

Hegel explicates the doctrine of conditional freedom ultimately by appeal to holism, and the mutual interdependence of
all the organic components (erroneously labeled "subject-object"
or "cause-effect") in an organic or systematic totality. As he
comments in the *Zusatz* to Section 158:

> It then appears that the members, linked to one
> another, are not really foreign to each other, but
> only elements of one whole, each of them, in its con-
> nection with the other, being, as it were, at home,
> and combining with itself. In this way necessity is
> transfigured into freedom--not the freedom . . . [of]
> abstract Negation, [but a much more positive and con-
> crete freedom]. From which we may learn what a mis-
> take it is to regard freedom and necessity as mutually
> exclusive. Necessity indeed, *qua* necessity, is far
> from being freedom: yet freedom presupposes neces-
> sity, and contains it as an unsubstantial element in
> itself.

> A good man is aware that the tenor of his conduct
> is essentially obligatory and necessary. But this
> consciousness is so far from making any abatement of
> his freedom, that without it real and reasonable free-
> dom could not be distinguished from arbitrary choice
> --a freedom which has no reality and is merely poten-
> tial. . . .In short, man is most independent when he
> knows himself to be determined by the absolute idea
> throughout. It was this phase of mind and conduct
> which Spinoza called *Amor Intellectualis Dei*.
>
> > (*Enc.* 158, *Zusatz*)

It is in this sense that Hegel consistently argues that what
is, is what ought to be (Phil. R., "Preface")--not in terms of
sanctioning uncritically any given situation, but instead discerning that all things are striving together toward a greater
realization of value. Thus any and all stages of existence,
however imperfect and unsatisfactory in themselves, are attempts
to actualize more perfectly and adequately an internal ideal pattern or structure in the world.

(iv) Hegel's discussion of Reciprocity forms the transition
to his treatment of the *Begriff* as the principle of freedom,
which we envisioned at the beginning of this section (GL 569-
571).[41]

> The Concept is the principle of freedom, the
> power of substance self-realized. It is a systematic
> whole, in which each of its constituent functions is
> the very total which the Concept is, and is put as in-
> dissolubly one with it. Thus in its self-identity it
> has original and complete determinateness.
>
> > (*Enc.* 160)

Complete freedom as self-determination thus resides only in the
Begriff. As Bernhard Lakebrink summarizes: "The Idea is its
own Cause and Purpose, or the Concept is 'the accomplishing
[fulfilling] of itself,' i.e. *Causa sui*. The Life of the pure
Concept is therefore Freedom itself."[42]

All existents to some extent embody the Concept. It is
immanent, and not external to the cosmic process. Yet the Concept or *Logos* is distinguishable from many of its finite manifestations in the cosmos. Thus can nature and human individuals
be said at once to "embody freedom" while not being themselves
fully free. In all its finite manifestations, freedom is limited
or conditioned by reciprocity. Only the Concept itself is fully
self-determining and free.[43] Indeed, the *Begriff* is the "principle of freedom," what Hegel terms the "concrete universal."

Thus freedom, for Hegel, entails more merely than the human moral freedom of choice or freedom of the will. Hegel fully intends that this definition of freedom is to be understood as the essence of all existence, the substance of the world. And the truth lies (as he is fond of pointing out) in realizing that this "Substance is Subject as well" (*Phen.* 10). That is, being (which is constituted by becoming) exhibits in that process of becoming what we would commonly refer to as the "subjective" quality of self-determination. Hence, in the *Logic*, Hegel demonstrates that freedom is constitutive of Being itself: he delineates a *metaphysical* freedom. *Esse est creare.*[44] With this final identity of the *Begriff* as the principle of freedom, it is not wide of the mark to suggest that the central thrust of Hegel's *Logic* is toward a study of freedom as the "concrete universal," actualizing itself in the world.

Section 4. Organic Mechanism in Nature

(i) Outline of Hegel's *Naturphilosophie*

Freedom has been defined as essential to the *Begriff*, the inner principle of teleological development of all reality. Nonetheless it remains to be seen *how* this formal definition translates into a meaningful doctrine of a freedom which is grounded on the teleological self-determination operant in the wider realm of nature. Our present understanding is still "subjective," formal and abstract (*an sich*; GL 708). We must, in Hegel's inimitable terminology, allow the Concept or Idea to "go forth freely from itself" and become "object to itself" (*Enc.* 244)[45] as the realm of nature, culminating in *organisms*. These most complex natural forms of organization exhibit self-sustaining, interdependent activity. Thus organisms, for Hegel, provide an intuition in non-human nature of the concept of *Geist*, that many-sided principle of creativity and community which becomes explicit in human societies, cultures and institutions.[46]

The course of Hegel's discussion of the "Objective Concept" and the immanence of that Concept in nature, is as follows. Freedom as teleological self-determination is the principal property of the *Begriff*. But, as we have seen, teleological self-determination is exhibited to a limited extent by any entity which is self-conscious, which is *an-und-für-sich selbst*. Hegel envisions the world in terms of "becoming," as an ongoing process of development and evolution.[47] *What* becomes, what evolves throughout, and what emerges from this process of development is ultimately "Mind"--self-consciousness, or "thought thinking itself." It is Hegel's passionate and overriding interest to understand both this process and its novel issue, for the principal property of this emergent Mind turns out to be its "concrete freedom."

In our treatment of Whitehead's theory, we saw that Whitehead accounted for the emergence of self-conscious mind in nature by his pan-subjectivist principle. Consciousness was not a phenomenon which came into being *ex nihilo*.[48] There is no dualism, no bifurcation of reality between nature and the perceiving mind. Rather, for Whitehead, some form of sentience or subjectivity is characteristic (though not necessarily dominant) in the atomic constituents of being, his "actual entities." The phenomenology of self-consciousness with which Hegel is so preoccupied is, for Whitehead, a sustained and consistent development consequent upon the more complex or "sophisticated" associations and groupings of actual entities (*vide supra*, p. 45, n.67).

This, of course, is a variation on the doctrine of "emergent evolution": the result of a process of development represents a sustained progression of forms through which a property or characteristic which was either immanent in, or in some sense a real possibility for the process from its inception is actualized or otherwise rendered fully developed. Variations on this doctrine are common to Whitehead, Alexander, Bergson--and, I would argue, Hegel as well. Admittedly Whitehead allows for a greater degree of spontaneity and randomness than do the other advocates of emergent evolution.[49] One must be reminded, however, that spontaneity in itself is not to be identified as the source of Whitehead's principle of freedom.[50] Furthermore, it is significant to note that sentience--which in the special case of human consciousness Whitehead and Hegel both identify as the source of novelty, spontaneity, creativity and freedom--is indeed "present from the beginning" in an elementary form in all actual entities, and is thus "emergent" (or more fully actualized) precisely in the sense described.

For Hegel, it is the *Begriff* itself which is objectified
and immanent in nature. His "Philosophy of Nature" is a description of its emergence in the progression of more complex forms
in nature, culminating in *organisms*, whose behavior is governed
according to their inner "concept" or Idea. As such, organisms
are subject to teleological description, within which mechanism
is sublated.

It is proper, I argue, to speak of Hegel's doctrine at this
phase of its development as "organic mechanism," indicating that
the mechanical and chemical functions which an organism performs
may be understood only in terms of the purposive organization of
those functions toward the survival and maintenance of the organism as a whole. Mechanical and chemical functions of the organism are organized according to this purpose, and are conditioned
further by the interdependence and reciprocal internal relatedness
among the organisms (i.e., within an organic *system*).[51]

"Organic mechanism" is thus the connecting link, the "critical threshold" in the transition from inorganic nature (nominally
subject, in Hegel's view, to mechanistic description) to the
realm of *Geist*, where events are described in terms of their
freedom and interdependence. Thus, an understanding of nature
is not peripheral, but rather integral to Hegel's whole system,
narrating as it does this gradual transition from necessity to
freedom (*Enc.* 381, *Zusatz*).[52]

This demonstration of the immanence of the *Begriff* in nature
is necessary, finally, to separate Hegel's doctrine from the various doctrines of subjective idealism. Kant, for example, seemed
to establish that the structure of knowledge--the order and connection of ideas--was in some sense only a subjective organization of the sensory manifold. "Objectivity" was achieved, not
by identifying that structure with the actual "things-in-them-
selves," but rather by postulating a "community of subjects,"
whereby all the individual percipients possessed a common set
of mechanisms for perception and for the consequent ordering of
those perceptions as knowledge.

For Hegel, this solution still seemed to presuppose a fundamental duality of mind and the world. If self-consciousness and
the process of acquiring knowledge could instead be shown as an
emergent and supervenient activity of the world-process itself,

then the structure of thought and knowledge discerned by mind
would be demonstrated merely as a reflection, or consciousness
of the structure of the actual world. The structure of thought
is the *Begriff*, the principle of freedom and of dialectical-
teleological development. In his analysis of nature, Hegel offers to demonstrate that "the dialectical principle active in
the sphere of thought is also the principle of natural development."[53] In our case, this also amounts to a demonstration that
freedom is at least immanent in the processes of nature, and
comes to its full, explicit realization in the supervenient development of human self-consciousness.

(ii) Mechanism, Chemism and Teleology in the *Logic*

The entire issue of determinism versus freedom, for Hegel,
turns on the alleged opposition of mechanism and teleology. In
Hegel's view, these last are not true opposites or contradictor-
ies. In the "Larger Logic," Hegel demonstrates that mechanism
is sublated (*aufgehoben*) in teleology (GL 734). The chief example cited is the behavior of living organisms, which can be seen
to employ and coordinate mechanical functions and processes according to an overriding internal pattern or purpose. The incorporation of mechanical functions in a teleological context as
the basis of organic activity is the principal justification for
my use of the term "organic mechanism" to describe Hegel's doctrine.

It is important to note that, for Hegel, "organism"--and
indeed, Life itself--represent ontological categories. This
generalized ontological category of life (*das logische Leben*)
is first distinguished from specific manifestations or expressions of life--viz., natural life (*natürliches Leben*) and life
"in so far as it stands in connexion with *spirit*" (*das Leben des
Geistes*; GL 762). These latter categories are the topics, respectively, of the "Philosophy of Nature" and the "Philosophy
of Spirit" in Hegel's *Encyclopedia*.

What perfectly general characteristics can be identified
as pertaining to life; or, more directly, what makes living
things *living*? This is the problem addressed in Hegel's *Logic*
by treating "life" as a "logical" (i.e., metaphysical) category.
The individual "units" or "quanta" of life Hegel calls "organisms" (not to be confused with biological organisms, which are

but one special case of the former). Organisms are distinguished by the immanence (or "innerness") of the Concept, which is Hegel's somewhat obscure way of indicating that "organisms" are intern- ally-governed, self-determining entities.

Mechanistic and deterministic models do not account for the behavior of organisms. Hegel argues that, from an external per- spective at least, an organism is certainly capable of purely "mechanical" behavior; but he adds, "to that extent it is not a living being. . . ." When an organism is regarded solely as a mechanical system subject to strict deterministic causality, "then the Concept is regarded as external to it and it is treated as a *dead* thing" (GL 766).

What characterizes a living entity is the immanence of its pattern or principle of organization of its activity.

> Since the Concept is immanent in it, the *purpo- siveness* of the living being is to be grasped as *inner*; the Concept is in it as determinate Concept . . . This objectivity of the living being is the *organism*; it is the *means and instrument* of the end, perfect in its purposiveness since the Concept con- stitutes its substance.   (*Ibid.*)

Organisms are characterized for Hegel (in a manner very similar to Whitehead) by process, immanent purposiveness, sub- jectivity and feeling, self-determination, "conditioned" or partial self-creation, and freedom.[54] "Organisms" are defined by Hegel so as to apply in the realm of nature to describe bi- ological entities (including human beings), as well as in the realm of *Geist* to characterize political and cultural entities.[55]

Organic mechanism is established in the *Logic* by considera- tion of three successively-more-complex descriptions of, or para- digms for, types of process or activity: mechanism, "chemism," and teleology. Mechanism is that relation which obtains among objects which are "complete and self-subsistent."[56] Accordingly, such relationships and interactions which such objects entertain are wholly external and "accidental" to the nature of the objects themselves.

> The character of *mechanism* [is] that whatever relation obtains between the things combined, this relation is one *extraneous* to them that does not concern their nature at all. . . .   (GL 711)

It is not entirely clear what examples Hegel intends of such objects and their mechanical relations. Not even tools or parts of machines will be capable of exhaustive explanation by "mechanism" alone, as we presently shall observe (see also p. 61, n.10 above). One may surmise from his discussions, however, that he envisions the normal physical "causal" interactions among the "corpuscular matter" of the physics of his day--inert stones, colliding billiard balls and similar objects which served as the examples of "matter" in classical (Newtonian) mechanics. In any case:

> The Object is immediate being, because insensible to difference, which in it has suspended itself. It is, further, a totality in itself, while at the same time . . . it is equally indifferent to its immediate unity.
> (*Enc.* 194)

Objects (or systems of objects) subject to purely mechanical explanation Hegel terms *begrifflose* (GL 715), i.e., lacking an internal concept or purpose. The essential feature of mechanism, as G. R. G. Mure notes, is that self-determination is absent: "each Object is a formal totality which is indifferent in its activity to its determination by other Objects."[57] Any given state or condition of a certain object or aggregate of objects cannot be explained solely by reference to that object or aggregate alone, but must instead assign a reason or *cause* of every state or phase to *other* objects. "Consequently, a principle of self-determination is nowhere to be found" (GL 713).

Hegel amplifies Hume's earlier skepticism concerning the adequacy of mechanistic or deterministic causality as a principle of explanation. Such explanations, Hegel argues, by their very nature involve us in an infinite regress. Since each object or event requires reference to another object or event to explain its own existence, it is impossible ultimately to give any coherent account of causality based upon mechanism alone (cf. *Enc.* 195, *Zusatz*).

> For this reason determinism itself is also indeterminate in the sense that it involves the progression to infinity [Hegel's "bad infinite"]; it can halt and be satisfied at any point at will, because the object it has reached in its progress, being a formal totality, is shut up within itself and indifferent to its being determined by another. Consequently, the *explanation* of the determination of an object and the progressive

determining of the object made for the purpose of the
explanation, is only an *empty word*, since in the other
object to which it advances there resides no self-
determination.   (GL 713ff.)

Hegel's interpretation of the weakness in the explanatory
power of mechanism seems to be its failure to admit of real reciprocal relatedness, including internal relations *among* objects
which are to some degree *constitutive of* those objects. In this
regard, when considering the Leibnizian "objects" or monads,
Hegel anticipates a later criticism by Whitehead that the faulti-
ness of Leibniz's theory lies in the fact that the monads are
"windowless" (cf. *Enc.* 194; GL 712).

By contrast, "chemism" (a peculiar intermediary phase between mechanism and teleology) is defined in terms of the relations or affinities among objects. Bare, self-subsistent objectivity is overcome in a (chemical) unity, which "conforms to the
Concept" (GL 729). This position, to a certain extent, is prefigured and explained in terms of mechanical objects which enter
into a larger relationship based upon "law." Here Hegel intends
the example of point-masses in a uniform force field (such as
the planets of the solar system in the sun's gravitational
field) all alike subject to Newton's Second Law of Motion (F=ma).
To a very limited degree, this uniform relationship of order can
be interpreted as constitutive of the objects thus related, in
the sense of establishing a uniform principle of organization
governing the processes of change and activity in which these
objects are involved. For Hegel, however, these "associations
of objects in law" entail a Concept which is still external to
the objects themselves (cf. *Enc.* 198; GL 721-725).

We might tend today to regard the elements of simple chemical processes as related precisely in this same way from the
standpoint of an atomic theory of chemical interactions (which
Hegel was not privileged to hold). That is, it would appear
that a simple chemical reaction could be explained in terms of
atomic elements undergoing differing molecular configurations
which are only marginally "constitutive" of the atoms themselves.
Thus a chemical process from our perspective seems to be no different from what Hegel has described above as a mechanical process exhibiting the "self-determining unity of law."

Hegel's own interest in, and reason for, distinguishing "chemism" as a category of relatedness distinct from mechanism is revealed in his discussion of oxidation-reduction reactions (cf. *Enc*. 355; GL 731).[58] Lacking an adequate atomic theory, it appeared that, during such reactions, otherwise inert, "self-subsistent" inorganic objects could effect changes in their own individual, internal constitutions in order to cooperate or participate in some sort of larger, external relationship. As this seemed to be the case, chemism became for Hegel most significant as a dialectical transition from mechanism to teleology. As Jeffrey Wattles comments:

> The chemical objects, which were originally taken to have immediate and straightforward existence, have that immediacy cancelled by the mediation of the two-fold chemical process. The object comes to be seen as mediated by process; the Concept is no longer identified with that object. As goal it has a new status, a status that Hegel calls freedom.[59]

These comments help to clarify the significance of Hegel's own movement from an inadequate mechanism to a more comprehensive mode of teleological explanation. We would not now, of course, see the transfer of electrons involved in oxidation-reduction reactions as holding much significance for this argument--and certainly not as supportive of self-determination or freedom! On the other hand, advances in nuclear and even in elementary-particle chemistry--involving chemical reactions which consist in the transmutation not only of elements, but also of the electromagnetic constituents of atomic elements--certainly support Hegel's wider contention that the relations into which objects enter must be viewed to some extent as constitutive of the objects themselves.

Whether this involves the sort of internal self-constitution which is identified with creativity or freedom is, at best, problematic. It is worth recalling that these factors were among the data of an emerging new scientific worldview which led Whitehead to affirm that such freedom and creativity characterize the whole of the actual world-process. We might refer here to Whitehead's pan-subjectivist principle, and assert that some nascent or germinal creativity and subjectivity must be present in even the most rudimentary events, in order to explain the gradual emergence of more complex manifestations of subjectivity and creativity in the more advanced, highly-structured "societies" of these events. There is, then, a certain fundamental agreement between Hegel and Whitehead on the point that a certain minimal degree of novelty and creativity must pervade the whole of reality. This is an idea which Whitehead was privileged to formulate with a particular rigor and cogency.

In any event, we are brought finally to Hegel's description of teleology, in which determination according to an object's own inner "concept" (i.e., self-determination) finally becomes explicit. In chemical and mechanical systems, the pattern or principle of organization embodied (whenever such was even in evidence) was seen finally as external to the object or system of objects. By contrast, the only necessity governing a teleological system is the internal "necessity" of behaving according to the system's own intelligible, characteristic structure (GL 734).

Hegel states explicitly in the "Lesser Logic" (*Enc.* 204) that his idea of "inner design" merely re-vitalizes Aristotle's ancient doctrine of entelechy ("actualized purpose")[60] as the inner generating principle of living organisms. Hegel suggests further that Aristotle's teleological doctrine of life in terms of this "Concept" or inner design was far in advance of "contemporary" (i.e., eighteenth and nineteenth-century) teleology, which was purely external.[61] Finally, in this same section of the *Encyclopedia*, Hegel suggests that the true significance of teleology or final cause as a model of explanation superior to (and sublating) mechanism and chemism is that it "cancels the antithesis between the objective which would be and stay an objective only, and the subjective which in like manner would be and stay a subjective only."

Thus for Hegel, as for Whitehead, teleology is the cornerstone of what Whitehead called his "Reformed Subjectivist Principle." That is, for both philosophers, the inherently purposive and creative character of all reality is precisely that which overcomes the false subject-object dichotomy, demonstrating that the principle of structure and creative development which the mind subjectively *observes* in the world is in fact the principle of intelligible (rational) order which objectively *is* in the world (*Enc.* 6).

In mechanism and chemism, as Mure notes, we saw the object or system of objects becoming more-and-more *für sich*. From the bare externality of mechanism, through the nascent spontaneity of chemical systems, the object "approaches teleological behavior: *viz.*, the systematic activity of that which has its end in itself."[62] Neither mechanism (nor chemism) nor teleology in itself is sufficient for a complete understanding of the worldprocess. Nor will Hegel allow that the world is somehow divided into "spheres of influence" where either efficient or final causation obtains.[63] The truth of the world lies in seeing that the essentials of efficient causation are preserved in the larger framework of the Hegelian-Aristotelian doctrine of "inner design." In this way

> the end-relation in general has proved itself to be in and for itself the *truth of mechanism*. Teleology possesses in general the higher principle, the Concept in its existence, which is in and for itself the infinite and absolute—a principle of freedom that in the utter certainty of its self-determination is absolutely liberated from the *external determining* of mechanism.
>
> (GL 737)

Teleological behavior is the principal characteristic of life, evident in those living structures in which mechanism and chemism are sublated in a higher unity. Teleology—behavior according to an inner concept—thus defines the transition of "objects" which have passed from bare objectivity (*an-sich Sein*) to subjectivity (*für-sich Sein*). Such objects Hegel classifies logically as "organisms" (GL 766).

Fully-developed subjectivity involves self-consciousness as well (*an-und-für-sich Sein*), and the teleological behavior characteristic of self-consciousness is (not surprisingly) a function of reason or wisdom (*Vernunft*). Indeed, Hegel argues that it is the function of reason, subordinating mechanical and chemical processes to its own end, to bridge the Kantian gap which exists between ends subjectively *entertained* and objectively *attained* in the world. Hegel describes the process by which subjective purposes, intellectually entertained by human agents, are realized, objectified, or made "concrete" utilizing external means (such as mechanical objects).[64]

In such cases, however, the end or purpose (while it surely antedates and transcends the means employed in its eventual realization) is not therefore totally external to the means of its own objectification. Rather, the end is all along immanent in the process of its realization.[65]

Consider the familiar example of a builder and his building. Surely the purpose of the builder--the "envisioned end-state"-- initiated the processes of construction. In Aristotelian lan- guage, this "final cause" or purpose is responsible for the "form of a building being imposed upon the "matter"--the "material cause"--of construction. For Hegel (as for Whitehead), however, the material available may alter the overall plan or purpose during construction, as well as influence the vision of the final use to which the finished product is to be put. The same is true for the complex factors of "efficient causation"--the workers, the building codes of the city, geographical constraints, and so forth. All of these interact *dialectically*, in a creative, but not necessarily benign or unpainful, tension. While the entire process is initiated and generated by its internal purpose or "Concept" (or "subjective aim"), the immanent purpose is itself clearly modifiable by the very process or processes which it generates.[66] The results, while objectifying a purpose or rea- lized end, may nonetheless differ from what the builder in our example originally envisioned. Thus, while purpose is *generative* for Hegel, it is neither external, nor is it finally and abso- lutely determinative. Instead, the whole is a truly creative process of becoming.

This doctrine of creative or emergent evolution is integral to--indeed, the sum and substance of--Hegel's organic mechanism. As Hegel himself concludes:

> The end does not merely keep outside the mechani- cal process; rather it maintains itself in it, and is its determination . . . It can therefore be said of the teleological activity that in it the end is the beginning, the consequent the ground, the effect the cause, that it is a becoming of what has become, that in it only what already exists comes into existence. .
> . .
> (GL 747ff.)

It is particularly helpful to explicate this summary in terms of Whitehead's more precise technical terminology. The teleological character of any organic event consists in the fact that its end or "satisfaction" lies in the actualization of its initial subjective aim. The concrescence of an actual occasion

consists in rendering definite, explicit and determinate what is
present or available from the beginning within the ensemble of
real possibilities for the outcome of a certain process. As the
"concept" or subjective aim is all along immanent in the process
of its own realization, it is (as we have seen) subject to modification and alteration by the very process it generates, even
as it guides the outcome of that process towards a novel unity
of definiteness. While it is true for Whitehead as for Hegel
that "only what already exists comes into existence" (in the
Whiteheadian sense of inherited data and initial subjective aim),
nonetheless freedom as creativity is exhibited in the self-determination of a teleological process which issues in a novel or
unique synthesis of inherited forms.

(iii) Organic Mechanism in the *Encyclopedia*

The unity of the Concept and its Object, first attained in
living organisms, Hegel terms the "Idea" (*Enc.* 213)--by which,
he explains, is meant the immanent determination of rational
structure (or *Logos*) in the world-process (cf. *Enc.* 214, 215,;
GL 754). "Life" as ontological category is itself the "immediate
idea" for Hegel (*Enc.* 216). The "percipient Idea," or the "Idea
which has being" Hegel further describes in the concluding para-
graph of the *Logic* as "Nature" (*Enc.* 244).

> The Idea, namely, in positing itself as absolute
> *unity* of the pure Concept and its reality and thus
> contracting itself into the immediacy of *being*, is
> the *totality* in this form--*nature*.   (GL 844)

We already have had occasion to note the major need and
justification for Hegel's treatment of nature. The discussions
of the *Logic* are "generalized ontology": uniformly applicable
to a variety of particular instances (and hence "concrete"), but
nonetheless in need of such application, objectification and
verification in the phenomenal world of nature and spirit. In
this latter sense it is true, as Errol Harris claims, that "the
logic, in spite of its proper claims to 'concreteness,' is, in
the last resort, an abstraction."[67]

The second justification follows from the first. Having
now reached an understanding of such essential notions as *Begriff*,
Geist, purpose and organism by (so to speak) working up from the
empirical considerations of nature, science and human experience,

it is now obligatory to go back to the beginning and re-examine these more everyday, immediate concerns and experiences in the light of this newly won knowledge. The subject-matter examined, for example, in the early sections of the *Phenomenology* and in the "Philosophy of Nature" is essentially the same. But the standpoint of the observer has changed dramatically as a result of his "voyage of discovery." The difference, Hegel suggests, is like that of an old man repeating the creed or dogma held as a child--but now "pregnant with the significance of a lifetime" (*Enc.* 237, *Zusatz*). Errol Harris helpfully summarizes this position:

> The mind first sees itself as the world come to consciousness and then sees the world as the process in and by means of which that coming to consciousness is brought about. Having found its own identity with the world in knowledge, mind goes back to the world as nature to view it as the process in and through which knowledge comes to be, and which, at the same time, comes to be the object (or content) of knowledge. As the process is throughout one of growing self-consciousness, it is a process at once of the emergence of the knowing mind and of the world's (the process itself) becoming known. Mind, in short, discovers its own immanent presence in Nature.[68]

Reason thus having been discovered as the actual principle of order and development of the world, Hegel's "Philosophy of Nature" proceeds to show how every phase of nature (up to the emergence of self-consciousness) is an implicit manifestation of this *Logos*, this principle of rational order.

At first reading, it might appear that the "Philosophy of Nature" holds no interest for the present investigation, since Hegel argues that "Nature exhibits no freedom in its existence, but only necessity and contingency" (*Enc.* 248). This would, on its face, appear to be an irreducible difference from Whitehead. On closer examination, however, we recognize that Hegel is trying to put some distance between his concept of nature, and that of contemporary Romantic philosophers, for whom nature was virtually deified as the realm of "sublime freedom." For Hegel the empiricist and humanist, however, nature does not represent a realm of mystery elevated beyond, and valued above the plane of human existence. It is instead a realm of stubborn and irreducible facts, the whole of which "confronts us as a riddle and a problem."[69] It is, further, no answer to the question, "What is

Nature?" merely to "chase down" certain of these facts in isolation. The task is instead to see how the totality of physical and organic phenomena fit into a larger cosmology which also takes account of the observer--not as something irreducibly separate and distinct, but as a participant which is also one of the products of the natural world-process.[70]

For Hegel, nature is that in which the Concept is immanent (*Enc.* 245). It is "the Idea in the form of otherness" or externality (*Enc.* 247). If there is any sense in which nature can be said to embody the Concept, the principle of freedom, then nature cannot be portrayed as wholly lacking in the kind of freedom which we have heretofore discussed: *viz.*, teleological self-determination. On the other hand, Hegel will not allow that nature somehow embodies a mysterious, contra-causal, "abstract" freedom which Romanticists attribute to it. Rather, for Hegel, nature is "only a natural mode of the Idea, [and] is at the mercy of the unreason of externality . . ." (*Enc.* 248). Hegel describes nature as "impotent" in that it "preserves the determinations of the Concept only *abstractly*, and leaves their detailed specification to external determination." He adds:

> This confusion of contingency, caprice and disorder with freedom and rationality is characteristic of sensuous and unphilosophic thinking. (*Enc.* 250)

Thus, Hegel's charge that nature is totally *devoid* of freedom may be set aside as merely a polemic against the naivete of Romanticism. His obvious concern, similar to our own, is to avoid the confusion of randomness and happenstance with freedom. Freedom involves creativity and teleological self-determination, all of which are embodied only partially and imperfectly ("externally") in nature. Nature itself, however, is "a living Whole." The importance of nature for Hegel is that it is a crucial stage on the dialectical path to Spirit, "the final goal of Nature," the self-conscious realm in which freedom as creativity becomes dominant (*Enc.* 251).

The main sections of the "Philosophy of Nature" essentially reiterate the generalized categories of mechanism, chemism and teleology. I have chosen to devote time to the treatment of these in the *Logic*, since this proceeds, as it were, unencumbered by certain nineteenth-century features of scientific detail, which we would find largely outmoded today. The "Philosophy of Nature" holds a three-fold significance for our argument.

(1) These treatments of scientific theory, grouped according to Hegel's ontological categories, serve to ground those generalized categories in empirical detail. Hegel's extensive treatment of technical aspects of physics, chemistry and biology reveal his thoroughgoing interest in and knowledge of the science of his day, and dispel the myth that his was a metaphysical system derived in abstraction from, in ignorance of, or even in outright hostility to the rapid advances of natural science.

(2) Hegel admittedly exhibits certain marked idiosyncracies in his interpretation of science, such as a decided rationalist (versus English empiricist) bias.[71] Hegel seems to prefer the ancient Greek mythical elements of earth, air, fire and water as more representative of the "concreteness" of physical elements than the criterion of "chemical simplicity" by which such pure and self-subsistent (and therefore, for Hegel, "abstract") elements as Oxygen and Hydrogen are regarded as primary (*Enc*. 281; cf. also Sections 282-285).

In fairness to Hegel, we find also a number of strikingly modern insights. Magnetism and electricity--the studies of which were still in their infancy in Hegel's time--are singled out as especially significant. These properties, while associated with individual physical objects, nonetheless transcend mere particularity. As "fields of force," magnetism and electricity bind together previously dispersed and "self-subsistent" bits of matter into a common association. In addition, electricity explicitly demonstrates that this "binding force" proceeds as a result of *opposition*. Electrical force is produced in the tensions of electrical "opposites," binding the opposingly-charged poles together ultimately in one electrical system. The single electric or magnetic pole could have no meaning or existence apart from its opposite (*Enc*. 309, 312, and esp. 313). In this way, Hegel's "physics of the total individuality" shows that, even at this level, individuality is ultimately sublated in reciprocity, interdependence and community--prefiguring on the human social level the transition from bare subjectivity to *Geist*.

Most remarkable in this vein, however, is Hegel's brief treatment of time. In the "Preface" to his *Phenomenology*, Hegel makes the suggestive remark that time "is the existent Concept itself" (*Phen.* 27), implying, in opposition to the later interpretation of Samuel Alexander, that the dialectical development of the immanent Concept *is* (or at least, may *also* be seen as) a temporal process.[72]

The Newtonian concept of time, popular in Hegel's day, asserted that time was an absolute and independent variable, a continuum "within which" physical events and processes took place. Time itself was to be seen as external to any individual process, permitting measurement of the temporal duration of that process by defining its beginning and end with reference to this absolute and external standard.

Hegel attacks this view in his "Philosophy of Nature," substituting the more modern explanation that "time . . . is Becoming directly intuited":

> It is not *in* time that everything comes to be
> and passes away, rather time itself is the *becoming*,
> this coming-to-be and passing away, the *actually
> existing abstraction*. . . .
> (*Enc.* 258)[73]

It is only the *Begriff der Zeit*, the concept of time, which is (like every concept) unchanging and hence eternal (cf. *Enc.* 258, *Zusatz*). Thus Hegel presents his principle of time in a manner analogous to Heraclitus' presentation of the principle of change: in a world of flux and process, it is only the principle of flux and process (or, in Hegel's case, the principle of time) which is itself unchanged. For such reasons, when tracing the contemporary rise to prominence of a concept of time in the philosophies of Whitehead, Bergson, Hartshorne and other "process philosophers, William Earle remarks: "I should date the conspicuous turning point with Hegel."[74]

(3) Hegel's section on "Physics" begins with physical force-field considerations of groups or systems of objects, and proceeds to chemical processes and interactions. Hegel narrates at this point the gradual transition to dominance of teleological behavior, made explicit finally in the concluding section of the "Philosophy of Nature" on "Organics."

This final section (most significant from the standpoint of the present argument) gives determinateness and definiteness to Hegel's discussion of the ontological categories of "organism"

and "Life" in the *Logic*. Hegel utilizes extensive knowledge of
the biology of his time, interpreted according to the classical
Aristotelian model of biological entelechy, to argue that self-
determination according to an inner Concept is the principal
common characteristic of all organic entities.

An organism, for Hegel, is a unifying activity. That is,
an organism is a self-producing process which attempts to syn-
thesize disparate elements into a concrete, harmonious unity.

> This *concrete unity* with self, self-produced into
> unity from the particularizing of the different corpo-
> realities, a unity which is the activity of negating
> this its one-sided form of reference-to-self, of *sun-
> dering* and particularizing itself into the moments of
> the Concept and equally of bringing them back into
> that unity, is *the organism*--the infinite process
> which spontaneously kindles and sustains itself.
>
> (*Enc*. 336)[75]

From the standpoint of the *Logic*, we have seen that this organic
process involves the coordination and sublation of mechanical
and chemical processes within the teleological self-maintenance
and perpetual synthesis of the living entity. In the "Philosophy
of Nature," Hegel proceeds to demonstrate how this model serves
to explain the distinct functions of plant and animal organisms.[76]

The section of the "Philosophy of Nature" on botany consists
mostly of lengthy *Zusätze* discussing in great detail then-conven-
tional botanical theory, with notable deference to the theories
of Goethe. Plants are indeed self-maintaining organisms (and
to that extent, teleological). But, for Hegel, they are only
rudimentarily so. The plant organizes its behavior solely in
response to its "other"--its environment. It does not seek to
shape or alter that environment with respect to its own needs
or purposes. Thus,

> the [plant] organism has its other, not within it,
> but outside of it, as a self-subsistent other; it is
> not itself its non-organic nature, but it finds this
> already confronting it as object, an object which it
> seems to encounter only contingently.
>
> (*Enc*. 346, *Zusatz*)

The distinct parts of the plant exist in only a loosely
inter-dependent relationship. Inverted in the soil, the plant's
roots will begin to sprout leaves, and the leaves, roots. Or,
severed from the plant, a leaf and stem are capable of sprouting

roots and eventually growing into a complete plant. Thus, to
borrow a portion of Bradley's phrase, the whole is in every part,
informing its function in the plant; but the parts appear only
casually related to the totality of the plant organism (cf. *Enc.*
345, *Zusatz*).

Thus, while plants in themselves exhibit at least a pseudo-
teleological behavior in their responsiveness to their environment, they represent for Hegel merely an incomplete, or as-yet-
inadequate phase of "organism."[77] Externality is more completely
overcome or "internalized" in what Hegel calls the "veritable
organism"--the animal--in which "the outer formation accords
with the [inner] Concept, so that the parts are essentially members, and subjectively exist as the One which pervades the whole"
(*Enc.* 349).

Let us recall that "organic mechanism" applies simply to
the functioning of an organism, which proceeds by sublating mechanistic functions to its own ends. It is in animal organisms--
and, of course, most especially in *human* organisms--that Hegel's
organic mechanism becomes fully explicit. Hegel suggests that
the animal organism "as living universality is the Concept." It
is the "microcosm, the center of Nature which has achieved an
existence for itself in which the whole of inorganic Nature is
recapitulated and idealized" (*Enc.* 352). The animal represents
a whole which cannot be fully represented by any of its constituent members in isolation (in contrast to plants). Each of
those constituent parts--body members, organs, and so forth--
may function as a *means* for the realization of ends serving *other*
parts of the organism or the whole organism. Each may also represent (on other occasions) an end to which the other parts and
functions in the whole serve as means (cf. *Enc.* 351, *Zusatz*).
This definition of reciprocal internal relatedness and interdependence is precisely what is entailed in the phrases "holism"
and "organism." And this is the essence of (inner) teleological
behavior as self-reference, self-maintenance, and self-determination.

Why then does Hegel not allow that animal organisms *other*
than human beings are "free" in the sense we have labored to describe? Animals, in eating, reproducing, and shaping their environment by Hegel's own definition act *purposively* for their

own benefit and maintenance. This is surely teleological self-determination as we have been describing it. The only absent condition, the "formal defect" of the animal (and the weakness of nature in general for Hegel), is that it is never *conscious* of its own activity as self-directed. Instead, as opposed to the higher-order functions of human beings, animals function only according to *instinct*.

> The difficulty in understanding instinct is simply this, that an *end* can be grasped only as an inner *Concept*, so that explanations and relationships stemming from mere Understanding soon reveal their ineptness in regard to instinct. The basic determination of the living being seized on by Aristotle, that it must be conceived as acting purposively, has in modern times been almost forgotten till Kant, in his own way, revived this concept in his doctrine of *inner* teleology, in which the living being is to be treated as its own end. The difficulty here comes mainly from representing the *teleological* relationship as *external*, and from the prevalent opinion that an *end* exists *only* in *consciousness*. Instinct is purposive activity acting unconsciously.
>
> (*Enc.* 360)

It now becomes apparent what Hegel has accomplished. His detailed application of the categories of the *Logic* in nature re-establishes teleology--what we are here terming organic mechanism--as the only acceptable model of explanation for *living* processes, and arguably even for complex, many-bodied *inorganic* processes in chemistry and physics as well. This is done, however, by a revival of the Aristotelian notion in biology of "inner teleology" or entelechy (development according to an inner teleological pattern or principle), rather than by revitalizing the trivial and discredited principle of external teleology. Hegel actually *denies*, in so doing, that consciousness is even necessary for behavior patterned according to inner purpose. Thus a link is forged between all forms of life--and possibly even of certain inorganic processes--in terms of their lesser or greater embodiment of the kind of purposive, teleological activity associated with organic mechanism. Such teleological self-determination does not qualify as "free" activity *only* because it is not *consciously directed*.

Ironically, Hegel, who is accused of being frequently vague and ambiguous, makes a more precise determination of "grades" of metaphysical freedom than does Whitehead. For the latter, freedom is equated with the creativity of teleological self-determination at the rudimentary or constitutive level of being. Hegel allows such teleological self-determination as the *ground* of freedom, but will not deign to call this activity itself "free" until it becomes fully self-aware--a phase which, for Whitehead, occurs only at the more complex, specialized "social" level of groupings of actual entities.

Why does Hegel place such a premium on self-consciousness as constitutive of freedom? The inner Concept, by which organic activity is determined, is *rational*. It is literally the *Logos*, or the Reason which *is* in the world. For Hegel, organisms are patterned after the Concept. They are rationally-ordered structures or, if you will, "self-actualizing ends" (*Selbstzweckmässigkeit*). While living things are *organische Gestalten* (organic structures), the structure is still external to the organism in a spiritual sense: while their behavior is determined from within by the structures or patterns they embody, the organisms themselves act instinctively, and have no control over their own internal constitution. Such determination, even though technically *internal* or *self*-determination, does not qualify even as conditional or finite freedom.

The point is not as obscure or contradictory as it may seem. The baser human volitions, for example--for food, rest, sexual contact and the like--form a perfectly rational, ordered and harmonious organic structure. Indulging these volitions or appetites permits the human (like any other organism) to maintain both its individual and corporate existence. Yet none would admit that the individual human, whose behavior was dictated solely by the interplay of these desires, qualified as a "free" being. As Spinoza had demonstrated in his *Ethics*, such "causes" of behavior, even when ordered (rational) and internal, still create a state of human bondage.

Freedom for both Spinoza and Hegel is a creative, determinative *power* over such internal structures afforded by a knowledge of their operation. Freedom is thus a property solely of Mind or *Geist*. For Hegel, further, to *think about* the rule of Reason in the world is to *be* Reason in the world, and so to be truly self-determining with respect to one's inner, rational "Concept" (cf. GL 56; *Enc.* 81). And this is the essence of the freedom which results from the coming-to-self-consciousness of organic mechanism.[78]

Section 5. Objective Spirit: the Realized Freedom of the Idea

(i) Human Freedom

We had occasion at the outset of this treatment of Hegel to discuss the difficulty of giving a precise, analytic definition of *Geist*. The critical factor which grounds Hegel's interpretation of this term, however, undoubtedly is seen in this gradual emergence of sentience in organic nature--a consciousness of the world, giving rise further to a consciousness of the phenomenon of consciousness itself. This is the point in the *Encyclopedia* at which nature gives rise to true freedom and spirit (*Enc.* 376).

While rejecting outright dualism, Hegel nonetheless feels that a critical threshold has been crossed with the advent of human consciousness. He writes: "it is only man who is thinking mind and by this, and by this alone, is essentially distinguished from Nature" (*Enc.* 381, *Zusatz*). With human consciousness, teleological self-determination becomes for Hegel a truly creative process. Not only is human action determined according to an inner Concept or rational pattern, but human mind, the organ of rationality, is, in essence, the creator and deviser of such purposive organization. A persistent theme of Hegel's thought from henceforth is that the essence and substance of Mind is freedom-- that *Geist* is "infinitely creative" (cf., e.g., *Enc.* 382, 384, 386, and their accompanying *Zusätze*).

Surveying all that has preceded and brought us to this threshold of human behavior, we are prepared to recognize that freedom is not merely an ontological state of being. Freedom is an *activity*, the reflexive activity of being *aware* of the on-going process which is one's existence in the world. This freedom is grounded in the "organic mechanism" which summarizes the teleological behavior of all living systems. The freedom of human agency, however, is not merely equated with this complex organic process of assimilation, synthesis, adjustment, response, growth, organization and self-maintenance according to a rational pattern or principle. It is instead a supervenient stage or phase of that activity: a stage at which that activity becomes reflexive, becomes aware of itself as determinative, and thus comes to be truly self-determinative through conscious decisions and acts. The inner Concept by which organic systems are observed to be ordered is through-and-through rational. But, for

Hegel, it is only in the human case that Reason becomes aware of itself as the factor organizing organic behavior. It is then a virtual identity to describe human beings as both rational and free. As Hegel remarks, such self-knowledge is the ground of genuine freedom, of "ultimate self-determing certitude." Reflexivity represents for Hegel "the realized freedom of the Idea" (Phil. R. 279).[79]

Comparison with Whitehead's doctrine proves useful in understanding the significance of this point. Both Hegel and Whitehead share a fascination with the creativity embodied in the ongoing process of teleological self-determination in organic structures. Both are convinced that this creative, quasi-causal process in some sense serves as the ground of our common experience and understanding of the term "freedom." Whitehead supplements Hegel's theory by demonstrating that this process is a generic quality of Being itself: it is universally pervasive and constitutive, rather than limited and restricted. Thus, Whitehead's theory aids in overcoming the last vestiges of subject-object dualism in Hegel's thought without injustice to any features of the natural world. Based on the preceding analysis, such an enterprise was surely Hegel's intention, and might well have been his unique accomplishment had the pertinent scientific data and theories been available to him.

On the other hand, we noted in our treatment of Whitehead that his theory was vague on the concept of the human moral self. That vagueness, of course, was shown to have certain advantages; and in any case, proceeded directly as a consequence of the factual "vagueness" of the physical "boundary" separating the "self" from its immediate environment. Hegel's theory, however, supplements Whitehead's doctrine by suggesting more precisely what it is that makes human life human. Hegel suggests the manner in which freedom in the human sense can be grounded in the creative process of organic mechanism, growing out of this as a supervenient phase of complexity. It is not merely the presence of rudimentary sentience (which, upon Whitehead's analysis, may be a common characteristic of Being itself), nor even of consciousness (which now is thought to characterize, in some degree, all living organisms) which constitutes freedom. Rather, it is the reflexive activity of consciousness--the organism becoming aware of itself as *subject*--which transforms teleological activity into full and genuine self-determination. And, for Hegel, this last phase marks the threshold of human moral behavior. As Richard Schacht notes:

> Hegel's point is relatively simple. One cannot really be said to be free so long as he is not explicitly aware of himself as being free. The consciousness of oneself as free is not itself a guarantee of true freedom: it may be only the illusion of freedom and is compatible with determinism. But it is a necessary condition of true freedom in that if one does not grasp one's actions as deriving from decisions and choices of one's own making, these actions cannot truly be said to be one's own. To act unhindered by others, and yet to do so unselfconsciously and without explicitly viewing one's acts as one's own, is to be free at most only in principle, or, in Hegel's terms, implicitly. Self-determination that is not self-conscious is a poor sort of freedom.[80]

The complementary nature of these two theories of freedom helps underscore the importance of what Hegel is trying to establish. The preceding discussion and quotation, however, simultaneously reveal that, once again, the task is not complete. There exists the possibility that even this self-conscious, self-determinative freedom may somehow be illusory, or at least dialectically-flawed. By way of dissenting from Schacht's suggestion, the danger is not from determinism (or mechanism) which has not so much been denied or opposed as entirely absorbed by Hegel's theory of freedom.[81] The problem instead lies in the possibility that even this understanding of freedom may be, in some sense, "abstract." This problem Hegel proceeds to tackle in the penultimate section of the *Encyclopedia* concerning "objective spirit," and in his expanded treatment of this section published as the *Philosophy of Right*.

In the *Randbemerkung* to Section 4 of the *Rechtsphilosophie*, Hegel comments upon the problem of the "freedom of the will," stating: "the proof that the will is free and the proof of the nature of the will and freedom can be established only as a link in the whole chain . . ." presumably referring to the chain of argument we have pursued to this point. "Will without freedom is an empty word, while freedom is actual only as will, as subject" (Phil. R. 4, *Zusatz*). Indeed, the whole of the *Rechtsphilosophie* is an analysis of the phenomenon of human free will in the

world. What, then, does Hegel intend by the will which is described thus as free?

Hegel is explicit here: "will is thinking reason resolving
itself into finitude" (Phil. R. 13). Without adopting his sar-
casm, we may feel compelled, as Karl Marx often felt, to trans-
late this passage into prose.[82]

Will is, after all, an ambiguous term, suggesting to some
a mysterious and irrational locus of desires in opposition to
the faculty of mind. For Hegel, of course, this cannot be the
case. What he intends throughout the *Rechtsphilosophie* by free
will is, quite obviously, the actual teleological process of
mind or reason formulating specific purposes (goals, wishes, desires) and attempting to objectify these—to actualize or carry
them through to some final realization or determinateness in
the world. "Free will" is a convenient acronym for this inter-
face of thought and action, of intellect and *praxis*. It is, as
Schacht notes, a less cumbersome formula than "thinking reason
resolving itself to finitude," but implies no new mysterious
faculty apart from the self-conscious self-determination which
we have outlined.

The free will "actualizes itself" in three ways, according
to Hegel, only the last of which will be seen to constitute true
or "concrete" freedom (*Enc.* 487; Phil. R. 33). First, there is
the immediacy of the "absolutely free will" (Phil. R. 34), the
same, dialectically-flawed entity encountered in the *Phenomenology* and *Logic*. This abstract or "negative" freedom is flawed
by its insularity and atomicity, by imagining that its acts are
absolutely spontaneous, uncaused, and independent. Hegel in
fact agrees with determinists that this sort of freedom is illusory (Phil. R. 29).

The earlier examples of this phase—the Master-Slave dialectic and the excesses of the French Revolution—are supplemen-
ted here by the view that the free will treats the world as its
own object, establishing its universal freedom through the acquisition of property. As such, interestingly, property is the
first external embodiment of mind's freedom (Phil. R. 41, *et.
seq.*). The process of this acquisition, however, leads dialectically (in Hegel's view) from the relation of the will to objects, to the more adequate relation of the will to other "wills"

(i.e., other owners of property, through the medium of the Con-
tract). This relation of will to will, between and among persons, is "the true and proper ground of freedom" (Phil. R. 71).
It is the beginning of that human interdependence and reciprocity, the realm of objective spirit, predicated upon trust and
the "consciousness that my interest, both substantive and particular, is contained and preserved in another's." Consciousness
of this reciprocity, argues Hegel, is true freedom (Phil. R.
268).[83]

This free relation of self to self ultimately is the substance and foundation of the organism of the State as embodiment
and guarantor of concrete freedom (Phil. R. 260). Initially,
Hegel suggests, the recognition that freedom is embodied in persons rather than things leads to the development of morality
(die Moralität), the internalized freedom of subjective will
(i.e., will conscious of itself as determinative in human activity; Phil. R. 106). It is at the level of morality--that is,
will seeking the good in and for itself--that freedom is first
made actual, for

> man wishes to be judged in accordance with his
> own self-determined choices; he is free in this rela-
> tion to himself whatever the external situation may
> impose upon him. No one can break in upon this inner
> conviction of mankind, no violence can be done to it,
> and the moral will, therefore, is inaccessible. Man's
> worth is estimated by reference to his inward action
> and hence the standpoint of morality is that of *freedom
> aware of itself*.
>
> (Phil. R. 106, *Zusatz*; emphases added)

In seeking to achieve and to do good, the moral or subjective will is acting, Hegel asserts, according to its own inner,
rational Concept. Hegel intends to convey the more formalistic
aspect of Aristotelian ethics--stressed in Kant's perspective
regarding the practical reason--that it resides in the nature
of the will to do what is right, and to seek what is good in and
for itself (i.e., the rational will is intrinsically good). The
distinction between good and evil, right and wrong as communica-
ted in ethical and religious principles should not, Hegel argues,
be seen merely in the form of external laws of authority to be
unquestioningly obeyed. Rather, the maxims of duty "have their
assent, recognition, or even justification in [the] heart,

sentiment, conscience [and] intelligence." This "subjective" or "moral" freedom, he suggests, is what is customarily intended by the term "freedom" (*Enc.* 503).

It is unthinkable for Hegel as it was for Aristotle to imagine the moral will as anything other than the seat of rational desire to realize the good. To be moral is to follow one's own intrinsic nature without impediment—and this surely is one possible meaning of moral freedom. Hegel is thus led to his famous judgment that the good is "freedom realized, the absolute end and aim of the world" (Phil. R. 129).

It would seem that this moral view of the world, involving the established freedom of the moral subject as teleological self-determination according to a rational, inward, moral Concept would suffice as a description of human freedom derived from, and in close analogy with the general doctrine of metaphysical freedom which Hegel has articulated. Indeed, such a definition of freedom is all that is customarily intended or required in moral argument. For our purposes, as well, this view of freedom closely corresponds with that developed by some Whiteheadian ethicists on the basis of his metaphysics. It would then appear at this juncture that our suggestion of similarity has been established.

For Hegel, however, this individualistic view of moral freedom is not in itself sufficient. It proceeds, as we have discussed (*vide supra*, pp. 58ff.), from the categorical self-certainty of conscience and the practical reason to the self-righteousness of Jacobi's "beautiful soul"—lacking in the understanding, compassion and forgiveness which Hegel saw as the proper final aim of the moral life (symbolized for Hegel in Christianity's doctrine of atonement through grace).

In addition, the Kantian view of moral teleology is ultimately external to the moral process itself. As Reyburn notes, "the free and moral will is not seen to be the principle of the world itself: it is something added to the world organizing it from without."[84] And this concept of external teleology, as we have seen, is not the view of teleology to which Hegel subscribes. The pattern or principle of organization of the world-process, be it moral or otherwise, must be "inner"—i.e., immanent in and in some sense generated by or dependent upon the very processes of development it enables.

In the case of ethics, as Hegel noted (*Enc.* 503), the principle of morality must never remain merely external to the moral agent, but must be internalized and justified. While *Moralität* seems to document this dialectical transition from externality to inwardness or subjectivity, it in fact reveals only the transferral of external authority from civil and religious law to the dictates of duty subjectively apprehended (presumably from God).

Hegel makes at this point his famous dialectical transition from *Moralität* to *Sittlichkeit*--the realm of "Ethical Life" embodied in the institutions of the family and ultimately the State.[85] The transition, of course, is from the realm of individuality and abstractness to community and concreteness--the life of *Geist* objectified in the world. In this sense, the transition is fully consistent with Hegel's own procedure.

The question which is intriguing for our purposes is, *why* is this transition necessary to an adequate understanding of freedom? Why does Hegel view concrete freedom as possible only in the ideal state? To this point, he has developed a doctrine of freedom as self-conscious, "quasi-causal" self-determination. His doctrine is remarkably similar to Whitehead's, as we have noted, and it is one which seems capable of answering all the traditional objections to, and questions about freedom normally raised in moral and metaphysical argument. Why continue on into the social and political realm, where many accuse Hegel of havin in fact *abandoned* a real doctrine of human freedom for a thinly-veiled form of (at best) benign authoritarianism?

Hegel's metaphysics is, of course, never far from its practical application, and the theory of moral teleology leaves us (in Hegel's opinion) with a practical problem. We cannot simply populate a nation or the world with moral individuals exercising their freedom *in vacuo*. The true moral dilemma lies not in justifying human freedom (which finally, for Hegel, is a self-evident characteristic of self-conscious life according to Reason). The moral problem lies in mediating the competing claims to right and goodness advanced by equally free, responsible and autonomous individuals. There must exist some structure for adjudicating these competing claims, short of compromising one or another's life or political liberty. The problem of mora freedom is, in short, one of constraint, finitude, fallibility, and the consequent need for a structure in which these may be overcome.

The overcoming or "adjudicating" of constraint and finitude through some sort of reciprocity or systemic interdependence is precisely what is accomplished in Hegel's "logical" and biological category of organism. The Hegelian doctrine which we have identified as "organic mechanism" narrates the process of synthesis of disparate, "self-sufficient" entities into an enduring and harmonious unity, in which each part or "member" is simultaneously an "end" for the supporting activity of the other members, and a means toward the maintenance of the whole. This symmetric reciprocity of the functions as ends and means in each member of the whole allows for maintenance of the individuality and the autonomy of each "part," while at the same time engaging the existence and activity of the parts precisely at the point of the uniqueness of their respective contributions in forging a harmonious unity which is characterized as much by these mutual relations among the parts as by the uniqueness of each part in isolation.

Thus it is no accident that Hegel describes the ideal state as an "organism" (e.g., Phil. R. 267) or as an "organic actuality" (e.g., Enc. 517). This is neither casual nor "trendy" use of language. It represents rather the deliberate, consistent application of a central systematic ontological category to the analysis of important problems in different areas of concern. In this case, the State is to individual moral agents what the biological organism is to inorganic matter and processes. In both cases, the individual atomic "units" are preserved and enhanced in a higher synthesis which is more merely than the sum of its constituents, and within which the constituents can both be and accomplish far more than they could in isolation. As the "abstract independence" of inorganic entities and processes is replaced by a concrete teleological self-determination in the biological organism, so is the "abstract freedom" of Locke, Rousseau, and the French Revolution given (in Hegel's opinion) a new, concrete reality--a more just and enduring order--by the participation in a community of moral agents. Abstract or "negative" freedom is transformed into the finite, concrete freedom enjoyed in conjunction with real mutual responsibilities. Hegel continually maintains that the will is truly free which "wills the [general] free will" (Phil. R. 27).

In the case of the "microcosm" of objective spirit--the Family--it is *love* which forges the bond of responsibility, through which individual dignity is preserved to a nobler common purpose (Phil. R. 158). In the state, the freedom and dignity of each member is preserved and insured in the relationship of *trust* which exists between and among the members (Phil. R. 268). It is only in this organic structure that the rights of all may be honored and protected.[86]

Thus the state is, for Hegel, the final actuality of the "ethical idea" of freedom, the domain of Right[87] actualized in the world (Phil. R. 257). Those reciprocal duties imposed by mutual responsibility to one another--seen in the realm of "abstract right" as *constraints* on freedom--become in the family and state the substance of free activity (Phil. R. 149). In the ideal state, these mutual responsibilities are institutionalized in the constitution and the just laws, the holistic understanding of which forms the appropriate subject matter for legal and political philosophy.[88]

Through understanding the state as organism, we are led ultimately to a full appreciation of Hegel's remark in the opening sections of the *Rechtsphilosophie*, that

> freedom is both the substance of Right and its goal, while the system of Right is the realm of freedom made actual. . . .
> (Phil. R. 4)

(ii) Objections to this View

Undeniably there are problematic aspects in such a "socialized" view of freedom. In our discussion of nature, for example, it was the organism as a whole which possessed the freedom of self-determination, rather than any of its constituent parts individually considered. This suggests by analogy that it is only the state as a whole which is "free," and not any of its individual members.

On one level it is true that Hegel argues for the sovereignt and autonomy of the individual nation-state as a whole organism. Freedom is invested in a symbolic or ultimate self, the monarch (Phil. R. 273, 275, 279). We might prefer a more modern term for the chief executive, but few would deny the practical necessity for having a voice to speak for the state as a whole upon occasion, in spite of the obvious possibilities (frequently exercised) for tyrannical abuse of this position. Hegel views the monarch as serving a unique function, during "the moment of ultimate decision, as the *self-determination* to which everything else reverts and from which everything else (i.e., the members of the state pursuing their distinctive lifestyles) derives the beginning of its actuality" (Phil. R. 275).

Several observations may be ventured concerning this problem. First, Hegel (like Socrates in the *Crito*) apparently views the state as the ground of an individual's freedom and existence. The state is that entity which nurtures and protects the individual, educating and cultivating him or her to a knowledge of his or her own freedom and responsibility.[89] Some organ or structure, Hegel might argue, must exist to represent the interests of the state as a whole (its collective will and desire). And at some points it is logical that the survival, well-being and freedom of that organism which grounds the finite freedom of its members must take precedence over the individual freedoms of those members.[90] One of Hegel's *Zusätze* suggests this difficulty:

> In times of peace, the particular spheres and functions pursue the path of satisfying their particular aims and minding their own business . . . In a situation of exigency, however, whether in home or foreign affairs, the organism of which these particular spheres are members fuses into the single concept of sovereignty.
> (Phil. R. 278, *Zusatz*)

Thus, it is *not* true that Hegel would deny privacy or individual freedom in the interests of the state. Indeed, he criticizes Plato for having done precisely this in the *Republic*, constituting the sole defect of an otherwise laudable vision (Phil. R. 185, *Zusatz*). It is true, however, that Hegel views the state, "the actuality of concrete freedom" (Phil. R. 260), as enjoying supremacy in an ordered hierarchy of freedom in which the state is viewed as an "external necessity" and higher authority than the sphere of "private rights and private welfare," whose "laws and interests are subordinate to it and dependent on it" (Phil. R. 261).

Marx, for one, found it difficult to countenance the identity and just subordination of the rights of individuals to the rights of the apparently bourgeois-style state which Hegel envisioned.[91]

Others, such as Kierkegaard, have seen in this theory yet another example of Hegel's continual propensity and willingness to swallow the real individual within some vast, totalitarian universal. I do not dissent from the very real concerns expressed in such criticisms. But it seems to me that the standard objections of existentialists, Marxists and other liberationists are directed finally against empirical particulars of the theory, rather than illuminating any serious flaw in Hegel's theory of freedom itself.

Indeed, Hegel's own doctrine of reciprocity or the "necessity" which is identical with freedom disallows such interpretations. According to this doctrine, the organic whole is conditioned by its real individual and semi-autonomous parts, even as the parts are conditioned by the aims and properties of the whole (see Section 6 below). It simply is not possible, then, for the state to exercise violent and destructive authority over its constituents. Such is neither the meaning nor the purpose of the organism of the state. No political entity which functions thus can expect to survive. It is inevitable that such an alienated and alienating structure will itself be negated with all the "fury of destruction" it has so unjustly exercised [cf. Section 2 (iv) above]. And in any case, such a structure is *not* a state, as Hegel envisions that ideal entity.

Hegel, for example, never suggests that "concrete freedom consists in the identity . . . of the system of particular interest . . . with the system of general interest [the state]."[92] He rather makes clear, I feel, that the "general interst" in some sense grounds the possibility of the particular, and for that reason, in cases of "exigency" (as he phrases it), the state may be entitled to overriding consideration. The fact that petty, posturing bourgeois dictators, misguided executives, corrupt legislators and civil servants, or tyrannical political oligarchies derive power and satisfaction from viewing their governments as states of "perpetual exigency" is more a theological commentary on the human condition than a political critique of Hegel's thought (or, for that matter, the thought of Marx or John Locke).

Likewise, I do not feel that Hegel ever intended anything like the popular lampoon of his thought, according to which real individuals are but cogs in the wheels of a vast spiritual mechanism. Nor is his state to be seen as the political institutionalizing of this atrocity. I have labored throughout to suggest that Hegel's notion of *Geist*, however complex and difficult, is profoundly ennobling, compassionate and reconciling in character. Life according to Spirit is not meant to destroy the individual, but to sustain and preserve the individual, while enabling individual existence at a vastly richer and more diverse level than could be managed in isolation. As Hegel himself suggests, such existence should be characterized by the "reconciliation and resolution of all contradictions" through faith, love, hope and the "comradeship of free men" (Phil. R. 359).

The fractious histories of the Christian church and the Muslim 'Ummah offer two examples of the profound difficulties associated with the practical application of this ideal of *koinoinia*, to be sure. But the inevitable chasm between the practical and ideal need not serve always as an indictment of the ideal. And if these institutions in our historical, social and cultural life which Hegel would identify as spiritual often tend to degenerate into a "bee-hive" mentality in which the freedom and dignity of the individual are suppressed rather than enhanced, then we must allow final responsibility to rest with the "bees." It does not seem to me possible for life according to *Geist* as Hegel envisioned it—characterized by love, trust and wisdom, forging bonds of mutual compassion and responsibility which both condition and enable individual freedom—to do the violence to the individual or to the concept of freedom in general that critics have suggested.

Ultimately, then, such criticisms suggest the well-known truth that philosophers make good visionaries and poor statesmen. But if Plato and Confucius failed in their respective attempts to actualize their visions of an ideal political order; and if, in our own time, we have witnessed the failure, the corruption, or the distortion of attempts to realize the political visions of Hegel and Marx, I maintain nonetheless that this proves nothing against the cogency and coherency of the visions themselves, nor against the lessons they purport to teach those concerned and entrusted with the day-to-day exercise of social and political affairs.

Finally it is true for Hegel--as for Plato, Marx and others
--that the vision of the state which guarantees individual freedom and rights is an ideal (although it is not thereby relegated
to the status of some sort of apocalyptic vision, devoid of attendant human responsibility). As Reyburn notes:

> The final end of the progress in history is not
> merely to develop this or that nation and achieve the
> purposes of some individual state. It is to bring
> forth mind itself as it is in its truth, *the* state as
> such. And the state, so comprehended, is not a bare
> abstraction, a mere essence; it is a concrete universal,
> the mind which expresses itself in moments which are
> themselves minds. . . .[93]

It is Hegel's own conviction that such an ideal political and
social order represents "the realized freedom of the Idea" (Phil.
R. 279).

Section 6. Concluding Remarks: Freedom and the Absolute

Despite its obvious importance, Hegel's theory of the state
is not the *terminus* for a complete understanding of his doctrine
of freedom. What was born in metaphysics returns through nature
and society to its own realm once again. In the arena of world
history, nation-states are born and pass away. The sequence of
their perpetual perishing narrates the gradual, and successively-
more-adequate embodiment of freedom as the concrete universal.
Freedom, argues Hegel, "is the sole truth of Spirit," and the
whole of world history "is none other than the progress of the
consciousness of freedom."[94]

Thus, the Concept embodied (however imperfectly) in each
nation-state or culture is that *Begriff* or Absolute Idea which
Hegel sees as the rational structure, the generative teleological principle of the world-process. And the essence of that
absolute idea as it is revealed in world history is none other
than freedom. The reflective mind, in studying the course of
the historical process, grasps this essential truth of the rational structure of the world as freedom. In so doing, mind
"lays hold of its [own] concrete universality, and rises to apprehend the absolute mind, as the eternally actual truth in
which the contemplative reason enjoys freedom. . ." (*Enc.* 552;
cf. *Enc.* 549). This Hegel describes as "the Mind's elevation
to God."

We had occasion at the outset of this treatment of Hegel to discuss the importance of theology and theological metaphor in his thought. Subsequently we have noted the importance of teleological explanation in understanding the processes of development in both the natural (i.e., non-human) and human world. Throughout, such rational patterns and principles as were found to enable the development and self-maintenance of all manner of organic entities were shown to be related to the general rational structure of the world-process as a whole--the *Begriff*, *Logos*, or Absolute Idea.

It comes as no surprise, then, to recognize that, in his discussions of the Absolute, Hegel has in mind the concept of God in history, working divine purposes in the actual world. We recognize further that, in the Absolute, the distinction we have maintained between *Begriff* and *Geist* appears finally to vanish. That is, the Absolute Idea is the rational Concept which has attained awareness of itself as Absolute Spirit, as "self-knowing truth" (GL 824, 844). The principle of freedom in the world is finally also the principle of reflexivity, self-consciousness and mutual or reciprocal relatedness. Hegel's ontology thus reflects in an ultimate way the very relationship we discerned empirically between freedom and self-conscious activity in the human moral sphere.

God is for Hegel, as for Whitehead, the ground of possibilities for the future, the ultimate reason for the definiteness of the world process, as well as the source of human freedom. Indeed, as William Earle suggests, it is precisely in the experience of freedom and self-consciousness in our own being that we derive "one of our clearest images of what something absolute might be."[95] But it is important to note that God is neither identical with the world process, nor is God wholly other than that process. Rather, God is transcendent in the literal sense of that term--i.e., spanning or "climbing across" the world-- including the world as an integral element of the divine nature.[96]

In this manner, while God's own primordial purpose (the *Begriff*) is the ground of the definiteness of history, the *Begriff* is *not* merely an external mechanism by which the world passively is generated. Indeed, while Hegel is not clear on this point, it seems evident that he intended that God's own

nature is in part consequent upon the activity of the world--
and (for Hegel) most especially upon human activity:

> God is God only so far as he knows himself: his
> self-knowledge is, further, a self-consciousness in
> man and man's knowledge *of* God, which proceeds to
> man's self-knowledge *in* God.
>
> (*Enc.* 564)

This suggests that the gradual emergence of self-consciousness and freedom in the world-process is in some sense the temporal attainment by God of the fullness of divine Being through
the emergent activity of the world. That growing role of reason
in the world finally is attained not so much through the political and cultural institutions of *objektiver Geist*, as through
beauty, reverence, and reflective thought which together characterize Absolute Spirit. Philosophy, the last and (for Hegel)
the highest of these is literally the realm of divine Reason
made actual and consciously determinative in the world. Since
the world is a product of the rational *Begriff*, this amounts
finally to a complete self-determination for the world. Philosophy is finally for Hegel, as it was for Aristotle, "the esoteric study of God and identity . . . the self-thinking Idea,
the truth aware of itself" (*Enc.* 573, 574).

By revealing finally the constitutive and determinative
role of reason in the world, philosophy is thus the medium by
which God makes freedom actual in the world. For philosophy
provides mind with the knowledge of absolute truth. And, for
Hegel, it is truth that shall set persons free.

IV. CONCLUDING SUMMARY

> Well, if *that* is what Hegel meant, then I agree
> with him! My problem is, I never could understand
> Hegel!
>   -Alfred North Whitehead-[1]

I have endeavored to present the relevant material on the
respective theories of freedom of Whitehead and Hegel in a manner which would highlight certain strong similarities between
the two doctrines. The course of our discussion has revealed
that human freedom, for both Whitehead and Hegel, is grounded
in the ongoing teleological process of self-determination characteristic of all "organisms."

With Whitehead's assistance, we are enabled further to
understand the logical category of "organism" and organic behavior as descriptive not merely of "living" entities, but of all
entities which are in any sense actual, no matter how "primitive"
or elementary. That is, this creative process in which the understanding of freedom is grounded is constitutive of Being itself.
"To be" is to be creative. To be inert, passive, uncreative
(or, in Hegel's terminology, wholly "self-subsistent," *an sich*),
is finally *not* to be in any sense actual.

Through Hegel's insight, in turn, we discern that the creativity which is universally pervasive and constitutive of the
actual world manifests itself in an ascending scale of ever more
complex forms, whose emerging essential nature is social and
holistic. The mode of human freedom, characterized by the reflexivity or self-awareness of this creative organic process
itself, is in fact one of the more complex, supervenient phases
of this scale--at once summarizing, preserving, fulfilling and
transcending the less complex phases of creativity.

Finally, when viewing the whole of the world process, Whitehead and Hegel both concur that the creativity of the world simultaneously exhibits an internal and limiting principle of rational
order, a *Logos*. This is to argue that the creativity which is
the essence of the universe is itself finally and fully explained
as the immanent teleological principle--the *Begriff*, Absolute
Idea, or primordial Principle of Concretion--coming to fulfillment

in each successive stage of that process. This rational principle or pattern of organization, however, is neither wholly external to the process of becoming, nor is it merely to be identified
as nothing more than the process itself. Rather, it is both.
This *Logos* is at once the transcendent end or goal of the process
itself: it is "the system or totality which is both a whole, and
one with the process. It is transcendently and eternally whole,
yet everlastingly self-realizing."[2]

Both Whitehead and Hegel concur further in giving to this
Logos a theological interpretation. Whitehead notes that his
concept of "enduring personality" as a series of terms in which
the succeeding terms "with some peculiar completeness sum up
their predecessors" has a correlate fact in the nature of God.
For Whitehead, "God's nature is an even more complete unity of
life in a chain of elements for which succession does not mean
loss of immediate unison" (PR 531). For Whitehead, the notion
of creativity thus leads to a doctrine of God as "an actual entity, immanent in the actual world but transcending any finite
cosmic epoch--a being at once actual, eternal, immanent and
transcendent" (PR 143). For Hegel, the notion of the teleological character of reality likewise yields a concept of the eternal, Absolute Idea "immanent in Nature" and at work within nature.
The essential features of the God-world relation are suggested
in the following *Zusatz*:

> In this case, there no longer stands, on the one
> side, an activity external to the object, and on the
> other side, a merely passive object: but the spiritu-
> al activity is directed to an object which has sponta-
> neously worked itself up into the result to be brought
> about by that activity, so that in the activity and
> in the object, one and the same content is present.
>
> (*Enc*. 381, *Zusatz*)

It is perhaps unfortunate from our point of view that Hegel
insisted on describing this crowning or culminating feature of
his thought as "the Absolute." As a traditional designation of
theism, it is entirely appropriate. Yet this term can (and
frequently does) suggest an image of immutable necessity, some
sort of cosmic or spiritual mechanism. Such an image stands in
marked contrast to Whitehead's notion of divine persuasiveness,
and appears inimical to any meaningful doctrine of metaphysical
freedom--apart from suggesting, as Spinoza had done, that God
alone is truly free.

We must bear in mind, however, that Hegel is rooted in Greek, and particularly Aristotelian thought. If there is any important role for determinism or necessity in his thought, it is the necessity of *reason*, of mind. It is virtually an article of faith with Hegel to maintain the final triumph or superiority of the "rational nature of things" over the blind, groping forces of passion, chaos, alienation and meaninglessness. Hegel speaks of this in the *Logic* as the "cunning of reason" (*Enc.* 209).

> Reason is as cunning as it is powerful. Cunning may be said to lie in the intermediative action which, while it permits the objects to follow their own bent and act upon one another till they waste away, and does not itself directly interfere in the process, is nevertheless only working out its own aims. With this explanation, Divine Providence may be said to stand to the world and its process in the capacity of absolute cunning. God lets men do as they please with their particular passions and interests; but the result is the accomplishment of--not their plans, but his, and these differ decidedly from the ends primarily sought by those whom he employs.
> (*Enc.* 209, *Zusatz*)

The necessity of reason is *not*, however, a necessity which predetermines the outcome of all process, any more than does the source of initial subjective aims in God's "Primordial Nature" necessarily imply a radical finalism or spiritual mechanism for Whitehead. Rather, for both, divine power is *persuasive* in the world-process by virtue of its rational evaluation of possibilities for that process. Hegel's cunning of reason is not a "trick." It represents instead the ever-present lure of the immanent *Logos* or rational principle towards greater order, harmony and unity.

God as Absolute Mind or Spirit thus functions as a lure towards the realization of rational purpose in the world precisely through the medium of autonomous human agency. Hegel himself refutes the charges of finalism and determinism brought against him in this regard. Discussing the realized end of purposive action, he suggests (in a manner thoroughly compatible with Whitehead) that such ends as are realized are themselves objectified, and become thus "a Means or material for other Ends, *and so on forever*."[3]

In order to preserve creativity and a meaningful doctrine of conditional or quasi-causal freedom, both Hegel and Whitehead

thus refuse to countenance either a radical separation of God
and the world or the absolute identity of God with the world-
process. For both it is in some sense true that the *Logos* is
to be seen, in Professor Harris's terms, as

> the source, the ground, and the creative principle
> of all things, immanent in all things and transcendent
> beyond all things--eternally real, eternally active, and
> everlastingly self-manifesting and self-realizing in the
> world.[4]

The basic similarities of their doctrines of God and of the God-
world relation thus serve to identify both the Hegelian and the
Whiteheadian metaphysical systems as panentheisms.[5]

We have marshalled evidence to demonstrate that, for both
Hegel and Whitehead, the similar "micro-ontologies" of teleological creativity serve to ground similar macroscopic doctrines
of conditional or finite freedom. We have seen, further, that
complete development of these doctrines led both philosophers
to adopt highly similar attitudes toward metaphysical theism,
and toward the relationship between their respective ultimate
or "absolute" metaphysical principles and the actual world. In-
asmuch as this has been accomplished, it would appear that the
central purpose of this essay as stated at the outset now has
been accomplished.

In particular, I would contend that we are now in a position
to understand why Whitehead himself finally was persuaded that
his work represented "a transformation of some main doctrines
of Absolute Idealism onto a realistic basis" (PR viii). Such
awareness, in turn, provides new insight into the comparison
which Whitehead drew between his doctrine of teleological creativity and Hegel's own doctrine--a comparison which heretofore
has proven somewhat enigmatic for Whiteheadian scholars:

> It is now evident that the final analogy to philo-
> sophies of the Hegelian school, noted in the Preface,
> is not accidental. The universe is at once the multi-
> plicity of *res verae* and the solidarity of *res verae*.
> The solidarity is itself the efficiency of the macro-
> scopic *res vera*, embodying the principle of unbounded
> permanence acquiring novelty through flux. The multi-
> plicity is composed of microscopic *res verae*, each
> embodying the principle of bounded flux acquiring
> 'everlasting' permanence. On one side, the one becomes
> many; and on the other side, the many become one. But
> *what* becomes is always a *res vera*, and the concrescence
> of a *res vera* is the development of a subjective aim.

> This development is nothing else than the Hegelian
> development of an idea.
>
> (PR 254)

Some readers may persist nonetheless in the opinion that
this entire essay represents little more than an exercise in
rank eclecticism--in inadequate and superficial synthesis, in
which certain significant differences between Hegel and Whitehead have been overlooked, minimized, or deliberately ignored.
It may be objected that I have given too "Whiteheadian" a reading
of Hegel, and/or too "Hegelian" a reading of Whitehead.

I do not deny (indeed, I stated explicitly in the Introduction) that the hermeneutic with which I approach Hegel has been
shaped and influenced by a prior acquaintence with Whitehead.
But I have tried to guard against merely reading Whitehead's
thought into Hegel's text (and vice-versa). Instead, I have
endeavored throughout to preserve the distinction and autonomy
of the two. Where certain similarities adduced appear surprisingly (and perhaps to some, questionably) strong, I would suggest
that the explanation lies in the fact that such affinities have
been present in the literature all along, rather than in the fact
that I have distorted the data to achieve my purpose. These similarities are indeed forceful when one deigns to consider them.

Moreover, where such differences do exist, it seems to me
on one hand (as in the case of Hegel's apparent rejection of
natural evolution; *vide supra*, p. 89, n. 47) that these are principally differences of historical context. They do not necessarily indicate irreducible metaphysical conflicts. On the other
hand, some allegedly "irreducible" differences (such as Hegel's
treatment of time; *vide supra*, pp. 102ff.) can be dismissed outright as based upon misinformation and clumsy or inadequate exegesis of primary texts.

Thus, while it may be true that upon occasion I have failed
to resist the temptation to overstate my own case, nevertheless
I feel that the comparisons I have outlined between Hegel and
Whitehead do in fact exist and may no longer be ignored. Rather
than engage in a further extension of this *apologia*, however, I
shall conclude by giving attention to the strongest objections
against the comparisons I have drawn.[6]

(i) First, with respect to the discussion immediately preceding: one might object that my ascription of panentheism to

both Hegel and Whitehead glosses over an essential distinction
of the "dipolar" theism of Whitehead from the more "traditional,
absolutistic" theism of Hegel. That Hegel's theism is neither
"traditional" nor "absolutistic" (by which is meant, I believe,
"absolutely determinative from the standpoint of divine omnipo-
tence and omniscience") has been, I trust, adequately established.
As to the "dipolar theism" of Whitehead's system, it is well to
recall that this term is Charles Hartshorne's, rather than Whitehead's own. As far as I know, only Hartshorne (and several of
his students) are, strictly speaking, "dipolar theists." Yet,
as Hartshorne himself has pointed out, there are many panenthe-
ists.[7] We are not, of course, arguing the identity of Hegel and
Whitehead with respect to theism, but merely their similarity.
Hegel's doctrine of internal teleology and the immanence in the
world-process of the teleological principle--which both generates
and is in some sense generated by that process--insures the mutual conditioning and active reciprocity of God and the world
intended by Whitehead's own doctrine of the Consequent Nature
of God.

The real question in my mind, given the similar panentheisms
of Hegel and Whitehead, is whether both philosophers have assumed
more than is necessary in utilizing the term "God" for their respective ultimate metaphysical principles. Use of the term "God"
to designate the immanent, conditioned, and conditioning *Logos*
that both systems require and demonstrate is, to be sure, completely congruent with the long tradition of philosophical theism.
Yet both Hegel and Whitehead intend far more than this by their
use of this term. Both in fact seem to identify their respective
Gods, whether symbolically or actually, with the God of religious,
and especially of Christian theism.[8] As I have suggested in both
cases, it seems to me that more than a few theologians might,
with all respect, prescind from this convenient identification.
More to the point, however, the latter tradition ascribes traits
to "God"--such as personality, "parenthood," love, suffering,
companionship, and other similar traits and activities--which
cannot be ascribed to the *Logos* purely on metaphysical grounds.
That is to say, while a panentheistic *Logos* appears necessary
to the systems of both Whitehead and Hegel, the more specific
image of, say, the Christian God does not. *Neither is the latter*

image proscribed in either metaphysical system. Both are, strictly speaking, indeterminate and completely open regarding this
modification.

It is simply the case that, at this point, one may with some
certainty draw that elusive boundary-line between theology proper
and philosophical theism. The trinitarian God of Christian theism, from whom both Hegel and Whitehead draw such evident inspira-
tion, belongs properly to the former realm and does not enjoy the
status of an internally-necessary truth provided to the *Logos*--
the *Begriff*, Absolute Idea or Principle of Concretion--in both
metaphysical systems. While this is a comparatively beningn observation in my opinion, it is one nonetheless of some importance
for "derivative" theological enterprises, such as process theology.

(ii) A second possible objection comes at the point of my
deliberate choice of the term "organic mechanism" to describe
the central features of Hegel's *Naturphilosophie*. This choice
may appear to "load the dice" in favor of a comparison with
Whitehead's doctrine of the same name in *Science and the Modern
World*. The force of this charge may be reduced somewhat by noting
that "organic mechanism" is more or less abandoned by Whitehead
in formulating his broader concept of a "Philosophy of Organism"
in *Process and Reality*.[9] For Hegel, my use of the term conven-
iently summarizes his description of the sublation of mechanism
within a higher organic unity, and therefore seems entirely appropriate.

The point of comparison of the two lies not so much in the
names chosen for their doctrines, as in the centrality of the
general category of "organism" for both philosophies. For both
philosophers this category, derived in dialogue with observation
of the natural world, serves to describe behavior which is neither
externally-determined nor contra-causal. I have used the phrase
"quasi-causal" on occasion to describe the manner in which "causal
efficacy" is admitted as *significant* in organic behavior, but not
absolutely *determinative*. This is the key to the concept of freedom which is developed on the basis of either a Whiteheadian
"Philosophy of Organism" or an Hegelian doctrine of "organic
mechanism." In the latter case, "organic mechanism" illuminates
Hegel's claim that freedom is somehow "the truth of Necessity"
(*Enc.* 158).

The category of organism as the ground of an understanding of freedom for both Hegel and Whitehead reveals that, in every finite process, there is an element of necessity to be considered. But this is not a necessity derived from the deterministic interpretation of causality envisioned by Laplace. Rather, as Errol Harris notes, this is a necessity

> which does not settle everything from the beginning, though it does prescribe determinate rules of procedure for the diversification of the system, proceeding from the central principle of organization. Novelty (as demanded by Bergson and Whitehead) is, therefore, not ruled out, but it is never capricious or irrelevant to principle.
>
> It follows that the necessity implicit in causation is not inimical to freedom of action at the level of intelligent mind. Here relevant variation is most labile and most characteristic of activity. Intelligent determination of action is precisely that which gives most scope for the exercise of discretion and untrammelled judgment; and so, by widening the range of applicability of the organizing principle governing the activity, it bestows upon the agent the sort of freedom that issues in responsible choice.[10]

Thus, the inevitable comparisons engendered by my use of the term "organic mechanism" for Hegel's doctrine are not unfair. Rather, these suggest the similarity of the very doctrines on which both Hegel and Whitehead ground their theories of the finite or conditional freedom which is the principal property of finite, self-conscious minds.

(iii) Nonetheless, one could object that, despite the similar use of organic categories to describe freedom, Hegel makes it quite clear that his theory of freedom is restricted to human beings (and to God) by virtue of their monopoly of self-consciousness. This is a difference between the two respective views of freedom, to be sure: one, I would add, which seems clearly due to the differing historical contexts. Far from suggesting an irreducible conflict, however, this difference highlights the way in which the two metaphysical systems inform and complement one another.

On one hand, with his doctrine of reflexivity (i.e., self-conscious activity) as a supervenient phase of organic mechanism, Hegel seems to pinpoint more precisely than does Whitehead just *what* form of teleological activity corresponds to freedom as we

commonly understand the term. Hegel's analysis parallels Whitehead's vague assertion that free activity is discerned by the
dominance of the mental pole in the concrescence of an actual
occasion. Hegel's focus on an understanding of the human self,
however, renders his analysis useful precisely at the point of
Whitehead's greatest weakness and ambiguity.

On the other hand, in this "age of ecology" we are perhaps
more prepared to shed our *hybris* and allow that other species
besides the human may exhibit freedom. Freedom does not simply
pop into the natural world from nowhere with the advent of human
beings. Indeed, with respect to the growth and development of
individual humans, we customarily equate freedom with the gradual
emergence or attainment of maturity and "full humanity." Freedom
is thus a task or achievement, and not merely some mysterious
state of being which is either fully present or wholly absent in
an organism.[11]

Similarly, with regard to the whole scale of organic forms
in nature, Whitehead's analysis helps us recognize that freedom
is an emergent trait in more complex organic forms. Its emergence
is equated with the emergence of consciousness and subjectivity,
particularly with the emergence of self-consciousness as the
supervenient activity of reflexivity.

Thus, freedom is (as is self-consciousness) a *continuous*
rather than a "quantized" variable, a function which seems to
attain a relative maximum in human behavior. The function falls
off sharply (but not abruptly) to negligible levels as we descend
the scale of forms, indicating that sentience (even if of only a
very rudimentary form) is never entirely absent in any phase.
This suggests that, with Whitehead's help, we are able to extend
Hegel's insight regarding the nature of freedom throughout the
scale of organic forms. Consciousness is a function whose value
(or "significance") decreases rapidly with decreasing complexity
of form, all the way down to the "primitive" or constitutive
elements of being (Whitehead's "actual entities"). In this way
we are enabled to comprehend the explicit emergence to dominance
of freedom in the more complex forms of the scale.[12]

(iv) I have suggested on several occasions that a principal
point of comparison for Hegel and Whitehead lies in their similar
stress on holism (or "organism") and reciprocal relatedness.

Professor Lewis S. Ford, in a forthcoming article analyzing certain contemporary developments in process thought, however, argues *against* this position.[13] He suggests instead that Hegel and Whitehead have in mind very different conceptions of "the whole."[14] Furthermore Ford adds that the internal relations which Whitehead specifies as constitutive among individual entities and between entities and universals, are in fact asymmetrical (unlike the case with Hegel), and therefore are not inimical to a meaningful doctrine of freedom.

The former suggestion--that Whitehead's pluralism entails a *less* inclusive and all-embracing concept of "the whole" than does Hegel's holism, seems to have much to recommend it. Each actual entity, in the duration of its concrescence, reflects or "summarizes" the whole universe. Thus it could be argued that "the whole" for Whitehead is a relative quantity: that there are, in fact, innumerable "wholes." Upon closer examination, however, Ford's alleged distinction between Hegel and Whitehead on this point cannot be sustained.

First: the objection regarding the concept of an "all-inclusive whole" (which Ford sees as compromising a doctrine of real individuals and genuine freedom) is properly leveled, not at Hegel, but at Bradley. The latter's concept of "the whole" as a mysterious, transcendent and all-embracing Reality--only imperfectly grasped by the finite mind--is often confused in English-language philosophy for Hegel's own doctrine.

Furthermore Whitehead (as Robert Whittemore points out) is far more indebted to Bradley (by Whitehead's own admission) than is commonly acknowledged by Whiteheadians. Hegel himself, as we have seen, is far less open to the charge of having articulated a concept of the whole which is destructive of genuine freedom. Indeed, Hegel's doctrine of finite human freedom arises as a consequence of his version of holism. In addition, Hegel's concept of discrete "organisms" likewise suggests the pluralistic nature of the "whole" which is reality: each organism, like each actual entity, is in some limited sense, at least, a "whole" in itself. And the world-process as a whole is not strictly unitary, but represents (as it does for Whitehead) a process of processes.

Ford's suggestion finally runs afoul of process theology itself, which has utilized the metaphor of the world as "God's

Body" to describe the immanent, yet transcendent nature of the God-world relation. This metaphor, in light of our previous comments on Hegel's theology, utterly undermines any attempt to drive a significant wedge between Hegel and Whitehead with respect to holism.

Secondly: we have had occasion in our discussion of Whitehead to note the significance of Whitehead's formulation of asymmetrical internal relatedness (*vide supra*, pp. 32-34). Whitehead's doctrine solves a legitimate problem for Hegel, by demonstrating how one can hold a significant doctrine of holism, including real internal relations among the "parts" within the "whole," without compromising freedom. In this sense, Whitehead's doctrine represents, not a difference, but an advance or modification upon Hegel's view--one which is completely compatible with the general metaphysical position described by both.

(v) Yet another objection may be raised against this enterprise by suggesting that Hegel and Whitehead are at opposite and irreconcilable extremes with respect to their advocacy of monism and pluralism, respectively. This is a familiar, but also a facile criticism. Some variations of absolute idealism, such as that of F. H. Bradley, may be open to the charge that they are entirely monistic.[15] I remain unpersuaded that Hegel's philosophy is as "monistic" as some critics have charged. If nothing else, his complex and highly pluralistic understanding of "concreteness" ameliorates this charge.

Whitehead on many occasions is willing to modify or qualify his allegedly "unqualified" pluralism. In discussing freedom as the "claim for vigorous [individual] self-assertion," for example, he imparts further meaning to the concept by suggesting that such freedom is productive of the "great Harmony," the "harmony of enduring individualities, connected in the unity of a background" (AI 362). Whitehead further discusses this dimension of freedom (with great "Hegelian" insight) by suggesting that "there is a freedom lying beyond circumstance, derived from the direct intuition that life can be grounded upon its absorption in what is changeless amid change . . . It is the freedom of that virtue directly derived from the source of all harmony" (AI 86).

Much of the fuss over the opposition of pluralism and monism, I further contend, is the result of a "category mistake." The metaphysical antithesis of monism is not pluralism, but dualism.

Advocates of monism are seldom engaged in the ridiculous task of denying all reality to the "many" forms of the natural world in favor of some underlying single reality. Nor are pluralists like Whitehead engaged in asserting the reality of the Many at the expense of any unifying features of the world-process. That process, as Whitehead himself asserts, is creative precisely by virtue of the Many striving ceaselessly to become One--and thereby being increased by one. For Whitehead, in addition, God is that "source of all [unifying] harmony," the principle of order, unity and purposiveness in the world.

The stress on One versus Many is merely a relative distinction. It is impossible to discuss the "Many" without specifying the nature and source of the obvious unifying or orderly principles which define the cosmos as a *uni*-verse. Likewise, as post-Parmenideans (such as Plato) discovered, it is difficult to talk with any intelligibility about the "One" without specifying the manner in which that One becomes Many.

"One and Many" are two starting points for metaphysics, the dialectical pursuit of which necessarily leads from one to the other, because they are interdependent concepts. Hegel perhaps stated this best in terms of his doctrine of truth. For our argument, the "truth" of "the One and the Many," like other forms of truth, is

> the circle that presupposes its end as its goal, having its end also as its beginning; and only by being worked out to its end is it actual.
>
> (*Phen.* 10)

The opposite of monism is dualism. Hegel and Whitehead both are engaged in a vigorous campaign against the dualism of Western metaphysics--whether of the ontological Cartesian type, or of the epistemic Kantian variety. Both result in what Whitehead termed "the facile vice of bifurcation" (CN vi, 30ff.): Mind and Matter, Subject and Object, Appearance and Reality.

Once again we may cite Bradley's position, in the latter portion of *Appearance and Reality*, that reality (as opposed to the appearance of pluralism and process) represents, for the finite mind at least, an imperfectly-knowable Absolute.[16] Hegel, however, held no such doctrine. Indeed, his organic mechanism would be unintelligible apart from the assumption of a rational

and knowable structure for the world-process. This amounts to a
denial of any distinction between appearance and reality--or, more
significantly, between reality in itself and our experience of it.
In this denial Whitehead, through his "Reformed Subjectivist Principle," of course concurs.

(vi) Focus on the teleological structure of process brings
us finally to the principal general feature of similarity revealed
in our study. George Kline has summarized this point of comparison as obtaining between the Hegelian "Concept" and the Whiteheadian "concrescence."[17] While helpful, I feel that this suggestion
is wide of the mark. The more precise comparison, I am persuaded,
is that obtaining between the Concept and the Whiteheadian "subjective aim."

Hegel clouds the issue with his unfortunate and imprecise
suggestion that the *Begriff* in its concrete existence may be
compared with "the 'I' or pure self-consciousness" (GL 583):
i.e., the Concept (according to Hegel) is the "subject itself"
(GL 64). What is more precisely supported in Hegel's sustained
discussion, however, is an understanding of the *Begriff* as the
pattern or principle of organization for organic activity, more
complex phases of which qualify as subjects or (as Hegel terms
them) "selves." A "self" is, for Hegel, any entity which functions according to its own inner Idea or concept, and is thus
determined by its own concept. The Hegelian "self" thus should
not simply be equated with its concept. The concept, rather, is
the teleological *principle* of subjectivity.

This description suggests an immediate comparison with the
Whiteheadian "selves" or concrescences, whose development proceeds as a consequence of their individual subjective aims. The
"subjective aim" is so called by Whitehead precisely because, in
each actual entity, it is the principle of subjectivity. Active
functioning according to its subjective aim is what defines the
subject as a subject. While it is thus the principal determinative and defining factor of a concrescence, the subjective aim
likewise is never merely equated with the concrescence as a whole.
It is instead that inner teleological principle of self-development whereby a concrescence attains its own novel unity of definiteness.

For Whitehead, the creativity and finite freedom which characterize the behavior of actual entities are grounded in their subjective aims. For Hegel, the finite freedom and creativity which are exhibited in self-conscious human organisms are grounded in the teleological self-determination which is the principal feature of the more general ontological category of "organic mechanism." That self-determination, in turn is likewise grounded upon the organism's inner "concept."

Finally for Whitehead, each actual entity is characterized by an initial subjective aim, derived from the primordial Principle of Concretion which characterizes the world-process as a whole. Likewise for Hegel, each inner concept exhibited in discrete organisms is derived from the Concept (the *Begriff* or Absolute Idea) which characterizes the world-process as a whole. Thus, I suggest that subjective aims are to the Principle of Concretion as individual "inner concepts" are to the Concept.

I have likened the Principle of Concretion and the *Begriff*, respectively, to the Greek doctrine of the *Logos*. It is a further common feature of both metaphysical systems that the teleological principle is not external to the process it generates, but instead is conditioned by that process. As we have noted, both Hegel and Whitehead endow the *Logos* with a theological significance by identifying it as "God." Whitehead in particular makes the dialectical (i.e., conditioning and conditioned) relationship between the *Logos* and the world explicit, stressing not only the "Primordial" (conditioning *Logos*), but also the "Consequent (conditioned *Logos*) Nature" of God. Hegel, as we have noted, holds to a similar doctrine (though less explicitly so). In this way, both Hegel and Whitehead are led consistently from an understanding of metaphysical freedom at the "microcosmic" level to a "macrocosmic" doctrine of a conditioning and conditioned God as the ground and guarantor of that freedom.

Henceforth Hegel and Whitehead must be seen as representing two schools or variations of one tradition of process philosophy.[18] The "process" schools are characterized mainly by their common recovery of the ancient Greek ideals of harmony and unity amidst real diversity, process and pluralism. Thus process philosophy is distinguished by the belief that reality throughout is one structured, constantly developing, interdependent whole.

CHAPTER I

[1]*Essays in Science and Philosophy* (New York: Philosophical Library, 1948), p. 10.

[2]*Hegel: A Re-examination* (London: G. Allen & Unwin, 1958).

[3]Victor Lowe, *Understanding Whitehead* (Baltimore: John Hopkins Press, 1962). Ivor Leclerc, *Whitehead's Metaphysics: An Introductory Exposition* (New York: Macmillan, 1958).

[4]This phenomenon is documented by James E. Will: "The Uses of Philosophical Theology in the Christian-Marxist Dialogue," *Union Seminary Quarterly Review* 26, No. 1 (Fall 1970) 19-42; "The Place of Ideology in Theology," *Journal for Ecumenical Studies* 15, No. 1 (Winter 1978).

[5]An example of this is the paradoxical statement that "die Wahrheit der Notwendigkeit ist Freiheit" (*Enc.* 158). One easily loses sight of the fact that Hegel is not using "necessity" in the customary deterministic sense at this point, but has *redefined* "necessity" in terms of his doctrine of "reciprocity" (see below, Ch. III, Sec. 3). This statement represents a deliberate play on words. The logical contradiction thus is not nearly so great as it seems.

[6]From the "Foreword" to *Hegel: The Essential Writings*, ed. Frederick G. Weiss (New York: Harper & Row, 1974), p. xi.

[7]One must exclude from this comparison, of course, the "systematic" commentary on *Process and Reality*, which comprises Part Three of *Adventures of Ideas*.

[8]Any philosophy qualifies as a "process" philosophy which: (i) stresses the primacy of change and becoming over static being or substance; and (ii) embraces some sort of holism, emphasizing relations among discrete entities in the system which are not entirely external to, but are in some manner constitutive of the individual entities which comprise that system (i.e., "real internal relations"); and (iii) discerns some sort of immanent pattern or principle of organization, generally exhibited in all such processes of change--in the terminology of Heraclitus, a *logos*. Secondary features resulting from these central principles include an emphasis on the importance of a doctrine of time; the development of a concept of nature within which the "natural" (i.e., nonhuman) world is "taken seriously"; and finally, a doctrine of metaphysical freedom. The differing "schools" of process thought may be distinguished by their differing treatment and relative emphasis of these central concerns. The centrality of these issues, however, distinguishes the process tradition from a variety of other philosophical traditions, such as analysis (broadly defined to include empiricism and logical positivism), existentialism, and transcendentalist or exclusivist forms of

philosophical theology (such as Thomism and neo-orthodoxy) which stress the radical distinction of God the creator from the world as created.

In this regard, Hegel and Whitehead are observed to stand as the two extremes of the process tradition, the means or intermediate schools being represented by pragmatism (including James, Peirce and Dewey) and "emergent evolutionism," or what I term "the biological tradition" (including Bergson and Teilhard de Chardin, and arguably Darwin and Herbert Spencer). Some of the connecting links among these discrete schools are represented by Boston Personalism (especially E. S. Brightman, whose decidedly Hegelian orientation led to views very similar in many respects to Whitehead's own), and the "English Hegelians" (arguably Bradley and Bosanquet, but more especially those for whom nature and time were of paramount significance, such as Samuel Alexander, R. G. Collingwood and Errol E. Harris).

[9]"Whitehead as I Knew Him," *Journal of Philosophy* 58 (1961) 505-516. Reprinted in *Alfred North Whitehead: Essays on His Philosophy*, ed. George L. Kline (Englewood Cliffs, N. J.: Prentice-Hall, 1963), pp. 7-17.

[10]Whitehead discusses his indebtedness, as well as his similarities and differences with Bradley from time to time in *Process and Reality*. A full analysis of this relation is given by Robert C. Whittemore, "Whitehead's 'Process' and Bradley's 'Reality'," *The Modern Schoolman* 32 (November 1954) 56-74.

[11]Professor Peter Bertocci relates an appropriate anecdote concerning Whitehead and Brightman, for which I am indebted to my own teacher, Dr. Tyler Thompson (himself a former student of Brightman's at Boston University). According to this account, Whitehead was giving a paper at a colloquium at which Brightman was present. At the conclusion of the session Brightman, a highly competent Hegelian, argued at some length with Whitehead to the effect that Whitehead's position in the paper just read was identical with that of Hegel. Whitehead was not initially receptive to this suggestion. After lengthy debate, however, Whitehead threw up his hands in frustration and exclaimed: "Well, if *that* is what Hegel meant, then I agree with him! My problem is, I never could understand Hegel!"

[12]Cf. *The Idea of Nature* (Oxford: The Clarendon Press, 1945/1972), pp. 14-16, 121ff., 136-141, 158-174.

[13]"External" teleology, of course, has been ridiculed by philosophers from Francis Bacon to Gilbert Ryle as "the ghost in the machine." Critics suggest that it is impossible to understand how a "future" (i.e., non-actual) event can causally influence the present.

Note that modified or "internal" teleology avoids these objections to traditional "external" teleology. The "ghost," if it still can be said to exist, now inhabits an organism or an organic, systemic structure, rather than a machine! With the contemporary replacement of the mechanical by the organic or holistic paradigm in physics and biology, teleological behavior is best explained as:

". . . action directed to (and by) the construction of some sort of whole or system . . . Ideally, every detail of such

activity is determined and molded by the pattern or design to
which it contributes. It is like a work of art, in which the
parts and the details are organized together, and are thus determined by the whole, not merely superadded one to another. The
pattern or structure is the prior principle, not the elementary
constituents. A teleological explanation is thus one which explains parts in terms of the whole, details in terms of the
structure to which they belong, structure in terms of its organizing principle, and process in terms of the pattern which it
brings into being. In such process the determining factor--the
teleological principle--is the implicit (or immanent) influence
of the organizing principle in every phase."
    Cf. Errol E. Harris, "Mechanism and Teleology in Contempo-
rary Thought," *Philosophy in Context* 2 (Cleveland: Cleveland
State University Department of Philosophy, 1973), p. 50.

[14]Cf. Errol E. Harris, *Nature, Mind and Modern Science*
(London: George Allen & Unwin, 1954/1968), pp. 416ff.

[15]"Organic Categories in Whitehead," *Journal of Philosophy*
34 (May 1937) 253-263. Reprinted in *Alfred North Whitehead:
Essays*, pp. 158-167.
    As we shall see, however, Hegel's dialectic is not "homo-
geneous" with respect to *Geist*. Indeed, the criticism is based
upon the fundamental misapprehension of Hegel as an unqualified
monist. For a discussion of Hegel's alleged monism, *vide* Ch. IV
below.

[16]*Philosophy* 31, No. 116 (January 1956) 36-54.

[17]"Philosophy and Faith: A Study in Hegel and Whitehead,"
*Our Common History as Christians: Essays in Honor of Albert C.
Outler*, eds. J. Deschner, L. T. Howe, and K. Penzel (New York:
Oxford University Press, 1975), pp. 157-175.
    A similar point regarding the importance and mutual similar-
ity of Hegel's and Whitehead's use and critique of religious symbolism is made in a master's thesis by James Robert Kuehl: *Actuality as Spirit: A Study in Hegel and Whitehead*, Diss. Northwestern University, 1964.

[18]"Life as Ontological Category: A Whiteheadian Note on
Hegel," *Art and Logic in Hegel's Philosophy*, eds. K. L. Schmitz
and W. E. Steinkraus (New York: Humanities Press, 1978), pp.
158-162. Also cf. "Concept and Concrescence: An Essay in Hegelian-Whiteheadian Ontology," Society for the Study of Process
Philosophies, American Philosophical Association Eastern Division
(Washington, D.C.: 28 Dec 1977).

[19]Edwards' point, in keeping with his defense of Calvinism,
was that one is therefore morally responsible as well. Cf. *The
Freedom of the Will* (Boston, 1754), esp. Part One, Sections IV
and V.

[20]"When is a Man Responsible?" in *Problems of Ethics*, translated by David Rynin (New York: Prentice-Hall, 1939). Reprinted
in *Free Will and Determinism*, ed. Bernard Berofsky (New York:
Harper & Row, Inc., 1966), pp. 54-63.

[21]Cf. "Freedom" in the *Oxford English Dictionary*, Vol. 4 (London, 1939).

[22]Pierre Laplace gave classic expression to the doctrine of determinism, especially in his *Essai philosophique sur les probabilites* (Paris, 1814): *viz.*, that all future states could, in principle, be calculated from a complete knowledge of present conditions. This concept is dismissed, for example, by Whitehead as one of the naive fallacies of "scientific materialism" which he criticizes in SMW 25, 148-156.

[23]The libertarian position regarding contra-causal freedom is defended articulately by C. A. Campbell, who disputes Schlick's claim that such freedom is illusory, or that the problem of freedom is merely a "pseudo-problem." *Vide* C. A. Campbell, "Is 'Freewill' a Pseudo-Problem?" *Mind* 60, No. 240 (October 1951) 446-465. Reprinted in part in *Free Will and Determinism*, pp. 112-135.

[24]For a full discussion of possible gradations or varieties of determinism in science and metaphysics, *vide* Errol E. Harris, *Foundations of Metaphysics in Science* (London: George Allen & Unwin, 1965), Ch. 22; especially pp. 476-82. *Vide* also Henry Pierce Stapp, "Bell's Theorem and World Process," *Il Nuovo Cimento* 29B, No. 2 (11 Oct 1975), 270-276; and "Theory of Reality," *Foundations of Physics* 7, Nos. 5-6 (1977) 313-323.

NOTES

CHAPTER II

[1]Cf. SMW 110ff., 113ff.; PR 74ff. Thomas F. O'Brochta defends the notion of freedom as one of Whitehead's "stubborn facts" of existence, arguing that, for Whitehead, "freedom is a necessary condition for the very intelligibility of human experience." *The Metaphysical Basis of Human Freedom According to Alfred North Whitehead*, Diss. Loyola University of Chicago, 1973, p. 7.

[2]This "recurrence methodology" is explained in PR vii. *Vide* also *Key to PR* 2. I term this recurrence "dialectical" in the Hegelian sense of successive particularization, leading finally to the adequate mediation and explication of a concept.

[3]Two recent articles suggest Whitehead's affinity with contemporary developments in science. The first supports Whitehead's doctrine that determinative explanations of causality are not sufficient to account for the futures of organisms because of an element of present decision. *Vide* J. M. Burgers, "Causality and Anticipation," *Science* 189 (July 1975) 194-198. The second, earlier article argues that the existence of "teleological" forces in nature is supported by recent developments in quantum mechanical theory. *Vide* J. M. Burgers, "The Measuring Process in Quantum Theory," *Review of Modern Physics* 35 (1963) 145-150.
    Cf. Whitehead's own discussion of the role of "purpose" in nature in his early theory of "organic mechanism": SMW 157ff.

[4]PR 38: "An entity is actual, when it . . . functions in respect to its own determination."

[5]Whitehead discusses the causal efficacy of the past without appeal to mechanism or determinism. *Vide* AI 81, 249; also PR 41, discussing the role of the "subject-superject" in its own internal determination, beyond the determinateness of the given data. Also cf. CN 73.

[6]Cf. Whitehead's own assessment of evolution in SMW 163ff.

[7]This follows from Whitehead's Ontological Principle, which holds that: (i) all entities shall be understood either as *actual* entities, or as in some sense derivative from, or abstractions of, actual entities (PR 113); and (ii) all entities which are actual--from God to "the most trivial puff of existence"--shall be subject to the same metaphysical description (PR 27ff., 168).

[8]Cf. John B. Cobb, Jr., *A Christian Natural Theology* (Philadelphia: The Westminster Press, 1965), p. 95: ". . . each occasion determines *how* it will take account of its predecessors, according to its subjective aim."

[9]By "intelligible," Broad intends a doctrine of freedom which may be utilized in support of a theory of moral responsibility. Cf. "Determinism, Indeterminism and Libertarianism" in

141

Broad's *Ethics and the History of Philosophy* (London: Routledge and Kegan Paul, 1952); reprinted in *Free Will and Determinism*, pp. 135-159.
    Whitehead, of course, strenuously *affirms* a theory of moral responsibility. Charles Hartshorne agrees with Broad that indeterminism alone is not sufficient for a meaningful doctrine of freedom, and should not be equated with it. Hartshorne demonstrates, however, that indeterminism and spontaneity, together with a notion of efficient causality in a quasi-determinative sense, are both *necessary* conditions for a doctrine of freedom. *Vide* "Freedom Requires Indeterminism and Universal Causality," *Journal of Philosophy* 55, No. 19 (11 September 1958) 793-811.

[10]Cf. Ivor Leclerc, *Whitehead's Metaphysics: An Introductory Exposition* (Bloomington, Ind.: Indiana University Press, 1975), p. 82: ". . . each individual actual entity arises out of a process of activity which is *generic* to all. Each actuality is thus an individualization of the ultimate generic activity."

[11]Cf. William A. Christian, *An Interpretation of Whitehead's Metaphysics* (New Haven: Yale University Press, 1959), p. 48: "Every actual occasion is a novel act of becoming. For the course of nature is a "creative advance" in which genuinely new things become. History never repeats itself in exact detail."

[12]Cf. MT 36, for example, where Whitehead describes the human intellectual entertainment of unrealized possibilities as an exercise in "outrageous novelty." What is described in the passage, however, bears closer comparison to "spontaneity" than to "novelty" according to the systematic definition of these terms.

[13]Cf. SMW 156, AI 249, 266.

[14]PR 159. Cf. AI 362, and 86: ". . . there is a freedom lying beyond circumstance, derived from the direct intuition that life can be grounded upon its absorption in what is changeless amid change. . . ."

[15]N.B. "Actual entity" and "actual occasion" are virtually synonomous terms. The former, however, refers more to the entity in general, while the latter emphasizes the temporal, concrescing aspect. For Whitehead, God as an actual entity is nontemporal, and therefore *not* an actual occasion. I use actual occasion interchangeably with actual entity when I wish to emphasize the temporal activity.

[16]This procedure follows Whitehead's suggestion (PR 196ff.) that the Philosophy of Organism may be understood in a "microscopic" sense, as the analysis of actual entities, and in a "macroscopic" sense, as the application of the former analysis to the wider concerns of experience in the actual world. It is in this latter, "macroscopic" domain that we shall encounter Whitehead's principal nonsystematic uses of "spontaneity," "novelty," and "freedom."

[17]AI 203, PR viii, ix. Cf. Leclerc, pp. 12-20. Strictly speaking, Leclerc is somewhat misleading in his generalization of Aristotle's search. The famous phrase from Book Z of the

Metaphysics (1028b2) reads: "The question that was asked long ago, is asked now, and always is a matter of difficulty, 'What is Being' is [more properly] the question 'What is substance?'" The term for Being as the ultimate matter of fact is indeed (as Leclerc notes) *ousia*. But that which Aristotle asserts as the proper thrust of the question is *hypostasis* ("substance"), meaning the essential nature of a thing, or that which "stands under" a thing as its truth, reason or cause. Leclerc is well aware of this issue, however, which he himself analyzed in an earlier article: "Whitehead's Transformation of the Concept of Substance," *Philosophical Quarterly* 3 (1953), 225-243.

[18]PR 228. Alternatively, Whitehead describes actual occasions as *sui generis* to indicate their teleological character: cf., e.g., PR 38, 131, 228, 380, 390, etc.

[19]Broadly speaking, Whitehead distinguishes three phases of a concrescence, whose analysis is "only intellectual" (PR 347): an initially receptive "conformal" phase, a subsequent supplemental and highly-complex "conceptual" phase, and finally the termination of the concrescence in the "satisfaction" of its subjective aim, at which point the entity becomes a datum or concretum, a potential for every new becoming. The discussion of these phases pervades the text of PR. For a useful and clear organization of this discussion, *vide* Professor Sherburne's *Key to PR*, pp. 36-71.

[20]"I use the phrase 'eternal object' for what . . . I have termed a 'Platonic form'. Any entity whose conceptual recognition does not involve a necessary reference to any definite actual entities of the temporal world is called an 'eternal object'. . . .Conceptual feeling is the feeling of . . . a definite eternal object with the definite extrusion of any particular realization" (PR 70, 372; cf. PR 32).

[21]*Key to PR*, p. 211.

[22]Cf. PR 380, 381. From the earliest inception of his "event metaphysic" Whitehead emphasized this special role of events as "fields of activity" creating new possibilities through their unique functions as the situations by which particular novel ingressions of "sense objects" ("eternal objects") were actualized in nature. Cf. CN 152ff., 170.

[23]*Key to PR*, p. 205ff.

[24]Indeed Whitehead (as did Leibniz) postulated the existence of these other "possible worlds" as a series of successive "cosmic epochs," the transitions to which might be governed by the gradual rise to dominance of alternative systems of natural law. Cf., e.g., PR 127. *Vide* also Collingwood, *The Idea of Nature*, p. 168.

[25]PR 374. This discussion constitutes a later addition (found in Chapters X and XI on "Abstraction" and "God" in SMW) to the original Lowell Lectures of 1925. Cf. especially SMW 230ff., 250ff., and 256ff. *Vide* also Lewis S. Ford, "Whitehead's First Metaphysical Synthesis," *International Philosophical Quarterly* (September 1977) 251-264.

[26]God, as Spinoza's one, underlying Substance is finally the only entity which is truly and completely *causa sui*. William Christian considers and rejects these objections to Whitehead's view of the function of God: *Interpretation of Whitehead's Metaphysics*, pp. 110ff. Donald Sherburne marshals Whitehead's own defenses against these charges: *Key to PR*, pp. 29ff.

[27]I am not confusing "subjective form" and "subjective aim" (cf. *Key to PR*, pp. 28, 244ff.). Rather, I offer the hypothesis that, at any moment it is possible in principle for an individual actual occasion to prehend a *Logos*, a rational, ideal structure of the world-process. I am identifying the different, unique "subjective forms" of this prehension occurring in every actual occasion as the individual "subjective aims" for each of those separate occasions.

[28]PR 34ff., my emphasis. Sherburne (p. 28) and Leclerc (pp. 68-71) *equate* being and becoming. William Christian (pp. 116-118) and Jorge Luis Nobo ["Whitehead's Principle of Process," *Process Studies* 4, No. 4 (Winter 1974), p. 275ff.] reject this view as doing away with a doctrine of real individuals. Instead, "process" must be understood as *producing* "being." As Whitehead notes, process and existence ("individuality") presuppose and require each other, for "in separation all meaning evaporates" (MT 133).

[29]PR 34: ". . . *how* an actual entity *becomes* constitutes *what* that actual entity *is*. . . ."

[30]If the data somehow *did* impart a basis for a selection or decision among themselves in the present moment, we would be faced with the case of a decision in the present being *effected by* entities which themselves were no longer *actual*. I perceive this as a violation of the Ontological Principle.

[31]Sadik J. Al-Azm, for example, accuses Whitehead of "radical finalism," arguing that the initial aim from God contains all that an actual entity must become. Thus, there is no room for freedom in Whitehead's philosophy. *Vide* "Whitehead's Notions of Order and Freedom," *The Personalist* 48, No. 4 (October 1967) 579-591.
    This is not entirely to the point: the above-quoted passage (PR 343) suggests that the subjective aim undergoes subsequent "modifications" in the process of its own realization. This may suffice to account for a limited or "finite" doctrine of freedom. The chief difficulty occurs over whether each occasion passively receives this initial aim from God, or whether the occasion itself instead actively prehends God's primordial envisagement of ideal order and harmony. In the former case, finite freedom *could* be portrayed as merely the dialectical interplay between the factors of divine determinism and the factors of efficient cause. In my opinion, this solution does not provide for "real subjective agency" in the occasion itself (see below, Section 4). I therefore shall suggest an alternative explanation in terms of the "nascent subjectivity" of the emerging occasion itself.
    In any case, the specific charge of "radical finalism" against Whitehead would appear capable of satisfactory resolution. Cf. Kenneth R. Merrill, "Whitehead on Order and Freedom: A Reply," *The Personalist* 50 (1969) 148-154.

[32]Newton, like many of his contemporaries, viewed the universe as an independent and self-subsistent creation of God: as William Paley portrayed it (reminiscent of Philo Judaeus), a "watch" created by a divine watchmaker. Newton, however, held that the continual intervention of God in creation was necessary to "correct" certain abberations and imperfections in the finite "mechanism" itself.

Whitehead's concept of God, on its face, seems to suggest a similar "continual intervention" of God in creation in order to maintain its functioning. This comparison should not be pressed too far, however. The important difference is that, while Newton and many of his contemporaries viewed the God-world relation as wholly "external," for Whitehead, in pronounced contrast, such "intervention" by God would come about precisely as a result of the *immanence* of God in the world. God limits the process of the world, which, in its turn, provides a consequent conditioning of God's own envisagement of ideal possibilities for the world. This holistic God-world relation, portraying the universe as, in some sense, "God's body," is *radically* different from Newton's theology.

[33]This despite John Cobb's attempt to explain relative or "finite" freedom wholly in terms of the subsequent "modifications" by the actual occasion of its own subjective aim. Cf. *A Christian Natural Theology*, p. 96. This explanation would preserve some measure of freedom, but still would appear to invoke God as a *deus ex machina* for the process of becoming (see below, Sec. 4).

[34]"Freedom in Whitehead's Philosophy," *Southern Journal of Philosophy* 7, No. 4 (Winter 1969), p. 413.

[35]Cf. Sherburne, *Key to PR*, pp. 245ff. and Leclerc, pp. 169ff.

[36]Cf. PR 243, 252, where Whitehead discusses this problem in terms of his "reformed subjectivist principle." This, together with the "principle of relativity" and the "subject-superject" doctrine, all follow from the Ontological Principle itself, which "accepts Descartes' discovery that subjective experiencing is the primary metaphysical situation which is presented to metaphysics for analysis."

Thus Whitehead's Ontological Principle repudiates the "subjectivist bias" and the variety of dualisms attendant upon modern and contemporary epistemology, such as subject-object, mind-nature, and efficient versus final causality. For a discussion of the significance of the Ontological Principle as a critique of epistemological dualism, *vide* Juliana Geran, *Whitehead on the Ontological Principle: A Critique of Early Modern Epistemology in Process and Reality*, Diss. University of Chicago, 1974.

[37]George L. Kline brings some order to this linguistic muddle with the suggestion that "post-concrescences" be labeled "concreta," replacing the vague and ambiguous use by Whitehead and Whiteheadians of "superject" and "superjective nature" for this stage. *Vide* "Form, Concrescence and Concretum: A Neo-Whiteheadian Analysis," *Southern Journal of Philosophy* 7, No. 4 (Winter 1969) 351-360.

[38]Borrowing the phraseology of Heraclitus and Aristotle, this is to suggest that every discrete, atomic event is characterized by an immanent *entelechy* (a "self-realizing end"), related in turn to a principle of rational, intelligible order discernable in all process--a *Logos*. See below, Ch. III, Sec. 2 (iii).

[39]*Vide* John B. Cobb, Jr. and David Ray Griffin, *Process Theology: An Introductory Exposition* (Philadelphia: The Westminster Press, 1976), and Robert B. Mellert, *What is Process Philosophy?* (New York: Paulist Press, 1975). Quotations are taken from the "Foreword" to the former book, p. 7. Cf. AI 192.

[40]This is especially true of Whitehead's earlier "organic mechanism" in SMW: *vide* especially pp. 116, 149-64, 212-220.

[41]William P. Alston, "Internal Relatedness and Pluralism in Whitehead," *Review of Metaphysics* 5 (1952) 535-558. Alston ignores the stress on "degrees of relevance" and the possibility of "negative prehensions"--both of which necessitate subjective decisions, and consequently must entail freedom of some sort.

[42]Donald Sherburne writes sarcastically: "An eternal object is supposed to bestow or withhold a specific, precise form of definiteness; but how can this be if every eternal object drags along with it, so to speak, the whole choir of eternal objects in virtue of the fact that its relationships to other eternal objects are *internal* relations?" *Vide* "Whitehead Without God," in *Process Philosophy and Christian Thought*, eds. Brown, James and Reeves (Indianapolis: Bobbs-Merrill, 1971), p. 327.

[43]*Ibid.*

[44]Cf. Charles Hartshorne, *The Divine Relativity: A Social Conception of God* (New Haven: Yale University Press, 1948), Ch. 2, "appendix." Cf. also Lewis S. Ford, "An Appraisal of Whiteheadian Nontheism" *Southern Journal of Philosophy* 15, No. 1 (Spring 1977) 31ff.

[45]Again I utilize the helpful terminology of George Kline, "Form, Concrescence and Concretum," *loc.cit.*

[46]Lewis S. Ford, "An Appraisal of Whiteheadian Nontheism," p. 32. The phrase omitted reads: ". . . preserves Whitehead's pluralism, preventing it from lapsing into the monism of absolute idealism." I shall *not* wish to defend Mr. Ford's programmatic assumptions that Hegel's organic mechanism is necessarily either monistic or deterministic, any more than I would care to support the similar attack on Whitehead, made on similarly-tenuous grounds by William Alston (p. 59, n. 2 above).

[47]*Whitehead's Metaphysics: A Critical Examination of Process and Reality* (Carbondale, Ill.: University of Southern Illinois Press, 1967).

[48]*Ibid.*, p. 194.

[49] *Ibid*. Cf. pp. 157, 159-163, where the charges of radical finalism and Platonism are clarified; and pp. 171-185, and 193-195, where the "privileged status" of eternal objects is held finally to undercut Whitehead's commitment to the freedom of real individual actual entities.

[50] Edward Pols, "Freedom and Agency," *Southern Journal of Philosophy* 7, No. 4 (Winter 1969), p. 416.

[51] Errol E. Harris, "Teleology and Teleological Explanation," *Journal of Philosophy* 56, No. 1 (1 January 1959), pp. 8, 11. *Vide supra*, p. 29, for John Cobb's similar exposition of this role of holistic teleological self-determination in the concrescence of an actual occasion ["Freedom in Whitehead's Philosophy," p. 413].

Lewis S. Ford, however, accuses Cobb in this article of imputing to Whitehead "symmetrical mutual relatedness" between parts and whole, which would compromise freedom. By denying any real significance to the genetic distinction between "earlier" and "later" phases of concrescence, argues Ford, Cobb seems to imply a symmetric internal relatedness between prior and consequent phases of concrescence—precisely the sort of holism which seems to endanger real freedom.

I have discussed the importance of asymmetrical relatedness as the modification of holism necessary for real freedom (*vide supra*, pp. 32-34). I concur fully with Professor Ford's concern, in essence, that "teleological self-determination" cannot be made intelligible as a doctrine of freedom apart from a thorough understanding of how the teleological principle is itself modified in exposition of "genetic successiveness": cf. "On Genetic Successiveness," *Southern Journal of Philosophy* 7, No. 4 (Winter 1969) 421-425.

Professor Cobb's concern seems to be a defense of the real subjective agency of an actual occasion *as a totality* against Pols' charge that the occasion is externally determined by the influence of eternal objects and God's primordial aim. Cobb does not appear to have considered the further significance of Ford's arguments for a complete understanding of the necessary modifications of the initial subjective aim.

[52] Pols, "Whitehead on Subjective Agency," *Modern Schoolman* 49, No. 2 (January 1972), p. 144.

[53] Pols, *Whitehead's Metaphysics*, pp. 113-125; esp. 113-115.

[54] Cf. Pols' own frustration with this issue: "Freedom and Agency," *loc. cit.*, p. 418.

[55] Cf. PR 327: "The present is the immediacy of teleological process whereby reality becomes actual." *Vide* also Lynne Belaief, *The Ethics of Alfred North Whitehead*, Diss. Columbia University, 1963, p. 72.

[56] Professor Ford's own current research into the development of Whitehead's thought suggests that Whitehead frequently abandoned, or moved beyond certain statements of his position without bothering to correct or rescind these. This is a further source of the conflicts encountered in his writing.

[57]"Can Whitehead Provide for Real Subjective Agency?" *The Modern Schoolman* 47, No. 2 (June 1970), p. 221.

This description is acceptable, but still seems to imply that freedom is composed of a dialectical interaction of the factors of efficient cause--in which case there is still no real subjective agency. This interplay is itself a *result* of the "decisions" effected with respect to the actual occasion's subjective aim--a unique and special "conceptual feeling." Cf. my remarks, p. 28, n. 31 above.

[58]Pols, "Freedom and Agency," *loc. cit.*, p. 418.

[59]*Ibid.*, p. 418ff.

[60]*The Ethics of Alfred North Whitehead*, p. 71.

[61]"Beyond Enlightened Self-Interest: A Metaphysics of Ethics," *Ethics* 84, No. 3 (April 1974), p. 202.

[62]Hartshorne argues that an emphasis on strong self-identity as the locus of moral responsibility is untenable. This represents an attempt to refute the major argument brought against Whitehead, that he cannot account for the persistence in time of the human agent to whom responsibility is to be ascribed. Cf., e.g., D. Browning, "Whitehead's Theory of Human Agency," *Dialogue* II (1963-64) 424-441. Cf. also Sylvia Ann Pruitt, *An Inquiry into the Ethical Implications of Whitehead's Metaphysics*, Diss. Emory University, 1970.

[63]"A single occasion is alive when the subjective aim which determines its process of concrescence has introduced a novelty of definiteness not to be found in the inherited data of its primary [conformal] phase" (PR 159). Thus, a living *occasion* is one which is dominated by its mental, rather than its physical pole. A "living society" is one which is constituted of living actual occasions.

[64]Donald Sherburne, "Whitehead's Psychological Physiology," *Southern Journal of Philosophy* 7, No. 4 (Winter 1969) 401-407; especially 404ff. Cf. also John Cobb and Sherburne, "Regional Inclusion and Psychological Physiology," *Process Studies* 3, No. 1 (Spring 1973) 27-40.

[65]Sherburne, "Whitehead's Psychological Physiology," p. 405.

[66]Belaief, *op. cit.*, pp. 98, 100.

[67]The phenomenon of consciousness and its importance for the understanding of human moral freedom are treated at length in Ch. III. Whiteheadians customarily view self-consciousness as a phenomenon of no metaphysical importance--a remarkable view, since it is obviously self-refuting (i.e., it is a metaphysical position formulated by the self-conscious mind!). This denial of importance to consciousness is hardly the point of Whitehead's antagonism toward the "subjectivist bias" in metaphysics--an antagonism, interestingly, which was shared by Hegel. This position *is* characteristic of Whitehead's earliest philosophical phase, when he claimed that "nature is closed to mind" (CN 4). As Whitehead himself came to see subsequently, however, the

metaphysical "problem" with respect to self-consciousness is--
not to deny its importance--but rather to formulate a theory
within which this important phenomenon may be viewed as a special,
or more correctly, a more complex supervenient phase of the process of nature itself.

[68]Belaief, *The Ethics of Alfred North Whitehead*, pp. 74ff.

[69]Thomas O'Brochta extensively and persuasively argues that
"Wisdom" is indeed the essence of *human* freedom as derived from,
or "built up" out of Whiteheadian actual entities. Cf. *The Metaphysical Basis of Human Freedom According to Alfred North Whitehead*; esp. pp. 242-281. Cf. also John Cobb's discussion of human
freedom as derived from actual entities, in which he concludes:
"Only where consciousness eventuates in self-awareness and self-
awareness comes to include awareness of a choosing among alternatives do we arrive at a clear instance of [predominantly *human*]
moral choice." *A Christian Natural Theology*, p. 97.

[70]Charles Hartshorne offers a lively discussion of such
phenomena, which plague more traditional models of self-identity
in ethical theory. Cf. "Beyond Enlightened Self Interest," *loc.
cit.*, pp. 201-210.

[71]*Freedom, Determinism and Responsibility*: *An Analysis and
Whiteheadian Interpretation*, Diss. Vanderbilt University, 1965,
p. 204.

[72]Cf. Lynne Belaief, *op. cit.*, pp. 81ff. *Vide supra* Ch. I,
Section 3.

[73]PR 339. Cf. Leclerc, *Whitehead's Metaphysics*, pp. 172ff.

[74]Obviously a "process ethics"--whatever the term finally
comes to entail--will be more a teleological than a deontological
or formalistic ethic. In this case, however, we can say with
some certainty that it is always "wrong"--or rather, one is always to be held *accountable* for acting in a manner so as *not* to
be serving simultaneously as "[his] brother's keeper."

[75]"A Whiteheadian Account of Value and Identity," *Process
Studies* 5, No. 1 (Spring 1975), pp. 35ff. *Vide* also Daniel Day
Williams, "Moral Obligation in Process Philosophy," *Journal of
Philosophy* 56 (1959) 263-270, where creativity with respect to
moral obligation is likewise viewed as an explanation of tragedy
and suffering. Williams, however, also came to view suffering
itself as a creative (or rather, *potentially* creative) process.
Vide The Spirit and the Forms of Love (New York: Harper and Row,
1968), *passim*.

[76]This observation is founded upon Whitehead's earlier view
that the theory of historical "causality"--based upon a clear
distinction in temporal series of past, present and future--no
longer can be sustained. Whence, "the passage of nature . . .
is only another name for the creative force of existence" (CN 73;
also SMW 163ff.).

[77]Only what is dominated by freedom is alive. Only what
changes and develops properly can be said to *be*. Changelessness

is equated with stagnation, decadence and perishing. Cf. AI 332; MT 107-109.

[78]Brown and Johnson both argue, with different emphases, that history is the realm of human freedom. Since human intentions and purposeful actions (according to Whitehead) *can* influence the flux of history, such efforts are *meaningful*, and represent rational undertakings. *Vide* Allison H. Johnson, "Whitehead's Philosophy of History," *Journal of the History of Ideas* 7 (1946) 234-249; and Delwin Brown, "Hope for the Human Future: Niebuhr, Whitehead and Utopian Expectation," *Iliff Review* 32 (1975) 3-18.

[79]This distinguishes Whitehead's view of history from others in the "process" tradition--e.g., Hegel and Teilhard de Chardin --who view history more decisively as a process *towards* some final state. Whitehead's thought, however, is not *inimical* to such views. Cf. Richard Hocking, "The Polarity of Dialectical History and Process Cosmology," *The Christian Scholar* 50, No. 3 (Fall 1967) 177-183.

[80]Cf. Hegel's similar views on "abstract" or "negative" freedom in Ch. III below.

[81]Cf. PR 143: "The notion of God . . . is that of an actual entity immanent in the actual world, but transcending any finite cosmic epoch--a being at once actual, eternal, immanent and transcendent. The transcendence of God is not peculiar to him. Every actual entity, in virtue of its novelty, transcends its universe, God included."

[82]Cf. Donald W. Sherburne, "Whitehead Without God," *The Christian Scholar* 50, No. 3 (Fall 1967) 251-272. *Vide* also John B. Cobb's "Critique" and Sherburne's "Rejoinder" in *Process Studies* 1, No. 2 (Summer 1971) 91-113. Cf. also Lewis Ford's careful refutation of Sherburne's approach to nontheism: "An Appraisal of Whiteheadian Nontheism," *Southern Journal of Philosophy* 15, No. 1 (Spring 1977) 27-35.

[83]Lynne Belaief provides a helpful and interesting discussion of Whitehead's own ambiguity in distinguishing God from the primordial "ultimate category" or principle of creativity. Cf. *The Ethics of Alfred North Whitehead*, pp. 34-43.

[84]For a provocative discussion of freedom and ethics without God in the tradition of process philosophy, *vide* Robert C. Neville, *The Cosmology of Freedom* (New Haven: Yale University Press, 1974). For further discussion of the issue of "God" as symbol and reality in process metaphysics, see below, Ch. IV.

CHAPTER III

[1]Cf. *Hegels Samtliche Werke* (Leipzig: Felix Meiner Verlag, 1923), Vol. 5, p. 417: "Über keine Idee weiss man es so allgemein, dass sie unbestimmt, vieldeutig und der grössten Missverständnisse fähig . . . ist also von der Idee der Freiheit" (my translation).

[2]Caroline Dudeck, *Hegel's Concept of Freedom as it Develops in the Phenomenology of Mind*, Diss. Bryn Mawr College, 1973, p. 3. George Lichtheim comments that Hegel's *Phenomenology* pictures reality as a sustained progression toward the realization of freedom, in contrast to the then-contemporary Romantic lament over freedom's loss. Cf. his "Introduction" to the J. B. Baillie translation of the *Phenomenology* (New York: Harper Colophon Books, 1910/1967), p. xxix.

[3]"Economic and Philosophic Manuscripts of 1844" in *Karl Marx: Selected Writings in Sociology and Social Philosophy*, ed. T. B. Bottomore (London: C. A. Watts & Co., 1956), p. 2. Cf. *Karl Marx: Early Writings* (New York: McGraw-Hill, 1963), p. 166: ". . . for socialist man, the whole of what is called world history is nothing but the creation of man by human labor . . . the evident and irrefutable proof of his *self*-creation."

[4]*Being and Nothingness* (New York: Washington Square Press Paperbacks, 1967), p. 707. This theme is developed at length in "Freedom: the First Condition of Action," pp. 539-619. In the *Phenomenology*, freedom is mentioned in connection with "negation" and the "labor of the negative." See below, Section 2 (iv).

[5]Hugh A. Reyburn, *The Ethical Theory of Hegel: A Study of the Philosophy of Right* (Oxford: The Clarendon Press, 1921). Cf., e.g., Richard Schacht, "Hegel on Freedom," in *Hegel and After: Studies in Continental Philosophy Between Kant and Sartre* (Pittsburg: Pittsburg University Press, 1975), pp. 69-94; and Thomas N. Munson, "Hegel's Political Thought," *The Monist* 48, No. 1 (January 1974) 97-111.

[6]*Phen.* 488, 491, 10. In the "Philosophy of Mind," cf. also *Enc.* 382 and *Zusatz*.

[7]J. N. Findlay, "Hegel's Use of Teleology," in *Ascent to the Absolute* (London: George Allen & Unwin, 1970), p. 131. For a thorough discussion of the Aristotelian character of Hegel's thought, *vide* G. R. G. Mure, *An Introduction to Hegel* (Oxford: The Clarendon Press, 1940), *passim*.

[8]It is *this* interpretation of teleology which is ridiculed by Francis Bacon, Moliere and Voltaire, among others. Hegel, in fact, *joins* their ridicule of such a notion of teleology, "which sets up for something absolute what is trivial and even contemptible in its content" (GL 736). Cf. my treatment of this issue, pp. 8f., 37ff.

[9] In addition to the references discussing this issue cited in the two previous chapters, *vide* also Errol E. Harris, "Hegel and the Natural Sciences," in *Beyond Epistemology: New Studies in the Philosophy of Hegel*, ed. Frederick G. Weiss (The Hague: Martinus Nijhoff, 1974), pp. 129-153. Cf. also Jeffrey H. Wattles, *Hegel's Philosophy of Organic Nature*, Diss. Northwestern University, 1973, pp. 1-4, 139-145.

[10] Hegel's argument is not in the least damaged by the now-contemporary argument--e.g., of behaviorists--that purposive behavior is epiphenomenal, accounted for wholly by the simulated activities of "servo mechanisms" and other such self-regulating, homeostatic devices which appear to exhibit teleological behavior by internal regulation or the performance of a goal-directed function. In fact, the fallacy of utilizing servo mechanisms to discredit teleological explanation (as Errol Harris has demonstrated) is that such arguments ignore the external design by which such devices are constructed in the first place. It is no argument to construct a device to fulfill a certain purpose or perform a certain task, and subsequently claim that, by acting purposively, the machine succeeds in discounting teleology as a proper model of explanation!
The purposive functions are not determined by the mechanism, but are presupposed by it. The very existence and operation of a given mechanism is dependent upon an envisioned purpose or design which is the prior condition of its construction and use. Cf. Errol E. Harris, "Mechanism and Teleology in Contemporary Thought," *loc. cit.*, pp. 49-55; and "Teleology and Teleological Explanation," *loc. cit.*, pp. 5-25.
In our present case, Hegel argues that, unlike mechanisms, organisms embody their own purposes. In contemporary terminology, these "purposes" are part of the patterned genetic heritage which governs their development and function--immanent in, and not external to the organism itself. Plant and animal organisms, however, are distinguished by Hegel from human beings in that the former are neither aware of, nor themselves in control of their purposive functioning.

[11] *Vide* GL 106-108, for Hegel's discussion of the importance of this term for philosophy. The archaic English term "sublate" is used upon occasion as a translation of the German verb *auf heben*.

[12] George L. Kline, "Some Recent Reinterpretations of Hegel's Philosophy," *The Monist* 48, No. 1 (January 1964), p. 37.

[13] Cf. Caroline Dudeck, *op. cit., passim.*

[14] These statements, and several which follow, reflect *Hegel's* view of Kant. I do not subscribe to that view in all its particulars. It seems to me apparent that a sympathetic appreciation of Kant's metaphysics as summarized finally in the *entire* critical philosophy (rather than from the standpoint only of the first, of even of the first and second "critiques") shows that, in many respects, Kant was not so far from Hegel's own views as Hegel himself apparently imagined.

[15]Hegel viewed the Roman empire and its emperor as the symbol of humankind's exchange of community for a vast, cosmic "individual," the "lord of the world" (cf. *Phen.* 290-294). In the *Encyclopedia*, and the *Rechtsphilosophie*, this stage is represented by the "Civil Society," a loose confederation of autonomous, "self-subsistent" individuals and organizations.

[16]This discussion occurs in the *Phenomenology*, but the precise phrase is, I believe, J. N. Findlay's. Cf. his "Foreword" to Miller's translation of the *Phenomenology*, p. xxiv; also Findlay's *Hegel: A Reexamination* (Oxford: Oxford University Press, 1958), pp. 124ff.

[17]Whitehead's doctrine of pan-subjectivity, through consistent application of his Ontological Principle, extends this holistic relation throughout the inorganic as well as the organic realm, as a consequence of the constitution of all entities by his "actual entities." Hegel encounters difficulties in attempting a similar extension of holism in his *Naturphilosophie*. See below, Section 4.

[18]Cf. GL 515ff.: ". . . the whole is equal to the parts and the parts to the whole. There is nothing in the whole which is not in the parts, and nothing in the parts which is not in the whole. The whole is not abstract unity, but unity as of a diverse manifoldness . . . But further, although the whole is equal to the parts it is not equal to them as parts; . . . The whole is not equal to them as this self-subsistent diversity, but to them together. But this their 'together' is nothing else but their unity, the whole as such."

Cf., e.g., Husserl's treatment of the "meaning" of phenomena in his *Cartesian Meditations*, and Maurice Merleau-Ponty's holistic description of perceptual experience in terms of the "meanings and motives" of the phenomena in which the observer is immersed as an element: *The Phenomenology of Perception*, translated by Colin Smith (London: Routledge & Kegan Paul, 1962), pp. 26-51.

The truth of Hegel's own assertion is admirably illustrated by a simple example drawn from quantum mechanics, of "two-particle" scattering. Let Ψ_1 and Ψ_2 represent the probability distributions for two identical particle-beams (e.g., two beams of electrons), each beam passing through a narrow diffraction slit (in practice, such a diffraction grating only can be achieved through scattering the beams off a crystal surface, the adjacent planes of the crystal serving as the diffraction grate or "slit"). The diffraction pattern for the first beam *alone* is given by the function $|\Psi_1|^2$, and similarly, the diffraction pattern for the second beam *alone* is $|\Psi_2|^2$. (That is, a photographic plate placed behind each slit would show a spherically-symmetric bright spot, tapering quickly away to darkness in all directions from the center of the spot.)

If classical dynamics and the nineteenth-century theory of matter were valid, each electron beam should consist of discrete, localized, "self-subsistent" atomic particles, and the simultaneous diffraction of both beams through their respective slits should produce, not one but two adjacent scattering patterns as described, with a combined intensity given by $|\Psi_1|^2+|\Psi_2|^2$. When this electron-diffraction experiment actually was tried, however, an "interference pattern," similar to that produced by two-source scattering of light waves, was produced, given by:
$$|\Psi_1+\Psi_2|^2=|\Psi_1|^2+|\Psi_2|^2+\Psi_1{}^*\Psi_2+\Psi_2{}^*\Psi_1.$$

*The atomic "particles" of matter behaved like waves in this experiment, interacting ("interfering") with one another. In this case, the "whole" system differed from or exceeded the sum of its two component "parts" precisely in the amount of the relational or "interference" terms $(\Psi_1*\Psi_2+\Psi_2*\Psi_1)$. Thus, a simple experiment in quantum "wave" mechanics demonstrates that the "whole is more than the sum of its parts."

[19]For Hegel, of course, this last phase of Spirit brings a true understanding of God: God *is* "Absolute Spirit," and "the esoteric study of God . . . is philosophy itself" (*Enc.* 573).

[20]The term is R. G. Collingwood's. Cf. *An Essay on Philosophical Method* (Oxford: Oxford University Press, 1933) Section III, esp. pp. 57-60, 86-91.

[21]This principle pervades Aristotle's biology and metaphysics. For specific instances of these discussions, in the order in which I treat them above, *vide*: *De Anima* II:1; *De Partibus Animalium* I:1; *Historia Animalium* VIII:1; *Metaphysica* V:4, XII: 4, 7, 9.

[22]*Vide* Spinoza's *Ethics*, Section V: e.g., Propositions I, VI, XVII, etc. Admittedly the "things" which Spinoza had in mind were primarily bodily emotions; and his "freedom" consists in a knowledge of (and hence a control over) the causes of behavior.

[23]There remains the critical question of whether, in Hegel's case, we are describing a *logical*, rather than a temporal process Hegel's scattered use of historical illustrations strongly suggests that he did not envision a logical process apart from its temporal manifestations. For a discussion of Hegel's theory of time, see below, Section 4 (iii).

[24]Such sweeping generalizations deserve some modest qualification. Tillich, for one, certainly did *not* refuse to engage Hegel's metaphysics! In this case, however, I feel that Tillich and other existentialist interpreters attach more significance than did Hegel himself to the latter's dialectical polarity of Being and Nothing. For Tillich, this opposition symbolizes the real existential threat of non-being: of annihilation, loneliness and death. It is simply not possible that Hegel was engaging such themes seriously in the *Logic*. For Hegel, Being and Nothing were merely two logical or conceptual categories whose apparent opposition was factually unreal, since neither concrete example nor intelligible meaning could be associated with either concept or category in isolation.

The first concrete thought is finally the *only* concrete fact for Hegel: that existence *is* "becoming, what Being is in its truth" (*Enc.* 88). The entire discussion, moreover, must be seen in the context of Hegel's ongoing criticism of the inadequacy of what he condescendingly termed "school logic." Many of the alleged contradictions and paradoxes in his terminology amount to little more than clever and deliberate word play, as I noted in Chapter I (*supra*, pp. 6f.). Hegel's attack on logic and analysis is a sport which contemporary philosophy has not yet outgrown The existential significance which Heidegger, Sartre and Tillich attach to these paradoxes, however, is not really the thrust or content of Hegel's own thought.

[25]One thinks at this point of the similar stress by Daniel Day Williams in his eloquent interpretation of Whitehead's thought, stressing the profound tragedy, as well as the creative hope which are together the result of human and divine suffering. *Vide supra*, p. 51, n. 75.

[26]We follow here the distinctions made by George L. Kline: "Some Recent Re-interpretations of Hegel's Philosophy," pp. 34-75; also his "Introduction" to his anthology, *Alfred North Whitehead: Essays on His Philosophy*; and "Concept and Concrescence: An Essay in Hegelian-Whiteheadian Ontology," typescript: Society for the Study of Process Philosophies, American Philosophical Association Eastern Division (Washington, D.C.: 28 December 1977).

[27]Wattles, *Hegel's Philosophy of Organic Nature*, pp. 44ff.

[28]GL 28. Cf. GL 50: "Logic is to be understood as the system of pure reason, as the realm of pure thought. This realm is truth as it is without veil and in its own absolute nature. It can therefore be said that this content is the exposition of God as he is in his eternal essence before the creation of nature and a finite mind." *Vide* also GL 58. This is, however, only a heuristic perspective, necessary to discover the essence of thought itself. The idea that Hegel continually adopts (as Kierkegaard claimed) a "timeless" or "angelic" perspective on truth (and thus, as Samuel Alexander implied, does not take time seriously) is *utterly* false. See below, Section 4 (iii).

[29]Cf. the analysis of "abstract freedom" in the *Rechtsphilosophie*, Sec. 35: "Personality implies that as *this* person: (i) I am completely determined on every side (in my inner caprice, impulse, and desire, as well as by immediate external facts) and so finite, yet (ii) none the less I am simply and solely self-relation, and therefore in finitude I know myself as something infinite, universal, and free."

[30]Cf. *Enc.* 24, *Zusatz*: ". . . freedom means that the other thing with which you deal is a second self--so that you never leave your own ground but give the law to yourself . . . In this case then we speak of dependence. For freedom it is necessary that we should feel no presence of something else which is not ourselves. The natural man, whose motions follow the rule only of his appetites, is not his own master. Be he as self-willed as he may, the constituents of his will and opinion are not his own, and his freedom is merely formal [i.e., "abstract"]. But when we think, we renounce our selfish and particular being . . . [and] allow thought to follow its own course.

[31]This enlarges upon the point made in the "Larger Logic," that "freedom is the truth of necessity" (GL 580). This argument, however, involves a slight (and deliberate) misuse of the term "necessity"--again as a result of Hegel's attempt to discredit the arrogance of formal logic. Strictly speaking, "necessity" is that which "determines absolutely." Hegel's obvious point is that the factors which are associated with "necessity" do *not* determine absolutely, but condition or limit abstract possibility.

[32]Cf. Errol E. Harris, "The Philosophy of Nature in Hegel's System," *Review of Metaphysics* 3 (2 November 1949), p. 223.

[33]Hegel's argument does not strictly imply that "essence *equals* existence." What he seems to deny is that essence or universals can have any transcendent or ontological status *apart* from some finite realization of these in actual fact.

[34]As we have noted (p. 68, n. 18 above), the whole transcends the sum of its parts at least by the sum of the relational terms. Whether transcendence means *more* than this is a problem Hegel and Whitehead both refer to in their arguments regarding some form of internally-necessary philosophical theism.

[35]This point is made by Joseph Aloysius O'Hare, in *The Meaning of Action in the Phenomenology and Logic of Hegel*, Diss. Fordham University, 1968. O'Hare argues that Hegel's *Logic* is a "progressive revelation of a metaphysics of process" which establishes creativity as the essence of finite being, and demonstrates that a teleological principle is immanent in and emergent from this creative process.

[36]Cf. *Enc.* 124, *Zusatz*: ". . . if we stick to the mere 'in-itself' of an object, we apprehend it not in its truth, *but* in the inadequate form of mere abstraction. Thus the man by or in himself is the child. And what the child has to do is to rise out of this abstract and undeveloped 'in-himself' and become 'for-himself' what he is at first only 'in-himself'--a free and reasonable being."

[37]This view is apparently espoused by J. N. Findlay, when he describes the transformation that an Hegelian outlook may bring upon the most ordinary of situations, and contrasts this with the apocalyptic triumphalism normally associated with Hegel's doctrines. *Vide* "The Contemporary Relevance of Hegel," in Findlay's *Language, Mind and Value* (London: George Allen & Unwin, 1963), pp. 217-231.

[38]In the *18th Brumaire of Louis Bonaparte*, Marx states: "Men make their own history, but they do not make it under circumstances chosen by themselves, but under circumstances directly encountered, given, and transmitted from the past." Quoting this passage, French Marxist Roger Garaudy concludes that it was not the concept of human freedom itself, but rather the individualistic, non-social and non-historical understanding of that term which Marx regarded as illusory. Cf. *Karl Marx: The Evolution of his Thought* (New York: International Publishers, 1967), p. 69.
We have had occasion already to consider Whitehead's distinction of real from pure potentialities, and the role of causal efficacy in his doctrine of freedom. Cf., e.g., Ch. II, Section 3 above.

[39]This, of course, is the proposition of absolute or objective idealism to which Bertrand Russell so strenuously objected. Cf. also the cautiousness of Whiteheadians regarding this issue; Ch. II, Sec. 3, pp. 58-62.
As explicated on similar grounds by Russell's teacher and colleague, A. N. Whitehead, however, the "holistic" assertion does not claim that in order to know one, particular thing one

must first know everything! That is obviously not possible. Rather, Hegel and Whitehead both assert the rather obvious truth, in refutation of a *pure* "logical atomism," that one's knowledge of a finite entity improves or increases directly as a function of the increased knowledge of the total system of entities and relations in which that particular "fact" is encountered.

[40]Cf. the "Outline of Logic" in *The Philosophical Propadeutics*, in which Hegel invokes the doctrine of reciprocity as the solution to the Kantian antinomy of freedom and determinism: "The true solution of this antinomy is *Reciprocity*; a cause which passes over into an effect has in this again a causal Reaction, by which means the first cause is reduced in turn to an effect or to a "Posited." In this reciprocity, consequently, is involved the fact that neither of the two moments of causality is for itself an absolute, but that it is only the *entire circle*, the *totality*, that is in and for itself." Translation of William T. Harris, in *Hegel: Selections*, ed. Jacob Loewenberg (New York: Charles Scribners' Sons, 1929), p. 122.

[41]Cf. J. N. Findlay's comment on this point in his "Foreword" to the Oxford University Press edition of Hegel's "Lesser Logic" (1973), p. xxii: "The 'truth' of the pattern of mutual necessitation . . . is said to be Freedom, in that free self-activity is what mutual necessitation (Reciprocity) dimly prefigures. . . ."

[42]"Freiheit und Notwendigkeit in Hegels Philosophie," *Hegel-Studien*, Beiheft I (1962), pp. 181ff.: "So ist die Idee Ursache und Zweck ihrer selbst, oder der Begriff ist ,das Wirkende seiner selbst,' ist ,Causa sui.' Das Leben des reinen Begriffs is mithin die Freiheit selbst" (my translation).

[43]This, of course, is Hegel's position. Curiously, it cannot be strictly the case. If reciprocity as he describes it really obtains, then the *Logos* or *Begriff* must itself be conditioned by the pluralistic process it generates. That is, the *Begriff* is *relatively*, but *not absolutely* free--it is *as free* of conditioning as an entity can be, by virtue of the fact that it is itself the pattern of that reciprocity which limits freedom. Hegel is well aware of the limitations imposed by the process on his "Absolute," as we shall see (*vide* Section 6 below). Nonetheless, he does not always make this point clear. Indeed, it is confused by his choice of the term "Absolute" as a final description of *Geist* and *Begriff*.

[44]Cf. GL 578: "Accordingly, the Concept is the *truth* of substance; and since substance has *necessity* for its specific mode of relationship, freedom reveals itself as the *truth of necessity* and as *the mode of relationship proper to the Concept*.

[45]". . . dass die Idee sich selbst frei entlässt." *Vide* J. N. Findlay, *Hegel: A Re-examination*, p. 268.

[46]Hegel provides an interesting theological metaphor to suggest why it is necessary to discuss nature as the determinate realm of the Concept: "God, as the living God, and still more as absolute spirit, is known only in his *activity*; man was early instructed to recognize God in his *works*; only from these can

proceed the *determinations*, which are called his properties, and in which, too, his *being* is contained. Thus the philosophical cognition of his *activity*, that is, of himself, grasps the *Concept* of God in his *being* and his being in his Concept" (GL 706).

[47]Much is made over Hegel's apparent *rejection* of the theory of biological evolution (cf. *Enc.* 249). This is less embarrassing when one realizes that evolution barely enjoyed the status of a credible theory in Hegel's day. One should recall as well the poignant remark attributed to Nietzsche: "Denn ohne Hegel kein Darwin."

In point of fact, biological evolution is the theory of natural development which is, in retrospect, most in accord with Hegel's own philosophy of nature, as Errol Harris persuasively argues. In agreement with that observation, it is perfectly consistent in the present essay to speak of "evolution" in connection with Hegel's *Naturphilosophie*. Cf. Errol E. Harris, "The Philosophy of Nature in Hegel's System," pp. 225-228; and "Hegel and the Natural Sciences," in F. G. Weiss, ed., *Beyond Epistemology*, pp. 149ff.

Nonetheless, Hegel did *not* advocate a theory of temporal evolution, and must not be credited with having done so. As Hans Querner observes, the procession of organic forms in the *Naturphilosophie* represents the dialectical development of the *Begriff*. The representation of a real historical process of development, by contrast, was explicitly rejected by Hegel. *Vide* "Die Stufenfolge der Organismen in Hegels Philosophie der Natur," *Hegel-Studien*, Beiheft XI (1974), pp. 153-163.

[48]It may be proper, however, to speak as Teilhard de Chardin does of an organic "critical threshold" above which self-consciousness comes to dominate the development of organisms. Cf. *The Phenomenon of Man* (New York: Harper & Row, 1965/1955); esp. Pt. III, Ch. 7.

[49]This is because Whitehead emphasizes the ensemble of real possibilities open for actualization by an actual occasion, rather than an immanent, germinal characteristic which is subsequently developed to maturity in the process of its own becoming, as Aristotle and Hegel seemed to emphasize.

[50]It is interesting to note at this point that some critics would object to this entire line of reasoning. Freedom may not be identical with spontaneity or contingency, but certainly requires these in some sense. And, unlike Whitehead, there is no room in Hegel's absolute idealism for a meaningful theory of contingency.

Hegel does discuss *Zufall* or contingency as an important category in the *Logic*. While space does not permit further consideration of this objection, Giorgio DiGiovanni has defended Hegel's use of contingency as entirely consistent, arguing that the Absolute (God) is to be seen as the source of contingency as well as of necessity. Cf. *Contingency: Its Foundation in Hegel's Logic of Becoming*, Diss. University of Toronto, 1970.

Dieter Henrich, a distinguished "Hegelkenner," also argues that chance and contingency are of great importance to Hegel in the *Logic* and the "Philosophy of Nature," in his demonstration that determinism is not an adequate or comprehensive model of explanation. *Vide* "Hegels Theorie über den Zufall," *Kant-Studien* 50 (1958-59) 131-148.

[51]Whitehead offers the classic definition of "organic mechanism" in his early metaphysical synthesis in *Science and the
Modern World*, suggesting that the behavior of "self-subsistent"
material entities is subject to influence by the larger, "holistic" situations which they together comprise: ". . . it remains
an immediate deduction that an individual entity, whose own life-
history is a part within the life-history of some larger, deeper,
more complete pattern, is liable to have aspects of that larger
pattern dominating its own being, and to experience modifications
of that larger pattern reflected in itself as modifications of
its own being. This is the theory of organic mechanism" (SMW
156). Cf. the longer exposition of this theory in SMW 115ff.

[52]Once again, Hegel's use of terminology precludes an un-
ambiguous comprehension of his argument. The "necessity" here
described is obviously the traditional "necessity" of causal
determinism, the linear "infinite regress" of Newtonian science,
and *not* what Hegel calls the "true" necessity of reciprocity,
which is *identical* with freedom, as described above (p. 86).
The "Philosophy of Nature" narrates the transition from the
former notion of necessity, to freedom.

[53]Errol E. Harris, "The Philosophy of Nature in Hegel's
System," p. 219. Cf. *Enc.* 6.

[54]Cf. George L. Kline, "Life as Ontological Category: A
Whiteheadian Note on Hegel," in *Art and Logic in Hegel's Philosophy*, eds. Kenneth L. Schmitz and Warren E. Steinkraus (New
York: Humanities Press, 1978), pp. 158-162. These common properties demonstrate that Hegel's organic mechanism exhibits
striking parallels with Whitehead's early metaphysical theory in
Science and the Modern World.

[55]Cf., for example, the *Philosophy of Right*, Sections 267
and 269, where Hegel refers to "the organism of the State."

[56]Bear in mind that Hegel's use of such terms in this context is pejorative and sarcastic. Hegel was saddled with a
Newtonian concept of "corpuscular matter"--the same concept
which Whitehead later would dismiss as "vacuous actuality" (cf.
PR 471, 43). Hegel could not fully accept this concept, but
was hard-pressed in his historical framework to deny it. His
recourse is to ridicule such "matter" as being of no real significance: i.e., "self-subsistent" and unresponsive to its environment. According to a *serious* use of such terms, of course,
nothing--not even the Absolute Idea--is completely "self-subsistent."

[57]*A Study of Hegel's Logic* (Oxford: The Clarendon Press,
1950), p. 238.

[58]Cf. Hegel's *Randbemerkung* to Sec. 335 in the "Philosophy
of Nature": "Certain chemical phenomena have led chemistry to
apply the determination of *teleology* in explaining them. An
example is the fact that an oxide is reduced in the chemical
process to a lower degree of oxidation than that at which it can
combine with the acid acting on it, while a part of it is more
strongly oxidized. There is here a rudimentary self-determination of the Concept from its own resources in its realization,

which is thus not determined solely by conditions which are already *outwardly* to hand."

[59] *Hegel's Philosophy of Organic Nature*, p. 61.

[60] The "soul," for example, is for Aristotle nothing more than the actualized and actualizing purpose or organization of the organic bodily processes--a refinement of the Pythagorean position. Cf. *De Anima* II:1.

[61] Cf. Hegel's criticisms of "external teleology," as noted above: p. 61, n. 8.

[62] Mure, *Hegel's Logic*, p. 247.

[63] *Ibid.*, p. 249. Cf. also Mure's *Introduction to Hegel* (Oxford: The Clarendon Press, 1940), Ch. III.

[64] Cf. GL 740-746. G. R. G. Mure offers the example of the "plough and the ploughman": the former is a mechanical object, subject to efficient causation in terms of its physical constitution and operation. Yet its existence and activity cannot be understood apart from the larger context of *purpose* which literally brings it into being and governs its eventual use. Cf. *A Study of Hegel's Logic*. p. 255.

[65] Cf. Jeffrey Wattles, p. 65: "Teleology proper is no longer simply a relation among a multiplicity of objects; it is an organization in which the end is realized through the means. There is a directionality to teleology that is distinct from the lack of direction in the mechanistic relation . . . In the teleological process, it is not merely the case, as it is in the chemical process, that at the end of the process a new condition or state of affairs has appeared. Rather in the teleological process that final state of affairs is the explicit development of what was already present in the beginning."

[66] Note that for Hegel, as a consequence of his stress on "organisms," it is not necessarily a *unitary* process towards a single end which is envisioned, but rather a process of finite (organic) *processes*. For a comment on Hegel's "monism" in relation to this issue of the plurality of process, see below, Ch. IV.

[67] Errol E. Harris, "Hegel's Theory of Feelings," in *New Studies in Hegel's Philosophy*, ed. Warren Steinkraus (New York: Holt, Rinehart & Winston, 1971), p. 75.

[68] "The Philosophy of Nature in Hegel's System," p. 224.

[69] Introductory *Zusatz* to the "Philosophy of Nature," Miller translation, p. 3.

[70] This view compares quite favorably with Whitehead's assertion: "Speculative philosophy is the endeavour to frame a coherent, logical, necessary system of general ideas in terms of which every element of our experience can be interpreted" (PR 4).

[71]Hegel was by no means unconcerned with the correspondence and coherence of empirical observation! He exhibits, however, an obvious preference for Kepler. The latter (Hegel argues) "proved" his laws of motion, while Newton's are only inductively demonstrated from experience. Also, argues Hegel, Newton's theories can be derived directly from Kepler's theories (*Enc.* 270).

[72]Alexander is generally held responsible for the remark that Hegel, vis 'a vis Bergson, did *not* take time seriously in his philosophy. In "Hegel's Conception of Nature" (*Mind*, old series: 9, No. 41 [1886]), Alexander argues that, while the logical Idea (*Begriff*) is a dialectical *process* it nonetheless represents "a history of ideas which form a process *not in time*" (pp. 499, 502; emphases added).
   Alan B. Brinkley, discussing "Time in Hegel's Philosophy" (*Tulane Studies in Philosophy* IX [1960], pp. 3-15), criticizes these claims of Alexander and argues against this thesis, suggesting instead that time is "the reality of the Concept" and thus "the *keystone* of Hegel's system" (p. 6). John Burbidge, in "Concept and Time in Hegel" (*Dialogue* [1973], pp. 403-422) argues that, for Hegel, time is the conceptual structure of becoming. In Hegel we thus find the harmonious integration of a dynamic character of time within a philosophical-conceptual system.
   J. N. Findlay divorces McTaggart's and Bradley's teaching on the "unreality" of time from that of Hegel. "Time, so far from being unreal, is the very form of that creative unrest which represents Spirit as it becomes conscious of itself" (*Hegel: A Re-examination*, p. 146).
   Finally, Sidney Hook argues in "The Contemporary Significance of Hegel's Philosophy" (*Philosophical Review* 41 [1932], pp. 237-260): "Although Hegel officially denies the reality of time, he recognizes its existence whenever he uses the words 'finite' and 'appearance.' Under the aspect of time the world confronts man as an *ever-enduring process*. Under the aspect of eternity the world is a completed system. But *to the process belongs metaphysical primacy*" (p. 249; emphases added).
   A full treatment of time in Hegel's philosophy has yet to be written. What may be once and for all written *off* is the uninformed criticism that Hegel "did not take time seriously."

[73]Cf. Whitehead's similar critique of Newton's theory, substituting as more adequate his own interpretation of Locke's observation that time is constituted by the "perpetually perishing" actual occasions (PR 126).

[74]"Inter-Subjective Time," in *Process and Divinity*, eds. Reese and Freeman (LaSalle, Ill.: Open Court Press, 1964), p. 285.
   With respect to Hegel's anticipation of contemporary scientific theory, Errol Harris argues further that Hegel asserted "the inseparable interdependence of space and time, and their essential union in motion," and that Hegel's "doctrine of light as the realization of space," together with his conception of planetary motion as "a single movement along a geodesic determined by the total configuration of the system" all anticipated relativity theory ("Hegel and the Natural Sciences," pp. 149-151).
   My own reading of the "Philosophy of Nature" has not persuaded me entirely that Hegel's eulogy of Kepler, or his doctrine

of light really bear such close resemblance to the contemporary
special and general theories of relativity. But the suggestion
itself is interesting, and is defended persuasively by Professor
Harris.

[75]Cf. Errol Harris, "Hegel and the Natural Sciences," pp.
139ff.: "Organism, the object of biological science, Hegel sees
as [a] new and further development of the Concept as it appears
to observing self-consciousness . . . He notes the looseness and
banality of its classifications, the vagueness of the "laws"
governing the influence of environment on the organism, and the
externality of the "teleological" relation postulated to explain
it. He himself has a much sounder conception of teleology as
self-maintenance, identified as purpose, of which the aim is
the organism itself. His whole conception and exposition of the
notion of organism is far in advance of his time."

[76]This after a brief discussion of "geological nature" which,
while well-informed as to geological fact, largely dismisses it
as "not pertaining to philosophy" (*Enc.* 339, *Zusatz*). Hegel proceeds with a further lengthy diatribe against evolution (*Enc.*
339-342).

[77]Or, as Wattles comments (p. 101): "The fact that each
part of the plant is potentially a whole, separate individual
indicates that the plant realizes only to a low degree the subjectivity which organizes its members into a higher unity."

[78]Cf. J. N. Findlay's *Hegel: A Re-examination*, p. 222,
where he argues that the behavior of any entity qualifies as
"freedom" for Hegel "only insofar as its begins to understand
or enjoy [its self-determination], since it is only in such
conscious enjoyment that things alien, dispersed and disparate
can be made part of a thing's being."

[79]In the case of both Hegel and Whitehead we have an elaborate justification of Aristotle's ancient insight that human
beings, as "rational animals," alone can be said to have the
causes of their behavior internal to themselves, and hence properly be described in the Greek sense as "free and responsible"
beings (cf. *Nicomachean Ethics*, Bk. III).
Cf. William Earle, "Freedom and Existence," pp. 52ff:
"Freedom thus is not something which floats into the natural
world from nowhere, supplying a new natural force on the same
level as those it is contrasted with; it is a modality of nature,
but a modality which adds a dimension to nature not reducible to
what was there before . . . [whence] the proof of freedom col-
lapses from the status of the radically problematic or hypothe-
tical to that of a self-evident truth . . . [Freedom] is nothing
but the reflexivity of self-consciousness itself, which in that
act of doubling back upon itself frees itself from the immediacy
of bare subjectivity . . . The assurance that I am free is identical with the assurance that I am self-conscious. And such
assurance is identical with reflexivity itself."

[80]"Hegel on Freedom," in *Hegel and After*, p. 86.

[81]Whence, as William Earle points out, doubting one's freedom is equivalent to doubting one's self-consciousness and rationality; it is a self-refuting skepticism. *Vide* "Freedom and Existence," p. 53.

[82]This particular unkind, but not wholly inappropriate remark precedes Marx's commentary on Section 262 of the *Rechtsphilosophie*.

[83]Cf. H. A. Reyburn's analysis of the relation of mind and freedom in *The Ethical Theory of Hegel*, p. 87: "The infinity of mind is its freedom. Freedom is not the mere absence of constraints, but is active self-determination. In truth nothing can be free from constraint except by mastering the world, for the world is one connected whole."

[84]*The Ethical Theory of Hegel*, p. 186.

[85]*Vide supra*, p. 66, n. 15, on the nature of "Civil Society," the dialectically-flawed phase intermediate to the microcosm of the family and its macroscopic counterpart, the organic State.

[86]Hegel thus argues, with Plato and Socrates, that the State is necessary to guarantee justice and freedom for all. Cf. *Enc.* 474: ". . . thus it was a true perception when Plato . . . showed that the full reality of justice could be exhibited only in the *objective* phase of justice, namely in the construction of the State as the ethical life."

[87]The German *Recht* can be translated as "right" or "law." The latter is more familiar to English audiences, but suggests, in my view, a negative notion of constraints and obligations without the corresponding positive dimensions of rights, protection and the possibilities for happiness thereby presented. For this reason I concur with T. M. Knox's decision to let the more awkward but suggestive term "Right" stand in translation of *Recht*, so as not to lose any of the richness of the original.

[88]Cf. Phil. R. 271: "The Constitution of the State is . . . the organization of the state and the self-related process of its organic life, a process whereby it differentiates its moments within itself and develops them to self-subsistence."

[89]Phil. R. 187, *Zusatz*: "The final purpose of education . . . is liberation and struggle for a higher liberation still. . . ."

[90]Though how, when, and in what fashion is destined to remain for all eternity a hotly-contested issue!

[91]*Vide* his commentary on Section 261 of the *Rechtsphilosophie* in Marx's *Critique of Hegel's Philosophy of Right*, translated by Joseph O'Malley (Cambridge: Cambridge University Press, 1970).

[92]Marx, *op. cit.*, p. 5.

[93]*The Ethical Theory of Hegel*, p. 262.

[94] "Preface" to the *Lectures on the Philosophy of History*, translated by J. Sibree, in *Hegel: Selections*, ed. Jacob Loewenberg (New York: Charles Scribners' Sons, 1929), pp. 359-361.

[95] "Freedom and Existence," p. 56.

[96] This, of course, is tantamount to arguing that Hegel, like Whitehead, is a panentheist. Robert Whittemore argues that Hegel is indeed a panentheist--that the very term itself was coined first to popular use, not by Charles Hartshorne, but by Hegel's contemporary K. C. F. Krause. Whittemore suggests that Hegel viewed the world as immanent in God, who transcends the universe as the Whole transcending the sum of its parts. Cf. "Hegel as Panentheist," *Tulane Studies in Philosophy* IX (1960), pp. 134-164.

NOTES

CHAPTER IV

[1]A *viva voce* remark. *Vide supra*, Ch. I, p. 8, n. 11.

[2]Errol E. Harris, "Science, Metaphysics and Teleology," in *The Personal Universe*, ed. Thomas Wren (Atlantic Heights, N. J.: Humanities Press, 1975), p. 36.

[3]*Enc.* 211; emphases added. Cf. this with Hegel's famous remark at the conclusion of *Die Philosophie der Geschichte*: "Bis hierher ist das Bewusstsein gekommen"--thus, as Collingwood notes, "nailing to the counter in advance the lie that [Hegel] regarded his own philosophy as final. . . ." Cf. *The Idea of Nature*, p. 174.

[4]"Science, Metaphysics and Teleology," p. 37.

[5]As far as I know, Professor Robert Whittemore of Tulane University was the first to document this aspect of the Hegel-Whitehead correlation. Cf. "Hegel's 'Science' and Whitehead's 'Modern World'," p. 46: "Both systems are thus--panentheisms, since for both God is at once the Reality, of which the universe in process is an appearance, and the self-creative source of that reality."

[6]The following discussion is based in part upon a paper which I read at the Eastern Division meeting of the American Philosophical Association: "Hegel's *Begriff* and Whitehead's 'Subjective Aim': A Response to George L. Kline" (Washington, D.C.: 28 December 1977).

[7]Cf., e.g., Hartshorne and Reese, *Philosophers Speak of God* (Chicago: University of Chicago Press, 1953). Interestingly (especially in a book of this title) while there are many references in the authors' exposition which obliquely refer to Hegel, there are no direct quotations or extended discussions of his treatment of God. The most suggestive reference, implying my point in the present essay, states that Hegel's theism "is equivocal on the issue between pantheism and panentheism" (p. 177).

[8]Robert Whittemore once again points out the similarities in this treatment: "God as Absolute Idea (Logic) is pictorialized as God the Father; as dirempted into otherness (Nature) God becomes God the Son; as reunited unity of self and other, God is God the Holy Ghost. [Hegel's] characterization is mirrored in the Whiteheadian system in the conception of God as primordial (Father), as consequent (Son), as superjective (Holy Ghost)." Cf. "Hegel's 'Science' and Whitehead's 'Modern World'," p. 46. *Vide* also Daniel Day Williams, "Philosophy and Faith: A Study in Hegel and Whitehead," and J. R. Kuehl, *Actuality as Spirit: A Study in Hegel and Whitehead*.

[9]Cf. Lewis S. Ford, "Whitehead's First Metaphysical Synthesis," *International Philosophical Quarterly* (September 1977), pp. 251-264.

[10]*The Foundations of Metaphysics in Science*, p. 477.

[11]*Vide supra*, p. 48 for our analysis of this dimension of the problem of freedom in Whiteheadian terms. In some cases, of course, the development is arrested and never reaches fulfillment. Indeed, philosophers as a class are customarily arrogant enough to suggest that it is only with philosophy and in the philosopher--the individual whose powers of self-reflective reasoning allegedly are most fully developed--that true freedom is fully realized!

[12]A recent doctoral dissertation utilizes a similar intuition of the significance of Whitehead's thought to develop a well-grounded theory of "non-human" rights. Cf. Susan B. Armstrong, *The Rights of Nonhuman Beings: A Whiteheadian Study*, Diss. Bryn Mawr College, 1976. See especially pp. 197-241.

[13]"Afterforeword: A Sampling of Other Studies," in *Explorations in Whitehead's Philosophy*, eds. Lewis S. Ford and George L. Kline (New York: Fordham University Press, forthcoming).

[14]Professor Ford, in private correspondence, adds that both Hegel and Whitehead likewise have very different concepts of "God." I have answered this objection in item (i) above.

[15]In all fairness we are well reminded that disciples of Sankara and Spinoza (among others) would not allow the pejorative connotations which this term entails when used as a negative criticism of a metaphysical system!

[16](Oxford: The Clarendon Press, 1893/1951), Part II, *passim*. By advocating such positions, Bradley and McTaggart gave the negative impression with which "absolute idealism" is associated in English-language philosophy.

[17]"Concept and Concrescence," *loc. cit.*

[18]See Ch. I, p. 8, n. 8 for a brief discussion of the distinct schools of process thought, in contrast with other traditions in philosophy.

BIBLIOGRAPHY OF WORKS CONSULTED

I.   Primary Sources

Hegel, Georg Wilhelm Friedrich. *Sämtliche Werke*. Herausgegeben von Georg Lasson. Leipzig: Felix Meiner Verlag, 1923.

_____. *Hegel's Phenomenology of Spirit*. Translated by A. V. Miller. Oxford: The Clarendon Press, 1977.

_____. *The Phenomenology of Mind*. Translated by J. B. Baillie (1910). New York: Harper Colophon Books, 1967.

_____. *Hegel's Science of Logic*. Translated by A. V. Miller. London: George Allen & Unwin, 1969.

_____. *The Logic of Hegel: Encyclopedia of the Philosophical Sciences*, Part One. Translated by William Wallace (1892). Oxford: The Clarendon Press, 1970.

_____. Hegel's Philosophy of Nature: *Encyclopedia of the Philosophical Sciences*, Part Two. Translated by A. V. Miller. Oxford: The Clarendon Press, 1970.

_____. *The Philosophy of Mind: Encyclopedia of the Philosophical Sciences*, Part Three. Translated by William Wallace. *Zusätze* translated by A. V. Miller. Oxford: The Clarendon Press, 1971.

_____. *Hegel's Philosophy of Right*. Translated by T. M. Knox. Oxford: The Clarendon Press, 1952 [1967].

_____. *Hegel: Selections*. Ed. Jacob Loewenberg. New York: Charles Scribners' Sons, 1929.

_____. *Hegel: The Essential Writings*. Ed. Frederick G. Weiss. New York: Harper & Row, 1974.

Whitehead, Alfred North. *The Concept of Nature*. Cambridge: Cambridge University Press, 1920.

_____. *Science and the Modern World*. Lowell Lectures, 1925. New York: Macmillan, 1925.

_____. *Religion in the Making*. Lowell Lectures, 1926. New York: Macmillan, 1926.

_____. *Process and Reality*. Gifford Lectures, 1927-28. New York: Macmillan, 1929.

_____. *Adventures of Ideas*. New York: Macmillan, 1933.

_____. *Modes of Thought*. New York: Macmillan, 1938.

_____. *Essays in Science and Philosophy*. New York: Philosophical Library, 1948.

II. Secondary Sources: Books

Armstrong, Susan B. *The Rights of Non-human Beings*: *A White-
    headian Study*. Diss. Bryn Mawr College, 1976.

Belaief, Lynne. *The Ethics of Alfred North Whitehead*. Diss.
    Columbia University, 1963.

Bradley, F. H. *Appearance and Reality*. Oxford: The Clarendon
    Press, 1893 [1951].

Christian, William A. *An Interpretation of Whitehead's Meta-
    physics*. New Haven: Yale University Press, 1959.

Cobb, John B. Jr. *A Christian Natural Theology*. Philadelphia:
    The Westminster Press, 1965.

_____, and Griffin, David Ray. *Process Theology*: *An Intro-
    ductory Exposition*. Philadelphia: The Westminster Press,
    1976.

Collingwood, R. G. *An Essay on Philosophical Method*. Oxford:
    Oxford University Press, 1933.

_____. *The Idea of Nature*. Oxford: The Clarendon Press,
    1945.

DiGiovanni, Giorgio. *Contingency*: *Its Foundation in Hegel's
    Logic of Becoming*. Diss. Bryn Mawr College, 1974.

Dudeck, Caroline Verna. *Hegel's Concept of Freedom as it Deve-
    lops in the Phenomenology of Mind*. Diss. Bryn Mawr College,
    1974.

Edwards, Jonathan. *Freedom of the Will*. Boston, 1754. Reissued
    in the "Library of Liberal Arts" series: Arnold J. Kaufman
    and William Frankena, eds. Indianapolis: Bobbs-Merrill,
    1969.

Findlay, J. N. *Hegel*: *A Re-examination*. Oxford: Oxford Uni-
    versity Press, 1958.

Garaudy, Roger. *Karl Marx*: *The Evolution of His Thought*. New
    York: International Publishers, 1967.

Geran, Juliana. *Whitehead on the Ontological Principle*: *a
    Critique of Early Modern Epistemology in Process and Reality*.
    Diss. University of Chicago, 1974.

Harris, Errol E. *Nature, Mind and Modern Science*. London:
    George Allen & Unwin, 1954.

_____. *Foundations of Metaphysics in Science*. London: George
    Allen & Unwin, 1965.

Hartshorne, Charles. *The Divine Relativity*: *A Social Conception
    of God*. New Haven: Yale University Press, 1948.

_____, and Reese, William L. *Philosophers Speak of God*.
    Chicago: University of Chicago Press, 1953.

Kline, George L., ed. *Alfred North Whitehead: Essays on His Philosophy*. Englewood Cliffs, N. J.: Prentice-Hall, 1963.

Kuehl, James Robert. *Actuality as Spirit: A Study in Hegel and Whitehead*. Diss. Northwestern University, 1964 [Master's Thesis].

Leclerc, Ivor. *Whitehead's Metaphysics: An Introductory Exposition*. London: George Allen & Unwin, 1958. [Bloomington, Ind.: Indiana University Press, 1975].

Lowe, Victor. *Understanding Whitehead*. Baltimore: Johns Hopkins University Press, 1962.

Marx, Karl. *A Critique of Hegel's Philosophy of Right* (c. 1843). Translated by Joseph O'Malley. Cambridge: Cambridge University Press, 1970.

_____. *Early Writings*. Translated and edited by T. B. Bottomore. New York: McGraw-Hill, 1963.

_____. *Selected Writings in Sociology and Social Philosophy*. Translated and edited by T. B. Bottomore. London: C. A. Watts & Co., 1956.

Mellert, Robert B. *What is Process Theology?* New York: Paulist Press, 1975.

Merleau-Ponty, Maurice. *Phenomenologie de la perception*. Paris: Gallimard, 1945. Translated by Colin Smith. London: Routledge & Kegan Paul, 1962.

Mure, G. R. G. *An Introduction to Hegel*. Oxford: The Clarendon Press, 1940.

_____. *A Study of Hegel's Logic*. Oxford: The Clarendon Press, 1950.

Neville, Robert C. *The Cosmology of Freedom*. New Haven: Yale University Press, 1974.

O'Brochta, Thomas F. *The Metaphysical Basis of Human Freedom According to Alfred North Whitehead*. Diss. Loyola University of Chicago, 1973.

O'Hare, Joseph Aloysius. *The Meaning of Action in the Phenomenology and Logic of Hegel*. Diss. Fordham University, 1968.

Pols, Edward. *Whitehead's Metaphysics: A Critical Examination of Process and Reality*. Carbondale: University of Southern Illinois Press, 1967.

Pruitt, Sylvia Ann. *An Inquiry into the Ethical Implications of Whitehead's Metaphysics*. Diss. Emory University, 1970.

Reyburn, Hugh A. *The Ethical Theory of Hegel: A Study of the Philosophy of Right*. Oxford: The Clarendon Press, 1921.

Sartre, Jean-Paul. *Being and Nothingness*. Translated by Hazel
E. Barnes. New York: Washington Square Press, 1966.

Schacht, Richard. *Hegel and After: Studies in Continental Philosophy Between Kant and Sartre*. Pittsburgh: University of
Pittsburgh Press, 1975.

Sherburne, Donald W., ed. *A Key to Whitehead's Process and
Reality*. New York: Macmillan, 1966. [Bloomington, Ind.:
Indiana University Press, 1975].

Stevens, Edward Ira. *Freedom, Determinism and Responsibility:
An Analysis and a Whiteheadian Interpretation*. Diss. Vanderbilt University, 1965.

Teilhard de Chardin, Pierre. *The Phenomenon of Man*. Translated
by Bernard Wall. New York: Harper & Row, 1965 [1955].

Wattles, Jeffrey Hamilton. *Hegel's Philosophy of Organic Nature*.
Diss. Northwestern University, 1973.

Williams, Daniel Day. *The Spirit and Forms of Love*. New York:
Harper & Row, 1968.

III. Secondary Sources: Articles

Al-Azm, Sadik J. "Whitehead's Notions of Order and Freedom."
The Personalist, 48, No. 4 (October 1967), 579-591.

Alexander, Samuel. "Hegel's Conception of Nature." *Mind* [old
series], 9, No. 41 (1886).

Alston, William P. "Internal Relatedness and Pluralism in Whitehead." *Review of Metaphysics*, 5 (1952), 535-558.

Belaief, Lynne. "A Whiteheadian Account of Value and Identity."
Process Studies, 5, No. 1 (Spring 1975), 31-40.

Brinkley, Alan B. "Time in Hegel's Phenomenology." *Tulane
Studies in Philosophy*, IX (1960), 3-15.

Broad, C. D. "Determinism, Indeterminism and Libertarianism."
Ethics and the History of Philosophy. London: Routledge
& Kegan Paul, 1952, pp. 195-217. Reprinted in *Free Will
and Determinism*. Ed. Bernard Berofsky. New York: Harper
& Row, 1966, pp. 135-159.

Brown, Delwin. "Hope for the Human Future: Niebuhr, Whitehead
and Utopian Expectation." *Iliff Review*, 32 (1975), 3-18.

Browning, D. "Whitehead's Theory of Human Agency." *Dialogue*,
II (1963-64), 424-441.

Burbridge, John. "Concept and Time in Hegel." *Dialogue*, XII
(1973), 403-422.

Burgers, J. M. "The Measuring Process in Quantum Theory." *Re-
views of Modern Physics*, 35 (1963), 145-150.

_____. "Causality and Anticipation." *Science*, 189 (July 1975), 194-198.

Campbell, C. A. "Is 'Freewill' a Pseudo-Problem?" *Mind*, 60, No. 240 (October 1951), 446-465. Reprinted in part in *Free Will and Determinism*. Ed. Bernard Berofsky. New York: Harper & Row, 1966, pp. 112-135.

Cobb, John B. Jr. "Freedom in Whitehead's Philosophy: A Response to Edward Pols." *Southern Journal of Philosophy*, 7, No. 4 (Winter 1969), 409-413.

_____. "The 'Whitehead Without God' Debate: The Critique." *Process Studies*, 1, No. 2 (Summer 1971), 91-100.

_____, Sherburne, Donald W. "Regional Inclusion and Psychological Physiology." *Process Studies*, 3, No. 1 (Spring 1973), 27-40.

Earle, William. "Freedom and Existence: A Symposium." *Review of Metaphysics*, 9, No. 1 (1955), 27-56.

_____. "Inter-Subjective Time." *Process and Divinity*. Eds. William L. Reese and Eugene Freeman. LaSalle, Ill.: Open Court Press, 1964, pp. 285-297.

Findlay, J. N. "The Contemporary Relevance of Hegel." *Language, Mind and Value*. London: George Allen & Unwin, 1963, pp. 217-231.

_____. "Hegel's Use of Teleology." *The Monist*, 48, No. 1 (January 1964), 1-17. Reprinted in *Ascent to the Absolute*. London: George Allen & Unwin, 1970, pp. 131-147.

Ford, Lewis S. "On Genetic Successiveness: A Third Alternative." *Southern Journal of Philosophy*, 7, No. 4 (Winter 1969), 421-425.

_____. "Can Whitehead Provide for Real Subjective Agency? A Reply to Edward Pols' Critique." *The Modern Schoolman*, 47, No. 2 (January 1970), 209-225.

_____. "Whitehead on Subjective Agency: A Response to Edward Pols." *The Modern Schoolman*, 49, No. 2 (January 1972), 151-153.

_____. "An Appraisal of Whiteheadian Nontheism." *Southern Journal of Philosophy*, 15, No. 1 (Spring 1977), 27-35.

_____. "Whitehead's First Metaphysical Synthesis." *International Philosophical Quarterly* (September 1977), 251-264.

_____. "Afterforeword: A Sampling of Other Studies." *Explorations in Whitehead's Philosophy*. Eds. Lewis S. Ford and George L. Kline. New York: Fordham University Press, forthcoming.

Harris, Errol E. "The Philosophy of Nature in Hegel's System." *Review of Metaphysics*, 3, (1949), 213-228.

_____. "Teleology and Teleological Explanation." *Journal of Philosophy*, 56, No. 1 (1 January 1959), 5-25.

_____. "Hegel's Theory of Feelings." *New Studies in Hegel's Philosophy*. Ed. Warren Steinkraus. New York: Holt, Rinehart & Winston, 1971, pp. 71-91.

_____. "Mechanism and Teleology in Contemporary Thought." *Philosophy in Context*, 2. Cleveland: Cleveland State University Department of Philosophy, 1973, pp. 49-55.

_____. "Hegel and the Natural Sciences." *Beyond Epistemology: New Studies in the Philosophy of Hegel*. Ed. Frederick G. Weiss. The Hague: Martinus Nijhoff, 1974, pp. 129-153.

_____. "Science, Metaphysics and Teleology." *The Personal Universe*. Ed. Thomas Wren. Atlantic Heights, N. J.: Humanities Press, 1975, pp. 24-38.

Hartshorne, Charles. "Freedom Requires Indeterminism and Universal Causality." *Journal of Philosophy*, 55, No. 19 (11 September 1958), 793-811.

_____. "Beyond Enlightened Self-Interest: A Metaphysics of Ethics." *Ethics*, 84, No. 3 (April 1974), 201-216.

Henrich, Dieter. "Hegels Theorie über den Zufall." *Kant-Studien*, 50 (1958-59), 131-148.

Hocking, Richard. "The Polarity of Dialectical History and Process Cosmology." *The Christian Scholar*, 50 (1967), 177-183.

Hocking, William Ernest. "Whitehead as I Knew Him." *Journal of Philosophy*, 58 (1961), 505-516. Reprinted in *Alfred North Whitehead: Essays on his Philosophy*. Ed. George L. Kline. Englewood Cliff, N. J.: Prentice-Hall, 1963, pp. 7-17.

Hook, Sydney. "The Contemporary Significance of Hegel's Philosophy." *Philosophical Review*, 41 (1932), 237-260.

Johnson, Allison H. "Whitehead's Philosophy of History." *Journal of the History of Ideas*, 7 (1946), 234-249.

Kline, George L. "Some Recent Reinterpretations of Hegel's Philosophy." *The Monist*, 48, No. 1 (January 1964), 34-75.

_____. "Form, Concrescence and Concretum: A Neo-Whiteheadian Analysis." *Southern Journal of Philosophy*, 7, No. 4 (Winter 1969), 351-360. Revised version forthcoming in *Explorations in Whitehead's Philosophy*. Eds. Lewis S. Ford and George L. Kline. New York: Fordham University Press, In Press.

_____. "Life as Ontological Category: A Whiteheadian Note on Hegel." *Art & Logic in Hegel's Philosophy*. Eds. Kenneth L. Schmitz and Warren E. Steinkraus. New York: Humanities Press, 1978, pp. 158-162.

_____. "Concept and Concrescence: An Essay in Hegelian-White-headian Ontology." Typescript: Society for the Study of Process Philosophies, American Philosophical Association (Eastern Division: Washington, D.C.), 28 December 1977.

Lakebrink, Bernhard. "Freiheit und Notwendigkeit in Hegels Philosophie." *Hegel-Studien*, Beiheft I (1962), 181-192.

Merrill, Kenneth R. "Whitehead on Order and Freedom: A Reply." The Personalist, 50 (1969), 148-154.

Munson, Thomas N. "Hegel's Political Thought." *The Monist*, 48, No. 1 (January 1964), 97-111.

Nobo, Jorge Luis. "Whitehead's Principle of Process." *Process Studies*, 4, No. 4 (Winter 1974), 275-284.

Pols, Edward. "Freedom and Agency: A Reply." *Southern Journal of Philosophy*, 7, No. 4 (Winter 1969), 415-419.

_____. "Whitehead on Subjective Agency: A Reply to Lewis S. Ford." *The Modern Schoolman*, 49, No. 2 (January 1972), 144-150.

Querner, Hans. "Die Stufenfolge der Organismen in Hegels Philosophie der Natur." *Hegel-Studien*, Beiheft XI (1974), 153-163.

Schlick, Moritz. "When is a Man Responsible?" *Problems of Ethics*. Translated by David Rynin. New York: Prentice-Hall, 1939, pp. 143-156. Reprinted in *Free Will and Determinism*. Ed. Bernard Berofsky. New York: Harper & Row, 1966, pp. 54-63.

Sherburne, Donald W. "Whitehead Without God." *The Christian Scholar*, 50, No. 3 (Fall 1967), 251-272. Reprinted in *Process Philosophy and Christian Thought*. Eds. Delwin Brown, Ralph E. James, Jr. and Gene Reeves. Indianapolis: Bobbs-Merrill, 1971, pp. 305-328.

_____. "Whitehead's Psychological Physiology." *Southern Journal of Philosophy*, 7, No. 4 (Winter 1969), 401-407.

_____. "The 'Whitehead Without God' Debate: The Rejoinder." Process Studies, 1, No. 2 (Summer 1971), 101-113.

Stapp, Henry Pierce. "Bell's Theorem and World Process." *Il Nuovo Cimento*, 29B, No. 2 (11 October 1975), 270-276.

_____. "Theory of Reality." *Foundations of Physics*, 7, Nos. 5-6, (1977), 313-323.

Vlastos, Gregory. "Organic Categories in Whitehead." *Journal of Philosophy*, 34 (May 1937), 253-263. Reprinted in *Alfred North Whitehead: Essays on His Philosophy*. Ed. George L. Kline. Englewood Cliffs, N. J.: Prentice-Hall, 1963, pp. 158-167.

Whittemore, Robert C. "Whitehead's Process and Bradley's Reality." *The Modern Schoolman*, 32 (November 1954), 56-74.

_____. "Hegel's 'Science' and Whitehead's 'Modern World'." *Philosophy*, 31, No. 116 (January 1956), 36-54.

_____. "Hegel as Panentheist." *Tulane Studies in Philosophy*, 9 (1960), 134-164.

Will, James E. "The Uses of Philosophical Theology in the Christian-Marxist Dialogue." *Union Seminary Quarterly Review*, 26, No. 1 (Fall 1970), 19-42.

_____. "The Place of Ideology in Theology." *Journal of Ecumenical Studies*, 15, No. 1 (Winter 1978), 41-53.

Williams, Daniel Day. "Moral Obligation in Process Philosophy." *Journal of Philosophy*, 56 (1959), 263-270. Reprinted in *Alfred North Whitehead*: *Essays on His Philosophy*. Ed. George L. Kline. Englewood Cliffs, N. J.: Prentice-Hall, 1963, pp. 189-195.

_____. "Philosophy and Faith: A Study in Hegel and Whitehead." *Our Common History as Christians*: *Essays in Honor of Albert C. Outler*. Eds. J. Deschner, L. T. Howe and K. Penzel. New York: Oxford University Press, 1975, pp. 157-175.